ARIADNE'S THREAD

To Michael, Martin & Janet

Ariadne's Thread

Through the labyrinth to Palestine and Israel

Eleanor Aitken

CORNELIAN PRESS

CAMBRIDGE

Copyright © Eleanor Aitken 1999
First published in 1999 by Cornelian Press
P O Box 997
Cambridge
CB3 7GG

Distributed by Gazelle Book Services Limited
Falcon House Queen Square Lancaster
England LA1 1RN

British Library Cataloguing in Publication Data
A catalogue record for this book is available from the British Library

ISBN 0-9535525-0-0

Typeset by Amolibros, Watchet, Somerset
This book production has been managed by Amolibros
Printed and bound by T J International, Padstow, England

Contents

Acknowledgements

For excerpts from 'Portrait: the man who snatched Adolf Eichmann', *Guardian*, 16th July 1977, © *The Guardian*, reprinted in Chapter Twelve and on the jacket.

Jacket photo provided courtesy of Agence France Presse.

For excerpts from *Blessed are the Peacemakers* by Audeh Rantisi, in Chapter Thirteen.

For excerpts from *Blood Brothers* and *We Belong to the Land* by Elias Chacour, in Chapter Sixteen.

Pain knows no national boundaries,
and no one can claim a monopoly on suffering.

Dr Haidar Abd el Shafi
in his speech at Madrid,
October 1991

For us, there is only the trying. The rest is not our business.

T S Eliot, *East Coker*

Preface

This book was conceived as an autobiography with a purpose; a purpose that seemed at the outset simple and straightforward, but which has turned out to be extremely difficult to achieve. It was to help ordinary people, like myself, a former schoolteacher, to appreciate the human cost incurred by the foundation and expansion of the State of Israel. I had had the opportunity to learn something of it on the spot.

When Israel celebrated its fiftieth birthday in 1998, the people of Palestine, as the country was called in the days of my youth, mourned the fiftieth anniversary of their dispossession, of their Catastrophe. It is axiomatic, I think, that to understand the present and so act sensitively for the future one needs to know and understand what happened in the past – or try to.

What happened in Palestine has been concealed, on the whole, from most Westerners with remarkable success. If there is ever to be real peace in the region there are first of all wrongs which must be put right as far as possible. Like the Balkans, the Middle East could be the flashpoint for another world war; and the nuclear threat still hangs over us all.

In my mid-twenties I started to be involved in struggles for human rights. One issue, one cause, led to another (the "labyrinth"). The thread of my story became intertwined with and then subordinate to the stories of other people whom I saw as victims of injustice, particularly when I reached the heart of the labyrinth: Israel/Palestine, the most intractable problem of all.

That happened on my first journey to the Middle East in 1972. My primary intention was to meet Soviet Jews on whose behalf I had been working and who had managed to emigrate to Israel. But I also visited Palestine refugee camps – and received a profound shock.

The early chapters of *Ariadne's Thread* are indeed autobiographical, to give readers something of my background and so enable them, I hope, to understand my approach to this thorny subject. Many people have helped me with this book. They will know how grateful I am to them and understand the reason why I do not name them. I alone am responsible for the views expressed. I apologise for any hurt or offence I may cause and for any mistakes I may unwittingly have made. I have tried to be truthful; but have found it very difficult to be a wholly impassive observer.

EA

Foreword

It was a snowy evening in 1972, my first term at Cambridge. I walked into the Friends Meeting House with apprehension: since arriving in England, I had seen nothing on television nor had I read anything in the press that remotely conveyed an accurate view of the Palestinians or their Nakba/Catastrophe. That evening, I was prepared for yet another desecration of history and identity in the "Palestine Exhibition" that had been publicised in the local press.

A very English woman was sitting behind a table, just a little younger than my mother, sipping hot tea, with blue eyes and a strong gaze. She smiled when I asked her how to go about the exhibition and simply pointed me to the hall. Nobody else was there. I walked around feeling her eyes on me: months later, she told me that she had sat wondering whether I would go up to her and support (or denounce, as some had) the idea behind the exhibition. As I looked at the posters and the photographs, I realised that the person who had prepared the exhibition had broken British and Western psychological and political barriers: that person had travelled among the Palestinians in their exile, had experienced the despair and humiliation of their homelessness, and had shared in their prayers, trials and tears.

That person was Eleanor Aitken.

On that evening, Eleanor gave me a thread which now has become her autobiography. *Ariadne's Thread* poses a powerful challenge to readers, whether Jews or Arabs, Palestinians or non-Palestinians. But mostly, it challenges Britons and Americans – the two peoples who have been most deeply involved, historically and currently, in the question of Palestine. The book traces the journey of a woman, who early in her life, recognised that personal fulfilment lay in helping those in need of food, political freedom or justice, regardless of race, ethnicity or religion. From her youthful days in London and Cambridge to her octogenarian widowhood, Eleanor has, unflinchingly and tirelessly, turned commitment into action, dedication into deed. When allied bombing in World War II left behind innumerable French victims, she was there with others to organise relief supplies, to cook and clean and serve. Years later, she joined in the anti-nuclear movement in England (long before such a movement became acceptable) and then made a little dent in the Iron Curtain by studying Russian, editing Russian poetry for English students and arranging programmes for visiting Soviet scholars and artists. She worked tirelessly on behalf of Greek political prisoners in the sixties, and later on behalf of Soviet dissidents, both Jews and non-Jews, and joined in the international outcry against their plight. For the last quarter of a century, she has been helping the Palestinians, not only by organising exhibitions and lectures, but by establishing and expanding Unipal. I have personally known many Palestinians whose careers and lives were improved as a result of Unipal's help.

To read her autobiography is to meet a 'child of God' in the sense that is presented in the Sermon on the Mount. For Eleanor has spent all her life in the service of others: indeed, before reading her autobiography, I did not know much about her because she never talked about herself or her family but about the people she wanted to help. At one time in Amman, Jordan, I took Eleanor and some friends to a restaurant: I wanted to show her some appreciation for what she was doing. Later, when I asked her whether she had enjoyed herself, she nodded but then added: 'You know, if we had eaten at home, we could have saved enough money to buy a whole lot of stamps for Unipal!' For Eleanor, the world centred not on the self but on the needy other.

Either Eleanor has a gene of compassion that very few of us possess, or else she has that 'inner seed' about which George Fox, the founder of the Quaker movement, spoke. For it is this breadth of her humanity, this divine seed, that comes through her autobiography as an admirable model of Christian realisation. Eleanor has lived the New Testament message with deep interiority and passion: yet she never speaks about her faith: she could be easily mistaken for a humanist or an agnostic. But I have not known anybody who has, as St. Paul preached, seen no difference between Jew and Gentile, male and female, European and Middle Easterner as has Eleanor.

This model of Christian selflessness and quietness will probably present an uncomfortable challenge to her readers. In particular, *Ariadne's Thread* will challenge all those in the West who see themselves as committed Christians, and who, while affirming a jingoistic millenarianism that celebrates the supposed fulfilment of prophecy in the state of Israel, deny Palestinian identity, history and rights. Eleanor shows the true path of the Christian in the Holy Land: not the path of the tourist who does not want to be irritated by the Palestinian refugee camps, or bothered about Palestinian exile, deprivation and injustice; Eleanor's thread will lead the reader to the despair of Palestinian men, women and children who see their homes blown up by Israeli forces, their lives thwarted by month-long curfews, their rights devastated by arbitrary measures that affect them only because they are Palestinian Arabs, Muslims and Christians alike. For the thousands of blithe Westerners who annually go on 'pilgrimage' to the Holy Land, Eleanor shows that there can be no holiness in a land that is repeatedly made unholy by the violence and arrogance of the Israeli occupiers. Only justice makes holy.

Ariadne's Thread leads through harrowing moments and round painful corners, into the rooms of Palestinian victims of Israeli torture as well as into the law offices of heroic Israelis who try to protect them. But as with Theseus, only Ariadne's thread can lead out of the monstrous darkness of the labyrinth into the freedom of truth.

Nabil Matar PhD Cantab
Professor of English
Florida Institute of Technology
July 1998

PROLOGUE

The road to Gaza

Ahmed Abdallah's story

"I was born in Klegat, a small village near Al Majdal (now Ashkelon). It doesn't exist any more; it was demolished by the Israelis. We were living in that village peacefully. The land – our land – is now used by an Israeli *moshav*[1].

"In 1948 I was about one and a half years old. Of course I don't remember the day we left. My mother has told me. Israeli[2] troops surrounded the village on three sides. They began to put pressure on the people to make them go from the fourth side, which was to the south. There was shooting, bombs, machine-gun fire. Our people were unarmed. So we went towards another small village. My family consisted of two brothers, three sisters, my mother and I. My father was already dead. A plane dropped bombs on us. My mother tried to protect me on every side – she held me tight in her arms. After a while, when it was quiet, she tried to collect the other children, calling, 'Fat'meh, Mohammed...Your little brother Ahmed is hurt, he's dying!' There was no answer. She laid me aside to go and look for them. She found she could not stand up. She crawled round. First she found Fat'meh, her eldest daughter. Fat'meh looked at her mother and said, 'Mother, I need water,' – and then died. After that she found Mohammed – dead. One after another she found my brothers and sisters – all dead. Then she lost consciousness.

"The news reached my uncles, who hurried to the spot. My mother was placed in a cart and taken to an Egyptian military hospital in Al Majdal. They thought I was dead, and I was put in another cart with the bodies of my brothers and sisters. They dug two graves: one for the boys, one for the girls. They were going to put me on the top of my brothers. They buried my eldest brother first. When they picked me up, someone held me where I was injured – and I cried out. They laid me aside and started to cover the other children. While they were doing so, the Israelis[2] attacked again and they fled.

1

"When they ran away it was of course only to hide somewhere and then return for me. There was an old woman from our village who had to come the same way as we had. She saw me. She found me crying and she held me and tried to comfort me. Then my uncles came back. She knew them, and handed me over to them. I was taken to an aunt, an old woman of about seventy years old. She really needed someone to take care of *her*. She didn't know much about caring for a little wounded child! We made our way slowly to Gaza. It took a very long time – months. In Gaza there were no medicines. Old methods were used to treat my leg. Everywhere there were people – refugees – sheltering under trees, because there was no place for them. All poor, with nothing. A friend of my father's took me to a hospital in Gaza. When the doctor saw my leg, he immediately decided to amputate it. My father's friend refused. He and my aunt discussed the matter. My aunt had some silver coins on her head covering, as was the custom. She cut them off. They took me to a private doctor – the only one in Gaza, Dr. Saleh Matar. He took care of me; he took the bits of shell from my legs – there were some in both. Two years passed. I was given special boots. I had not seen my mother. She was still in that military hospital, thinking all her children were dead. No one visited her there; everyone had come on to Gaza. She had been severely injured, and did not want to live, believing she had lost all her family. She refused to take any medicine. No family, no home, nothing was left for her in life, she thought.

"The Red Cross brought her to a hospital in Gaza. It doesn't exist any more; it was an emergency hospital. There she was told that her youngest son was alive. She began to ask for medicine, and left the hospital quickly, on crutches. When she found me it was as if she found a new spirit, a new life. She hugged me, and kissed me. We started the most difficult period in my life. An injured child. An injured mother. No house to live in. All the people in the same situation. We lived with my aunt in a little shed with a straw roof.

"When I was four, I went with my mother to collect animal droppings in the street. We sold this for manure for the orange groves. We got a penny a day, sometimes two, even four or five. We could buy bread. Every day we did this. We carried on like this till UNRWA was set up in the early fifties.

"UNRWA gave us a tent. It was like a palace to us. Even when it snowed! Yes, it snowed in Gaza for the first time and the last time. My mother got other work – in the orange groves, doing people's washing, working as a servant. She felt this very badly. She was the daughter of the *mukhtar* (like a mayor) of our village. She had been a landowner, a lady in her village. I went to school when I was six, and did well. When I was twelve, I was able to earn something in the holidays and help my mother.

"UNRWA gave us a small shelter, one room. The camps were being set up. Toilets – latrines – were in the street, for everyone to use. No electricity, no water supply. But we were content.

"In 1965 my mother got a job as a cleaner in Shifa Hospital (the "government" hospital – then under the Egyptians). I was coming up to *tawjihi* – the school leaving certificate.

"Then in 1967 the Israelis came and occupied the Gaza Strip. I passed my examination and was accepted for teacher training at the UNRWA training centre in Ramallah on the West Bank; and, when I graduated in 1969, I got a job in an UNRWA school as a teacher of English – and till now I work as a teacher. More than twenty years. But I remember, when I got my first wage and brought it to my mother, I said, "Mother – the first fruit of the tree you planted!" She looked at me and refused to take the money. "I looked after you and made you a man," she said. "I don't want your money. I want you to bring my family back to me." I understood. She wanted me to marry and have children. I did not dare to say, "No." I wasn't planning to marry. I was only twenty-three. But I knew how she was suffering. I looked for a wife, a wife who would understand and respect my mother. I found a good wife. I have eight children: five girls, three sons. They have different names from my mother's children – but she insists on calling them by the names of her children! I never leave her alone. If she is alone, the tears come to her eyes. I know what she is thinking of. Quickly I say to the children, "Go, go to your granny." They run to her, put their arms round her. She smiles. I explained to them about the names. They understand. She lives with us, of course. If she asks for anything, whatever it is, I bring it to her. I'll look after her always."

Ahmed still lives and works in Jabaliya camp at the northern end of the Gaza Strip, where he is now a head teacher. There is always a warm welcome in his home there for anyone who comes in friendship, whether Jew or Gentile; but he still bears the scars on his legs where he was wounded as a baby when with his family he was driven in 1948 from his native village during the Zionist "War of Independence". His story has been related here as he told it me.

Ismail Faggawi's story

Ismail, also a teacher of English, is a thoughtful, sensitive man with intellectual interests. He lives with his wife and children in a tiny house in Khan Younis camp near the southern end of the Gaza Strip. In a corner of his little sitting-room is a small bookcase crammed with books. He has set his heart on upgrading Palestinian education – on making it more "learner based", and more appropriate for Palestinians. In 1992 he was awarded a British Council scholarship to study in Edinburgh, and has completed an MA in Education.

"Our home was in Jaffa, but I was born in exile – here, in the Gaza Strip. My mother and father told me what happened. Jaffa faced the same fate as Deir Yassin and Qibya. The Jews had some military settlements round Jaffa, and when their opportunity came they shelled the town. We, the civilian population of Jaffa, were unarmed. Our family's house was not strongly built, so they tried to find a shelter. But they failed. Then someone told them, "We can escape by the sea." They gathered together with their neighbours and went down to the beach, where the small Jaffa port is. My mother told me that she saw Jaffa families with their children and old men and women getting into boats. They sailed south in the direction of Majdal. The sea was rough. She saw a boat turn over and the people drown.

"My grandfather ordered the family back and they made their way home through the shelling, which was coming from one of the Jewish settlements near Jaffa. He learnt there was a truck going to Majdal, and that the British army was patrolling the road to the south and allowing the Palestinians to leave. So they got into the truck and came here. Thousands and thousands of Palestinians came down to this sandy area: to Khan Younis, to Rafah. They had to live between land and sky. There were no houses for them, no shelter, no food. Quakers came to help these miserable people – with wheat, fish, blankets. Then UNRWA started to help the Quakers."

My own road to Gaza, to Jerusalem, and elsewhere in Palestine took over half a century, with many twists and turns on the way.

But my journey began in an inward sense, in India.

---

1   A non-collective settlement.

2   Ahmed uses the word Israeli which is what he grew up with. It is a slight anachronism. At the time he speaks of, the State of Israel had not yet been declared.

CHAPTER ONE

An Anglo-Indian childhood;
the origins of an idea

The procession of bullock carts wound its way down the mountain, jungle on either side of the road. From an open space on the right, I could see, from where I was sitting in one of the carts, other mountains rising like pyramids from a wide, flat plain. It must have been very early in the morning, for it was slowly getting light. Inside the grown-ups sitting near me I could sense a feeling of sadness. It was in me too. We were leaving Kodaikanal in the Palni Hills, South India. I had been born there two years before, in 1917, the year of the Russian Revolution and the Balfour Declaration: two events which left a heavy imprint on the rest of the century, and in a peculiar way influenced my own small destiny.

My next memory is also one of twilight, but it's evening and in England and I am in a strange place, alone except for the woman holding me by the hand, and the feeling is no longer one of just sadness but of acute misery. Two huge dark yew trees stand by the garden path leading up to a grey stone house. I had just been left by my parents in the village of Uley, in a valley of the Cotswolds. Here I was to stay, apart from one break, for the next six years.[1]

Mrs Phillips of the Gables, Uley, took in "Anglo-Indian" children to make a living. She was the widow of an Indian Army officer, and preferred little boys to little girls, "gals" as she called us. I had a painful longing for my parents. They were somewhere behind the trees along the crest of a hill the other side of the valley. When would they come for me? I was often caned, often humiliated. Still very small when "taken short" on the stairs, I screamed as the pee cascaded down the bare oak staircase. It was a moment of terror. The expected beating came, and I was sent to bed as an additional punishment. My punishments were often doubled in some way.

I had to start lessons at three years old. They were pain and grief to me. Rows of pot-hooks with a grey slate pencil on a grey slate…When not quite the right shape, they had to be rubbed out and I would have to start again, and again – squeak, squeak. And the reading! I found that very difficult indeed and would cry a lot during lessons. Eventually, I was tried out on a book called *Reading without Tears*, which I found more difficult and tear-provoking than ever. It had horrid little people crawling about the capital letters; but the reader I remember most clearly was one which started off with a picture of an ox. "I am by the ox. He is on the ox", etc. What exactly *was* an ox? We only knew about bulls and cows. All the pictures were very old-fashioned. Even in those days little girls didn't wear black stockings with long-sleeved white dresses, and people didn't go about in gigs. So when in my reading I came to the word "gig", I was stuck. Inevitably, I was taken to the room where the cane was kept lying in the white cupboard inside the door. The worst moment was watching it being taken out. However, in spite of the difficulties, by the time I left the Gables reading had become my refuge.

And the Gables had its compensations. There was a large and beautiful garden, and beyond it a field sloping down to a stream with golden kingcups and geese: we heard their cries first thing in the morning. Twice a day, morning and afternoon, we were taken for a walk, up the hill to the top of the "Bury" (a long hill with an ancient burial ground at the top); through woods and fields and along quiet lanes: in springtime looking for the first violets, celandines, and primroses – triumphant when we found a four-leaf clover, a six-petalled primrose or a white violet: they were supposed to bring luck. And in those days there were fields full of cowslips – so many that we could make cowslip balls. In autumn we could go nutting along the hedgerows. Where are the hazelnuts now? Sometimes, when our walk led past the blacksmith, we would dash ahead so that we could watch him if he was at work bashing a red-hot shoe, sparks flying. There might be a great cart-horse which would patiently lay a hoof onto the blacksmith's leather apron to have the new shoe fitted.

There were no bedtime stories, except as a treat on Sunday evenings. Mrs Phillips would first of all gather us round the piano and we would sing hymns, and then she would either read to us from a big illustrated book, *The Life of Jesus of Nazareth*, with pictures of Palestine and Palestinians (as I now realise) in their "biblical" i.e. their traditional dress, or she would tell us stories herself both from the Old and the New Testament. In winter we were able to enjoy her sitting-room fire for the stories; in summer we sat on the lawn. I suppose that it was this that first gave me the idea, when about five, of becoming a missionary and of "doing something for poor and unhappy people". That was what Jesus of Nazareth did...

The establishment had its pets: two white bull-terriers and sundry cats. My favourite was a black female cat called Kitty Kumbly, who used to come to bed with me. In winter she was a boon, warming the ice-cold sheets. One pitch-black night I felt something very strange in the bed – small, squirming, slimy things. I began to throw them out. As fast as I threw them out, they returned. It was a nightmare. The following morning at breakfast Mrs Phillips announced that Kitty Kumbly had had a litter of kittens and I had been very cruel. Each child could have one of the kittens "except Eleanor, because she doesn't know how to look after animals". Then indeed, I felt the sting of injustice. Like most small children I loved animals, particularly cats. I hadn't realised what was happening, never having seen kittens actually being born; and the room was in total darkness. There was of course no electricity in the house and we children were not allowed candles and matches by the bed.

One winter we were invited to a fancy-dress party in a neighbouring village. My parents had sent me a beautiful little pink sari, with silvery borders. Mrs Phillips had taken it away, but I looked forward to wearing it at the party. At the time, a girl of my age, Esmé Penny, was staying for a while at the Gables (children came and went, but I stayed on forever, it seemed). The evening of the party arrived. I was given a black Old Mother Hubbard dress to wear; Esmé, my sari. She looked very pretty in it and was much admired. Old Mother Hubbard did not get a look in. Esmé became very excited, and tore around so that the sari came loose and part of it dragged on the floor. Old Mother Hubbard trailed after her miserably. "Please, Esmé, my sari! It's getting trodden on!" The sari was given back when I left the Gables, and sixteen years later came in very handy for a school play, in my first job as a teacher.

When I was about six, there came a big change in my life at the Gables. My parents had long leave from India. They brought back to England year-old twins, Jack and Jill, who were installed in an upstairs room at the Gables with a very kind village woman as their nanny.

Our father was in the ICS, the Indian Civil Service. In 1919, when I was brought home, it was not considered good for children's health to keep them in the tropics: not only on account of the heat, but because of the diseases against which there was then no protection. There was vaccination for smallpox but no immunisation for cholera, bubonic plague, or for other deadly fevers that strike unexpectedly, and no antibiotics.

"Every mother was forced to make a choice between children and husband…a major sacrifice either way; and the children learnt that most dreaded of 'Anglo-Indian' customs – separation from one's parents at an early age."[2] Usually they did not suffer this trauma before the age

7

of five; but in 1919, when I was brought back, there had been anti-British riots in the north and my father was afraid they might spread southwards. Perhaps it was British families that suffered as much as anyone in the days of Empire. My two elder sisters, "Bobbie" and Nancy, had some years before been parked in England. My elder brother Michael, who had stayed in India with his parents because of the war returned to England when I did, to go to prep. school. I was the fourth child and I think the supply of relatives and friends to take responsibility and provide a home when needed had been exhausted by the time my turn came to be left. The twins were fortunate in having their own Nanny.

Our parents had no home to come back to on that long leave, and as life "on the Continent" was cheaper then than in England, they took us all – six children and Nanny – to France and then to Switzerland. First we stayed in Touraine. It was a beautiful summer, with fruit galore of every kind. Walnuts were dropping off the trees which lined the country roads around our pension. The vineyards were laden with grapes, and there were peaches, pears and plums. In the nearby village of Bouret there was the smell of wine being made.

From Touraine we went to Switzerland, to St Cergue in the Jura Mountains. In the fields pale autumn crocuses appeared through the first powdering of snow. Across the Lake of Geneva stretched the chain of high Alps. In the evening we would watch Mont Blanc and its fellow snowy peaks turn a rosy pink in the sunset.

The twins, Nanny and I returned to the Gables. Nanny greatly improved my lot there. She used to buy out of her own money luxuries for the twins such as butter and oranges, of which there were none downstairs, and then invite me up to share in her bounty; and before we all left the Gables she did something about my clothes. "You have no summer clothes at all. That won't do," she said, and she made me straight off five cotton frocks – all in the same simple style, but in different colours. I was thrilled.

Mrs Phillips had a daughter, a nurse. After working in Cairo for a time, she brought home a beautiful white donkey, which in due course produced a foal. The white Egyptian donkeys in Gaza have always reminded me of those first white donkeys I knew. We had one wonderful walk with them, going far afield, up the hills and onto the plateau to the big, wide world. When we were tired we had rides on one of the donkeys.

A child's early years are probably the most formative of its life. Did not the Jesuits say, "Give us a child till he is seven years old"?

The Gables gave me two good things which have remained with me: a fellow-feeling for those unjustly treated – a feeling which grew with the years to be a passion; and a great love of the countryside. I have wished so much that children doomed to live in big cities, shanty towns, and refugee camps could have the chance to feel grass under their feet, climb trees, and watch the sunset behind the hills and fields. In later years it was sometimes possible, with help from other people, to give to a few such children some contact with the natural world of which they had been deprived. When I was married, with children of my own, we had some of the same age from the slums of London to stay with us for short holidays in the summer; and when Unipal[3] started, real summer camps were organised for children from the refugee camps in the Gaza Strip, with outings, and bathing in the sea.

In 1926, when I was nearly nine, we left the Gables. Our mother had come home for good. She was not well, and I think she felt it was time to look after her children herself.

Once again we had no home of our own, so the twins and Nanny and I went with her to stay in a guest-house in the Severn valley. The countryside, though flatter than that round Uley, was green and lovely, and I was allowed to wander in the fields by myself. But most of the time I read. The various story books edited by Andrew Lang were fascinating, particularly *The Arabian Nights*. My mother gave me lessons: history and handwriting. She was determined I should write better, and for a time I did.

One day an amazing thing happened. I spilled something down one of my new dresses, but no beating followed. My mother just told me to go and change. Surprised, I asked her, "Aren't you going to punish me?"

"No," she replied. "It was an accident."

This was something new.

From my mother I began to learn about our father's work in India.

Once, during an epidemic of bubonic plague in the district for which he had responsibility, the inhabitants of a village had to be evacuated to allow the complete elimination of the rats which spread the disease through their lice. It was reported to him that villagers were going back to a certain hut at night. He decided to investigate himself. When he went in he found a little girl who was very sick: she had both smallpox and plague; so he picked her up in his arms and took her to where she could get proper treatment. He had been vaccinated against smallpox at least twenty times. "I had it done in front of the villagers whenever there was an epidemic," he told me, "to give them the courage to have it done too." It was very distressing, though, to learn that he felt in the course of his duties as a magistrate that he had to obey the law and condemn to death someone who had committed a murder. (It is only comparatively recently, in 1969, that capital punishment was abolished in UK.)

He had a strong sense of duty; and this virtue once brought its own reward. To return to India after leave during the war he had had a choice – to go by a slow boat which would extend the risk of being torpedoed, but would get him back to work on time, or take a fast boat which would surely reduce the risk, but which left England later and arrived late in India. He chose the slow boat. It was the fast boat which was torpedoed.

He came home a few months after our mother. Without his wife to look after him he had become very ill. Never strong, having had asthma since boyhood as a result of whooping-cough, in India he developed malaria too, attacks of which came on even long after his retirement. Towards the end of his service he was to have had a plum job – that of Collector of Madras city, the equivalent of Commissioner in North India. But he had incurred the wrath of the State Governor – for having objected to the imposition of what he thought was an unjust tax on the poor. As punishment he did not get his promotion but was sent up country to a malaria-ridden district instead. There he was so ill that he was obliged to return to England – a few months short of twenty-five years' service: and so with a reduced pension. Consequently, we were rather hard up.

Our parents had to find somewhere to live where the climate would be suitable for his health. They took lodgings in Seaton, south-east Devon.

That autumn Nancy and I went to a boarding school in Sandgate, Kent. It had a strange Latin name, "Conamur" – "we try". Nancy and I did not fit in well. We never had the right school uniform. For some reason, my mother, who after more than twenty years in India was something of a Rip van Winkle, had remembered the fashions of her youth and had knitted me long black woollen stockings, which I hated, for everyone else wore brown ones. I was often ill, and at the end of the year begged my parents not to send me back.

It was about this period that I was sent to stay with grandparents, just before we started at Conamur and then in the holidays.

Our paternal grandfather, Charles Reilly, had a bushy white beard and a loud voice: I found him an irascible and alarming old man. Formerly a gifted architect, he had designed the first underground restaurant in London – mastering the difficulties of drainage, plumbing and ventilation, new at that time. In payment he was offered a lump sum or shares in the company. Unfortunately for his descendants, he chose the former. The company, hitherto unknown, was Lyons! He bought a beautiful old Jacobean house in Upminster, opposite the church. Today it would have been preserved as part of the national heritage; but, sadly, a row of shops has taken its place. In the large old-fashioned garden was a cedar tree under which Byron was said to have composed part of *Childe Harold*. Two of his four sons became distinguished – one, Chief Justice of Mysore State in India; the other, a well-known Professor of Architecture. Their sons in turn did well and received knighthoods, one of them a peerage as well. But our branch of the family never had such distinctions. Our father was just a very intelligent and well-educated *good* man; his Victorian sternness was tempered by real kindness.

Our maternal grandfather, Robert Dunthorne, had been an art dealer, with a show-room at 5 Vigo Street, off Regent Street, and was a friend of a number of well-known artists of the time – Whistler, Watts (who painted my mother's portrait) and others. In fact, there are several portraits of our mother in the family by different artists. I have an etching of her by Helleu; she is playing the violin with the bow at an impossible angle. Another friend was Alfred Gilbert, the sculptor, who created the statue of Eros that stands in the centre of Piccadilly Circus. He made a beautiful little bust in ivory of our Uncle Gordon, the youngest of the Dunthornes, as a gift to our grandparents.

Grandfather had come of Norfolk farming stock. As a boy of twelve he had started work in London as shop assistant to a pawnbroker, sleeping at night behind the counter. A combination of business flair, discernment in pictures, transparent honesty, and a warm personality eventually had their reward – he became a rich man. As was the Victorian custom (cf. Soames in the *Forsyte Saga*), he built a fine house with a huge garden outside London. He had been dead some years when I stayed there. Grandmother, I am sorry to say, was a bad-tempered, selfish woman; my mother told me she gave her hell over her engagement to father. I have a reproduction of a portrait of her (she too had a reputation for beauty), but I cannot put it up because of the evil expression on her face, an expression of hatred.

I remember her brother, our great-uncle Emery Walker, as a kind hospitable man. He used to give a party every year for friends and family on "boat race day", when Oxford and Cambridge university crews compete on the Thames. His garden ran down to the river, so we had a splendid view. Uncle Emery was an engraver, typographer and antiquary and a close friend of the more famous William Morris, to whom he was adviser for the Kelmscott Press. It is said he had an important hand in the great improvements in printing and book design that have come about this century. His house, 7 Hammersmith Terrace (which now has a blue commemorative LCC plaque on the outside wall) was full of Morris designs; on wallpapers and furnishings. Morris is reported to have said that he regarded that day lost on which he did not see Emery Walker; and Uncle Emery nursed him during his last illness.[4] Our great

11

uncle had a magnificent library, and was generous in allowing its use to others. My elder brother had the run of it and borrowed books on heraldry which interested him at the time. The library was purchased recently by the Cheltenham Museum and Art Gallery.

What first brought Morris and Uncle Emery together was "a common desire to improve the lot of their fellow man":[5] they first met on their way home from a Socialist meeting in Bethnal Green. Uncle Emery became the secretary of the Hammersmith Socialist Society, started by Morris. George Bernard Shaw lectured for it and said that it provided "a platform on which every Socialist was proud to speak".

Our mother had studied art at the Slade School and was a contemporary there of Augustus John, later a well-known portrait painter. His behaviour alarmed and shocked her. She and a friend, she said, had once had to barricade themselves in a room to escape his amorous advances. She was good at draughtsmanship, and came higher than Augustus John in an exam on anatomical drawing, which must have given her particular pleasure. Apart from fine art, she had other accomplishments – piano, violin, languages, and writing. From the proceeds of some stories for children, written when she was nineteen, she bought a beautiful bureau, of which I am now the lucky possessor.

After I left Conamur my father took his turn for a while in teaching me: setting me sums, and the whole of one of Macaulay's *Lays of Ancient Rome* to learn by heart. By then, he had bought a house in Seaton. It was full of books: an education in itself; and I read what I wanted: the Tarzan and William books, Scott (we had a complete 1832-4 edition), Thackeray, Jane Austen. For Tarzan and Jane Austen I had an equal passion. *Pride and Prejudice* I read standing in my pyjamas on the bare bedroom floor with my hand on the light switch by the door in case I heard my father's footsteps on the stairs, for there was a strict rule about early bed and lights out. Dickens I did not much care for in those days; but there was a complete, bound edition of his periodical *All the Year Round* in several volumes, so I read Wilkie Collins's *The Moonstone* in its original serial form, in double columns of small print. After "to be contd." one chased up the next exciting instalment. And there was a very special complete edition of Shakespeare from William Morris's Kelmscott Press, on hand-made paper, with Morris's designs in the margins. I wonder if we children appreciated enough how lucky we were with such a library in the house – or, indeed, with so much else we had.

There was also Arthur Mee's *Children's Encyclopaedia*, from which I learnt the notes of the piano, and then went and strummed at the home of a friendly neighbour. I kept begging our father to get a piano and allow me piano lessons; but other things, which the whole family could enjoy, had to come first: a wireless – how unbelievable it was that one could hear music from Rome coming out of that strange little box! It contained "accumulators" – jars with knobs on top and a liquid inside. From time to time they had to be taken to the shop to be recharged. Then came an ancient Morris Oxford tourer, with a hood which went up and down, and perspex windows which slotted into holes in the body-work. When the perspex split, it was mended with sticking plaster. Then the *Encyclopaedia Britannica*. At last, when I was thirteen, there was a piano – a grand! For two years I had piano lessons with rather a dry, dull teacher. I passed on what I learnt to my younger sister, Jill.

The house itself was quite extraordinary. One day, when we were still in lodgings, I had been wandering on the beach by myself, when, looking up, I had noticed what seemed like a fairy castle on the cliff above me. It had battlements and turrets, and was a lovely golden yellow. I could hardly believe my eyes. It was two-thirds of that "castle" that my father had bought! In reality the whole affair was three cottages thrown together, with the battlements and turrets added as a kind of decoration. Inside it was a mixture of very poky rooms and enormous ones, connected by passages; on the first floor by a little gallery. There was a veranda with a long balcony above, and bedrooms facing the sea. One could spend hours gazing out into the bay: even when calm, the changing colours fascinated. When the fishing boats came in to the beach, one of us would run down and buy herrings for dinner. In autumn and winter we were battered by south-westerly gales and the walls got very damp from the salt spray. There were little gardens front and back: true to cottage tradition the front one for flowers – though it had a miraculously prolific loganberry; the back garden for vegetables and fruit. That had a *blue* rose.

The school the twins and I were sent to eventually was a private school about ten minutes' walk up the hill. Basically a boarding school for girls from affluent families, it accepted a few day-girls – rather looked down on by the boarders. However, I did enjoy the lessons and eventually the games, though I was no good at lacrosse for a long time. When at last I had learned to catch and throw with the crosse, I loved it. Of all outdoor team games it is surely the best. The ball travels through the air, not along the ground, as in football and hockey. Lacrosse, given its name by French settlers, originated over 500 years ago with the Iroquois Indians.

In Seaton my father, although not strong, still managed to do work for the community. He was elected onto the Town Council and I can still see in my mind's eye the covered garbage lorry that he instituted (there had been open carts before) with printed on both sides, "Burn your refuse, save your rates". Perhaps he had in mind the Indian way of disposing of rubbish by burning. It was long before the days of plastic and the plethora of wrappings that we now have. Seaton was then something between a fishing village and a small country town. When we first arrived there, it still had a horse bus that took travellers from the railway station to their individual addresses.

For all his interest in the Council, what our father cared most about was the League of Nations. He was not quite a pacifist, (and my mother most certainly was not); but he had a hatred of violence and he worked hard for the League of Nations Union. An excellent speaker, he once came to the school, where I listened to him with pride. The other girls were very impressed too, but horrified when he referred to the Armed Forces as "having to train young men to kill". Many of the girls had brothers or relatives in them. I do not think they had given a thought to what the job could involve; they were just enamoured of the prestige of uniform and rank.

Our mother, too, tried to help the wider community, though she was very limited in what she could do, by her own frequent ill-health and the fact that she had a large brood to care for and a rambling, inconvenient house to run. She did most of the cooking herself, and abhorred anything ready-made or tinned. She also made most of our clothes. Washing was done by hand; the ironing with flat irons heated on the kitchen stove, like Mrs Tiggywinkle's, and then slipped into a metal "shoe".

It was the time of the Great Depression and the Hunger Marchers; and I heard for the first time the word "unemployment". It had a sinister ring. Soon a couple of young men, unemployed Welsh miners, turned up to help my mother in the house. It was the only way she could provide some work for those needing it; and it was an unmitigated disaster. One incident sticks in the memory. The kitchen was a long way from the dining-room, down a passage, so we had a bell, and when the first course was finished it was rung so that the second course could be brought in by whoever happened to be in the kitchen. The second course was on its way and we heard a thump at the door. Presently it opened with a resounding clatter. A tray containing the "afters" emptied its contents on the floor – china plates smashed, sticky baked apples rolled in every direction. After only four days, the two boys disappeared suddenly. I had a glimpse of them hurrying up the road with a suitcase between them. Poor fellows! Poor parents!

Next, we had an unemployed Welsh miner and his wife, and they lasted somewhat longer. The husband sat in the kitchen. He was large and lethargic, and his wiry little wife did the work. She was very depressed. So my mother's efforts to help the unemployed in this way were not exactly successful. What was perhaps more so was what she did for the succession of men who came to the door needing food and cast-off clothing. She never turned anybody away empty-handed, always giving the caller a meal and frequently some garment that was not wanted. Unfortunately, on one occasion she gave away in error my father's best hand-made Indian boots.

Our family life at Seaton could not be called happy. We children came together from very different backgrounds and were strangers to each other. We were strangers to our parents, too, and they to us. Being hard up added to difficulties: doctors' bills and the cost of medicines were a constant worry.

In 1932, when I was fifteen, we moved to London. My brother Michael wanted to become a doctor, and needed to go to medical school. I sorely missed the countryside and the sea; but a new and exciting world was opening up.

---

1   Laurie Lee's *Cider with Rosie* takes one back to just such a village at the same period.

2   ed Charles Allen, *Plain Tales from the Raj*, Deutsch/ BBC 1975.

3   See Chapter Eleven.

4   Philip Henderson, *William Morris: his Life, Work and Friends*, Thames & Hudson.

5   R C H Briggs, *Sir Emery Walker, a Memoir*, 1959.

CHAPTER TWO

London: school and university

My younger sister and I were fortunate in being able to go to the North London Collegiate School, which had a high academic reputation. It meant working hard, but I loved it. The school had been founded in 1852 by Frances Mary Buss, a pioneer in women's education; and was considered a kind of sister school to Cheltenham Ladies' College, founded by Miss Beale, the posh school where my two elder sisters had boarded.

It was here that I discovered the joys of theatre, and that I could act. Though I revelled in comic parts, the most memorable occasion was when I was given the title rôle in a play written in verse by one of the staff, with a tragic Greek subject, *Andromache;* Jill still remembers this as the one occasion when she felt proud of her sister. When I became a schoolteacher, I found how immensely useful drama is in language teaching.

Once a week we used to go for the whole day to Canons Park, Edgware, where we were able to play hockey and netball as well as have lessons; and in the summer there was a pond for us to swim in. Waiting in the underground train at Edgware before it started on the return journey, we would amuse ourselves turning somersaults on the hangers – then leather loops. We could swing with our feet in the loops behind us before dropping down. Sad to say, a guard eventually discovered us and put a stop to this pleasant exercise.

Canons was an eighteenth century mansion with extensive grounds and had been the seat of the Duke of Chandos. Our lessons there included class singing. I used to try to imagine during singing lessons that perhaps it was in that very room that Handel composed when he stayed at Canons with the Duke. I am greatly indebted to those lessons, not that I could ever sing, but for what I learnt from them otherwise. After the move to London, my parents had to my great grief stopped my piano lessons so that Jill could have some; they said she had "a better touch". (So that's what came of my teaching her to begin with!) And they could not afford to pay for lessons for us both.

In London, my father found more good works to occupy him.

When in India, my parents had been in general on more friendly terms with missionaries and with Indians than with either colleagues in the ICS or other British people of a colonialist type. They did not frequent "the club", where most British residents in India would spend their evenings. My mother became interested in work for the deaf and dumb, teaching them knitting; and in various projects to help poor women to become self-supporting. In London my father linked up with the CMS (Church Missionary Society) and used to give talks on their behalf. My intention to become a missionary was reinforced and I tried to teach in Sunday School; but, since for weeks I was only allowed to observe, and not take a class myself, I gave up from boredom.

However, my father's main social work was as a visitor to Pentonville Prison. I vividly remember visiting with him a prisoner's family living in one room in a very damp basement. He took us all one day with the children of that family to Bertram Mills' circus, and laid on a fabulous tea afterwards at Lyons Corner House in Tottenham Court Road. My brother Michael kept the company amused at table with jokes and games and tricks.

Jill and I had not been long at the North London when Hitler came to power and the repercussions began to be felt in England. We entertained in our home some of the first refugees; to begin with, political ones: Social Democrats. One day I was asked to take two on an outing to show them something of interest in London; so we went to one of my favourite haunts, Parliament Hill Fields and Kenwood. Kenwood had recently been left to the nation and the house had a fine collection of pictures, including paintings by Vermeer and Rembrandt. The grounds reminded one of the country. We walked down Leighton Road to Kentish Town where we took a tram to the terminus at the Fields. On the way back the two Germans started to talk about the war that was coming. I simply could not believe them. I really did not understand much about what was going on.

Two other incidents stand out from my school days at the North London. A young man came to speak to us in the Upper Sixth about the wonderful things that the Jews were doing in Palestine: how they were pioneering, redeeming the land, making a home for a persecuted people. They were "returning to Zion". I was very interested and, when I got home, told my parents. To my surprise, for they were very concerned about the Jews in Germany, they were shocked. My mother asked, "Whatever is Miss Drummond thinking of?" (Miss Drummond was the headmistress). "Doesn't she know that there's another people living in Palestine?" It was the first inkling I had of what Zionism really meant. Looking back, I realise that my parents were quite unusual people. Although my father had been in the Indian Civil Service and dedicated to his work, he was not without sympathy for Indians who longed for freedom and independence. He once said to me, "Every right-thinking Indian wants us out." But he would have been devastated by the way independence came about in 1947: in haste, with partition and its tragic consequences. And the ICS in his time rightly enjoyed considerable respect.

It never numbered, the whole of the time the British were in India, more than about 1,400 – yet it governed a vast sub-continent: administered justice; dealt with famine and epidemic; and as far as possible prevented inter-communal friction and violence. It was certainly exploitative; sometimes harsh; but it was never cruel – as the army could be, as in the Amritsar massacre – and it was virtually incorruptible. To accept gifts of fruit or flowers was allowed; but my mother, as she told me, was chary even of doing this.

There was, at least among some ICS members, a genuine spirit of service, with the aim as it was expressed, of "preparing the Indians for self-government". Today, of course, that sounds patronising. Certainly, my parents were not colonialists in the usual sense of the word, and they had an understanding of what settling *en masse*, permanently, in another country would mean; and "redeeming" the LAND at the expense of its inhabitants was something which roused their indignation.

And, while we were at the North London, Mussolini was in power and announced that the Italians had a right to empire in the same way as other European countries, including Britain. He had his eye on Abyssinia (Ethiopia). The shock duly came. One day, on my way home from school, a poster outside the newspaper shop caught my eye: ADOWA BOMBED. That meant war. I hurried home, crying, and told my father. He sat stunned and silent. The League of Nations talked of collective security and there were rumours of sanctions; but nothing effective was done. The Italian fascist invasion and occupation of Abyssinia was barbaric. Bombs and mustard gas (the cruel forerunner of napalm and phosphorus) were used indiscriminately on civilians as well as the Abyssinian armies (Abyssinia had no airforce); and there was a three-day wholesale massacre of the inhabitants of Addis Ababa, the capital, as well as elsewhere in the country. Although the League had branded Italy as the aggressor, the British and French governments managed to prevent any action being taken to impede the Italian conquest.[1] As was to happen years later in the Israel-Palestine conflict, Westerners chose to support the strong rather than the weak; the latter, less well-known, less well understood, were not valued in the same way. The Emperor of Abyssinia, Haile Selassie, appealed in person to the

League in Geneva, but unavailingly. We saw in the papers photographs of his sad, low-key arrival in England as a refugee.

There was an inspiring French teacher at the North London: Caroline Senator. She was Jewish, and was in charge of the Jewish prayers that took place separately every morning from our assembly. The Jewish girls, about a third of the total, came in for notices at the end. She was my favourite teacher, and one of the best, if not *the* best teacher I have ever known. Even fifty years later I found very little in methods of teaching a foreign language that I did not learn from her then. She knew how to encourage us to think for ourselves, never spoon-feeding us, and she was able to instil a love of literature, especially of poetry and the music of poetry. I believe she was one of the most respected teachers in the school, and loved by many, including myself. So, though I am not really a linguist, it was thanks to Caroline Senator that I did French at university, with English as a subsidiary subject.

Our old school building in Camden Town was bombed during the war. Afterwards it was rebuilt and another "sister" school, Camden High School, moved in while the North London moved out entirely to Canons Park, where new buildings were added to the mansion.

In my last years at the NLCS I was befriended by an old friend of my mother's: Rosa Whitlaw – a remarkable woman. She told me that when she saw me come back from school one day, dog-tired, carrying a heavy satchel and a hockey stick, she had felt I was a child in need! She invited me to stay with her at "Periwinkle", a little old cottage in the Chiltern Hills, not far from Stonor. The countryside all round was unspoilt. "Auntie Periwinkle" became my life-line. I would stay with her for a week or two every holiday till the end of my time at university; and invariably for a few days before important exams. Solitary rambles in the hills restored health and spirits; and Auntie Periwinkle introduced me to the luxury of reading at meals. At supper-time on winter evenings we would sit with a book propped up in front of each of us, a paraffin lamp between us in the middle of the table to read by, a log fire in the grate. She was a gifted painter and knew several languages, Italian in particular; but apart from a governess in childhood she was self-educated. In her youth she had longed to be a doctor; but her brother, good for nothing as he appeared to be, must have everything spent on him: she, after all, was only a girl. She came nearest to her ambition during the First World War, when she was a VAD – a volunteer nurse caring for wounded soldiers. She would often reminisce about that. If she had had the chance, she would have gone far in the medical or any other profession where her gifts could have been used, I am sure. Over the centuries how many millions of intelligent, talented women must have been similarly prevented from making their own contribution to society, and how many still are, wherever you look! When eventually Auntie Periwinkle came into some money, she used it in a way characteristic of her: she founded a home for unmarried mothers to bring their new-born babies to – to regain their strength, learn something about motherhood, and have their confidence restored. It was long before "permissive" society norms. She had a warm, generous heart, as well as a brilliant mind.

Her cousin was married to the poet, Walter de la Mare, and we often went to have lunch at their house: a rare privilege for a schoolgirl. Mr de la Mare's conversation sparkled with poetry and wit – which was never malicious. The gaze of his blue eyes was penetrating; but one knew he was not looking for weaknesses. To me he was immensely kind. One day, he led me to a cabinet full of tiny objects sent him by admirers all over the world after the publication of his book *Memoirs of a Midget*. He took out a minuscule violin and put it in my hand. I promptly dropped it! Mr de la Mare picked it up – mercifully it was unharmed; but I was covered with confusion. Without saying a word, he took out something else and put that too in my hand. It was an object lesson never to be forgotten on tact, and on how to give an offender a second chance.

Knowing Walter de la Mare personally made me interested in his poetry and stories. Once I wrote a short story closely modelled on his style, which was published in the University College magazine. Unknown to me, Auntie Periwinkle sent him a copy. I was mightily relieved and pleased to hear that he liked it. Walter de la Mare's poetry is a poetry of the imagination, expressive of himself without being in any way self-centred. It seems to me to contain something of Wordsworth and something of Coleridge; but most of all a child-like wonder at creation, especially at the beauty of the natural world and the mystery that lies behind it. The last verse of *Fare Well* has haunted me:

> Look thy last on all things lovely,
> Every hour. Let no night
> Seal thy sense in deathly slumber
>   Till to delight
> Thou have paid thy utmost blessing;
> Since that all things thou wouldst praise
> Beauty took from those who loved them
>   In other days.

My ambition had been to go to Oxford, where my father had been at St John's; but my parents could not afford to send me there. In those days there were no student grants. State Scholarships were few and far between; no one in my year at school had one. To attempt an open scholarship for a place at one of the very few women's colleges (two in Cambridge, four in Oxford and no mixed colleges) was not even considered. I went to University College, London – progressively co-educational – which was within reach of home. The school had been generous to me. For my last two years there I had been given a scholarship, and, on leaving, a small exhibition which helped with the fees at UCL. My parents gave me a tiny allowance to spend on fares, books, stationery, lunches, clothes, club subscriptions, etc.: £39 a year (£3 every four weeks). To my dismay, I could not afford the 2/6*d* subscription for the Drama Society. I walked part of the way to college as a rule to save 2*d* on the bus, and economised on everything, buying the cheapest Woolworth's paper for lecture notes and essays. It was narrow lined and rather "see through". As I squashed up the words and wrote on both sides, not surprisingly there was once a remark written at the end of an essay – "your handwriting, though not exactly bad, is *very* difficult to read!"

London then had one great advantage over Oxbridge for a modern language student. We were obliged to go to the country of the language that we were studying for at least six months, including a term at a foreign university. I went to Grenoble; but spent as much time in the mountains as in the lecture rooms. For part of the vacation I stayed with a French friend with whom links have been maintained to the third generation of our families. During my last years at school I had started the habit of going to France in the holidays to stay "au pair", looking after children and/or giving English lessons, usually the latter. Every year while at UCL I went to a Burgundian family, who took me with them when they went on holiday: once to the French Alps, where we had long expeditions. The most memorable was up and over the Col de la Seigne into Italy, twenty-five to thirty miles. We set out the previous day, and spent the night in a mountain hut. At three o'clock the following morning we started out in the dark, with a guide, reaching the Col in time to watch the sunrise spreading a glow over the French peaks behind us, and gradually dispersing the mists among the Italian peaks ahead. Then we went down into a long valley running parallel with the Mont Blanc range, past a dozen glaciers to Courmayeur, and a sumptuous Italian lunch at the foot of one of the glaciers.

But for two summers running the French holidays had to be cut short by the threat of war. In 1938 there was Munich, when Chamberlain, by sacrificing Czechoslovakia to Hitler, gained a year's respite for Britain to prepare for the emergency. One hoped in vain that war would be averted altogether; but in 1939 it became a reality.

In the autumn of 1938, I became acquainted with a Christian Jewish refugee from Germany, when she offered me a chocolate as we were going up the stairs to the library at college. We soon became friends and remained so for more than thirty years. Her family had twice been refugees. They were Latvian but had lived in Moscow; and being a banking family, at the time of the Russian Revolution they had fled to Berlin. With Hitler, they had had to move again. But they were not impoverished refugees. When I first met Irene or Irina (she liked to be called Irina, having been born in Moscow), her father was somewhere in Latin America looking after, I think, his banking interests there; while she was with her mother in lodgings in London.

Irene's mother was very worried about a couple of Jewish friends who were desperate to get out of Germany. The British Government required £100 per person to be guaranteed before any refugee was allowed asylum in the country (£100 equals £2,900 in 1998). Moved by her anxiety I organised help amongst students and, with the permission of lecturers, all of whom were sympathetic, a box went round in every lecture and students dropped in their 2ds, 3ds or 6ds, week after week – whatever they had pledged beforehand. In this way, we raised the required amount; but it took a long time, at the end of which we heard that the Jewish couple in question had managed to emigrate to South Africa. We contacted a refugee agency and they advised us to use the money to help a Czech girl who, after the Nazi invasion of Czechoslovakia, was stranded in London and could not go home. She had the opportunity to join a Czech community in Calcutta, but she needed money for the voyage and other expenses. So Milada Sikorova had the sum collected from our tins and our best wishes. Sadly, we had no further news of her. Many people did what they could for Jewish and other refugees at that time, often having them to live in their homes. People were generous and welcoming; but (as now) the government was not. How many Jews perished, simply because £100 could not be raised in time to save them, will never be known.

To my delight, I learnt I had a place in Oxford for my postgraduate teacher's training. A dream was to come true.

Meanwhile, in the summer of 1939 London children were being evacuated, and volunteers were called for. As I had had to return early once again from France, I volunteered, and went with a primary school from St Pancras. Never shall I forget that journey. Helpers were each allotted a compartment full of children. They were all labelled and carried gas masks. We did not know where we were going. There was no corridor, and not long after we had started, one of the kids wanted to go to the loo. Then they tried to climb into the luggage racks. However, we reached our destination without mishap. It was 3rd September 1939, the day war was declared, and unusually hot. All the children wanted when we arrived and they tumbled out onto the platform at Kettering, Northants, was to have a drink and find the toilets. We were taken off to an official reception centre in a school, and local housewives picked the children and volunteers who were to be billeted on them at government expense. A young schoolteacher asked me to go and live with her, along with two small boys. I was there for a month. Kettering is an ugly town, with drab, regimented streets. One of my first jobs was to go round visiting the little evacuees to see how they were getting on. I came across two small boys locked in an embrace on the pavement crying their eyes out. What was the matter? "Where are the green fields?" they wailed. These unfortunate children had been told they would be going to a lovely country place and would see woods and fields, things that they could not see in the treeless streets of St Pancras, and that that would make up for their having left their Mums and Dads at home. At another port of call two small boys made me understand they were very happy: "She don't arf make some good puddins!" But at another the hostess was very angry. The children had wetted the beds, they were dirty, I was to find them another billet.

I was supposed to combine the evacuation experience with the teaching practice required before the training course began. Actually I did very little teaching; but I tried my hand at nature study because I could take the children out on rambles in the countryside round Kettering. This they loved. We collected leaves and autumn berries, and the children drew pictures and wrote it up the next day.

In Oxford the students on the course were mainly from Oxford University, but in the hostel where I lived we were from universities as far afield as Edinburgh, China, and Cape Town. I felt an immense sense of freedom during this year away from home. The young men, knowing that they would have to join the Forces at the end of their course, were determined to enjoy themselves. For the time being, it was only the "phoney war" (1939-1940). Frank was chairman of a Social Committee, and I was its secretary. We organised cycle rides in the countryside round Oxford, then unspoiled by the by-pass, and other modern structures. Frank and I arranged a dance – my first – and in June, as term drew to an end, he invited me to a ball. It was a simple wartime affair in New College dining hall, with the windows blacked out, and ending at midnight. There was a lovely moon; so Frank took me afterwards in a punt on the river. It was beautiful, romantic, and completely proper.

Of the theoretical part of the course I remember only one sentence, but that one, vividly. At the end of his impressive introductory lecture the Principal, M L Jacks, said, "…and let us remember that all our work is *sub specie aeternitatis*" (as I understood it, "seen from the perspective of the eternal"). With that, he picked up his papers and swept out of the lecture theatre. When I came to write my dissertation on the teaching of French, I wrote – sincerely, if somewhat sanctimoniously – that I saw it as a contribution towards international understanding and towards better relationships with fellow human beings: and therefore towards the fulfilment of the second of the great commandments, "Thou shalt love thy neighbour as thyself".

In the late summer of 1940 an intensive bombardment, the "blitz", started on London and other towns. We had made an "Anderson" shelter in our garden: a deep oblong hole with a corrugated iron roof curved over it and earth piled on top of that. It was exceedingly damp inside. My parents refused to use it, preferring the risk of being killed in their beds to the certainty of catching pneumonia. The shelter eventually filled with rainwater. Other members of the family were abroad (Michael, a doctor in the RAF, Jack in the Navy) or in distant parts of the UK. I slept first under the dining-room table which was very solid, and then in the kitchen, where a couple of pillars had been put in to support the ceiling, and a wall had been built outside the window as protection against blast.

I found the blitz a great strain. Every evening as dusk fell the siren went; and then the bombs began to drop all around us. It could be very noisy. What if the house were hit? Would we live till tomorrow? At the end of September I was glad to leave the air raids behind; but carried away with me a nagging anxiety for my mother and father.

My first job was in Northampton.

Though I was in full-time teaching for only four years (for many years in part-time later), what I discovered about teaching – the teaching of a foreign language in particular – determined the nature of the main work of my life, which began only well into middle age, when I was fifty-five.

1 Wilfred Thesiger, *The Life of my Choice*, Flamingo, 1995, pp 220-238.

CHAPTER THREE

First teaching jobs; first encounter with Quakerism

Ruth Marsden at Northampton High School for Girls was the ideal headmistress for a beginner-teacher. When she had appointed me, she had said, "You will be in charge of French throughout the school." She was throwing me in at the deep end. Most of the week at home before term started I therefore spent weeping from apprehension, so that my parents were alarmed. The reality was tough, but immensely rewarding.

Miss Marsden advised me, "Be kind and polite to the girls and they will be the same to you." She was right. And I wanted them to *enjoy* French, to learn both to speak it and to read it for pleasure. Miss Marsden allowed me to change the dull, old-fashioned course book the school was using for one that was more fun and would mean better results; and I managed to build up a small library of French story-books in each classroom, appropriate to the level of the pupils in them. I felt rich on £215 *per annum* in spite of having to pay back money borrowed for my teacher's training. The books really were read – and French came on fast as a result. We had acting in the classroom and out of it.

This, I learnt, was an adventure for the girls. The Upper V performed a French play for the school at the end of my first term. Mary, who took the principal part, said, "We've had no drama in the school before. It's marvellous!" In the summer, another Mary, in the Lower IV, took the part of the princess in *La Belle au Bois Dormant, (The Sleeping Beauty)* performed in the garden on Open Day. My child's pink sari served well as a pretend hedge of roses surrounding her.

Then there were the songs. Tape-recorders did not then exist, so in break or the lunch hour a few of the class to be involved would gather with me round a piano and we would learn a song. As I could never sing in tune myself, I relied on others to lead the singing. It was fun and seemed to work. Once, though, in the middle of *Ma Normandie* (which has a delicious but difficult melody) a solemn, bespectacled little girl raised her hand: "Miss Reilly, aren't we singing just a little bit flat?" We certainly were.

There were some outstanding teachers on the staff. An Irish painter, Alicia Boyle, with a strong, colourful personality, taught Art; Phoebe Jackson, English. Phoebe, ten years my senior, was new with me, and did much to boost my morale, as she had taught before. She was also to take some of the junior French. Both she and her husband were poets. When Phoebe arrived one morning with a poem in her head, Miss Marsden gave her permission to miss the first lesson in order to write it out. Phoebe and Alicia did much to educate me for Life, which I needed badly. They also took me along to Russian lessons with an emigrée Russian lady, and we were soon joined by Magda Clarke, the History teacher (now elderly and deaf, she has become a distinguished flower painter). We felt the need to learn the language of this people who had become our allies and of whom we knew so little.

After I had been at the school a year, Miss Marsden said we needed an extra French teacher. When two candidates came for interview, she asked me to try out their French. Janet Margesson I liked immediately. We talked about French literature, especially Flaubert and *L'Education Sentimentale*. Our views seemed more or less to coincide; and as she had been partly educated in Paris her French was better than mine.

Her father was a Conservative Cabinet Minister, and she had been brought up by governesses before continuing her education in Paris and at Cambridge University. She herself, however, was an active member of the Communist Party. I once went to a Party meeting in town which she chaired, and was tickled that members of the audience addressed her very respectfully as "Madam" instead of "Comrade" or even "Madam Chairman", as was the way in those days. She had an aristocratic bearing and accent. Never having been to school she had difficulties with discipline at first; but in the end I think she was beloved by everyone. Once she confided to me that she had a passion for beautiful clothes; but what she turned up in at school was sometimes remarkable. One winter morning she arrived wearing sandals and thick woollen socks with holes through which a big toe protruded on each foot. I suggested she change over the socks; but still the big toes stuck out. I guess there was some ribaldry in class that day.

Janet was one of the most brilliant, idealistic, and loveable people I have ever known. My daughter was named after her.

Drama soon took off in a big way at the school. Phoebe was helped in this by a flamboyant new English teacher, Julian Flaxman, who eventually went on the stage herself (and then, I heard, was so disgusted at what women were expected to do to make a career in the theatre that she became a Catholic and then a nun).

Julian dramatised Jane Austen's skit on the eighteenth century sentimental novel, *Love and Freindship* (*sic*: written when the author was

26

seventeen and still shaky in spelling). It was performed by staff for the rest of the school, Julian and I taking the parts of the silly young friends; and was hilarious.

My parents had stayed in London in spite of the air-raids. However, as soon as possible after my arrival in Northampton, I managed to find them lodgings, first in the town and then in a village nearby, so they could have a rest for some weeks.

One evening, when I phoned them after they had returned to London, I realised something was seriously wrong. My father was very ill, and my mother sounded exhausted. I begged Miss Marsden to give me a few days' leave so I could go and help. She did not like it. It was the summer term and my pupils would shortly be taking School Certificate and Higher ("O" and "A" Levels). But she relented, and I took the next possible train. When my mother opened the door, she looked aghast – afraid I had come to be looked after too. At that very moment my father was needing oxygen, and she had been unable to open the cylinder. Mercifully I managed to, under her instructions.

The air-raids had stopped for the time being; but our nights were disturbed by doors banging in the deserted, half-destroyed houses just opposite us all along the street. My mother and I decided one morning to put a stop to this. Entering one house after another like a couple of burglars we somehow fixed the offending doors. After that the nights were quiet.

For the rest of the term I would dash for a train at four p.m. every Friday, returning to Northampton on Sunday evening. Eventually my father had to go into hospital. He was never to be at home again.

One Sunday evening I was sitting in the train at Euston waiting for it to leave for Northampton. Gazing out of the window onto the platform I saw three people in conversation – an Indian and a middle-aged couple. They were talking Russian. Just before the train moved, the Indian sat down in the seat opposite me. I had a little book of Russian poetry to read on the journey; but I was still a beginner. Stumped for the meaning of a word in a poem by Lermontov, I ventured to consult him – for he had been speaking Russian fluently. He was able to help, and we got into conversation. He was a medical student on his way back to Birmingham, where he was living at Woodbrooke, the Quaker college; and he had spent two years travelling and working in the Soviet Union before the war. That interested me a great deal.

A few days later a little parcel arrived for me at the school. It contained Müller and Boyanus's Russian-English dictionary; and had a note inside – "from Sadashiva Shenai". So began for me a momentous acquaintance. ("On rencontre des gens bizarres / Dans les trains et dans les gares," teased Janet.) We met in London; Shiva came to

Northampton. He asked me to marry him, and I said, "Yes." For a time we were very happy. Then the skies fell.

My parents were horrified. Their friendship and respect for Indians did not, apparently, stretch to their countenancing the marriage of their daughter to one. (I might have known. Nancy had had a similar experience. But she and I were far apart in every way, and I was too young and too absorbed in other things to take it in at the time.)

They mustered their troops. Uncle Charles, the Professor of Architecture, was asked to talk to me and Shiva. Then a judge, an old friend from Indian days, had a turn. Next, a bishop. I had been invited during the Christmas holidays to spend a few days with an old friend in Southwell. The bishop there was our former acquaintance, Canon Barry of St John's, Smith Square, London, the church we used to attend (bombed in the war and now a concert hall). I was invited to lunch at the Bishop's Palace and there had another lecture. He asked me an astonishing question: "What do you think you'd feel like if you gave birth to a dark-skinned baby?" I should have answered, "So what?" but was too shy to say anything. Worse was to come. My elder brother, Michael, on leave from the RAF, took me to have lunch at his favourite restaurant in Soho, the "Shanghai". But it was no treat. He gave me a drubbing which, inevitably, reduced me to tears. To him I was just an idiot, and he was at pains to prove it to me in whatever way came to mind. "I suppose you think we should negotiate for peace?" he asked aggressively. Unconditional surrender was what the government and most people wanted at the time. I was afraid that that path would lead to yet more killing, suffering, and destruction. But negotiate with *Hitler*? I could only answer miserably, "I don't know."

"You see!" said Michael. "You don't think anything through. You don't *think* what marriage to an Indian will mean."

Perhaps he was right in relation to me; I shall never know. He was certainly right in one respect. I had not thought through the question of whether we should negotiate or not. If I had, I would have realised that to demand "unconditional surrender" was both unrealistic and cruel. At that time there was someone trying desperately to get politicians and public to see this – the "reluctant soldier", William Douglas-Home, younger brother of Alec, later to become Conservative Prime Minister; himself later to become a celebrated playwright. He stood three times for Parliament in by-elections as an Independent, on a platform of anti-unconditional surrender, and for the British government to announce its war aims and its peace terms. Though he did not win a seat in Parliament, he gained a great deal of support. Such an announcement, he was convinced, would encourage anti-Nazi elements in Germany. That there were such elements was eventually shown, but too late, by the July 1944 plot against Hitler, confirming Mr. Home's theory – later proved correct – that "approaches had been made at various times to find out what the Allies' war-aims were regarding those in opposition to the Führer's policy".[1] What patriotic soldier or citizen, in any country, would accept "*unconditional* surrender"? Would *we* have?

I wish I had known at the time more about Mr Home's efforts. What he has written about his feelings in the run-up to the war expresses very clearly my own inarticulate ones before the war started and as it progressed.

I felt the soul of mankind was being stifled…in the wealth of nationalistic speeches, in the flag-waving, and in the daily denunciations of those who were about to become our enemies, I searched – ever more hopelessly and ever more despairingly – for some detached, impartial, neutral voice, which by its mass appeal to human nature, might have stilled the roar of airplane engines and the rumbling of tanks, and held the dogs of war in leash. That voice, if it had spoken, must have been the voice that spoke beside the sea of Galilee; the speakers should have been the bishops, priests and deacons of the Church – the theme, the wild, impractical ideal inherent in the Gospel. Thus there would have spoken, in the midst of war – the voice that crieth in the wilderness without whose sound the world becomes a wilderness without a voice.[2]

But no such voice came from the Church, and the world seemed to have become a jungle with men bent on killing each other. (And now, what voices from the Church are raised against our ugly trade in arms, twenty per cent of the world's total, which fuels the wars spawned by previous ones?)

The pressure on Shiva and on me continued. By that time my mother was ill as well as my father. She had had a coronary thrombosis. Neither of them bullied me; but they made their feelings plain. I was bewildered and uneasy. Although twenty-five, it was my first real love affair. Was I doing the right thing? Shiva, not unnaturally, was upset and annoyed. Eventually we agreed it was best to part.

Two years later, Shiva came to my wedding – to someone else.

I left Northampton and took a post teaching French and English at a school which purported to be co-educational – Wanstead County High School, London E11. I was anxious to widen my experience and have more challenging work. Northampton High School was too nice. Wanstead certainly was an experience! Boys and girls sat separately in classrooms; lined up separately when they changed rooms; had different playgrounds; boys went by their surnames, girls by their Christian names. Men and women teachers had widely separated staff-rooms on different floors and most of the masters had been rejected for the Forces. They were not Conscientious Objectors to military service. A few behaved objectionably.

Walking down a corridor to take a Vth form French lesson one morning, I saw one of the boys peeping out of the door, on the look-out for my arrival. A master was walking in front of me and had not seen me. He went straight up to the boy and slapped him in the face – for nothing. I was appalled and angry, and tried (unsuccessfully) to make him apologise to the boy.

Being a young newcomer, I had been given the most difficult form in the school to be in charge of: the C stream of thirteen to fourteen year olds, not of the brightest, and at the turbulent age of adolescence: the kids no other teachers wanted. For the first time I had difficulty with discipline – especially when trying to teach English, in which I had had then no experience. The struggle it was – taking *As You Like It* with that form! The boys in particular took a delight in teacher-baiting. I realised they did not look upon me as a human being at all. Something must be done. So at weekends I got onto my bicycle and visited my pupils' homes, mainly in Dagenham and Romford, starting with that of the most difficult boy of all. He stared at me, chatting with his parents over a cup of tea. There was, as if by miracle, no more trouble. After a few such strenuous but successful weekends I felt the visits were no longer necessary. But a year at that school was enough.

Restless again, I decided to try primary teaching – and teach *children*, rather than *subjects*. The Inner London Education Authority, The ILEA, would fit me in somewhere, I was informed.

But air-raids then started again. The staff used to take it in turns to spend the night at the school to "fire-watch" in case incendiary bombs fell on the roof. We had had to do the same in Northampton, though nothing ever happened there; nor did it for a long time in Wanstead. One night in the spring of 1944, however, the whole horizon was aflame. Then, in the summer, came the V-bombs.

Cycling back after school to my lodgings in Ilford I would watch them as they droned overhead, then cut out and suddenly drop. There would be an explosion, and a cloud of dust. One evening as I turned into the road where I lived I saw the corner house had become a heap of rubble. My landlady had already fled, taking her small son with her, and I was living alone. After a time, Friends at the local Quaker meeting took pity on me. I stayed with them, and in the evenings when the siren went we would carry our bedding down to the vast, smelly, communal shelter that had been dug out under the park. As the summer term drew to an end we heard there were plans afoot to re-evacuate the schools. A letter from the ILEA announced that under the circumstances I could not be promised a job. I had already given in my notice at the High School, so I was soon without work and without anywhere to live.

Our family house in North London had been sold in 1943. My father had died that spring, and my mother, who needed to be looked after, was living in the same nursing home in Morden where she and my father had spent together his last months. The other members of the family were scattered far and wide, so I visited her as often as possible. On summer Sundays during the war with little traffic, it was easy (apart from the tramlines) to cycle across London from Ilford in Essex to Morden in Surrey and back again in the day.

I had become interested in the Society of Friends (Quakers) while still in Northampton, and, soon after starting my job at Wanstead, had been accepted into membership.

My interest in Friends had come about after the shattering episode over Shiva, when I became more keen that ever to fulfil the old dream, and work in India.

I had applied to the Church Missionary Society, been interviewed and, it seemed, approved of. And then came the forms: blue forms, with such questions as "What do you believe about the Trinity?" There were large spaces for answers to a number of questions on dogma. How, I wondered, was this relevant to the people of India? Anyway I could not answer the questions satisfactorily in my own mind, let alone write them clearly on paper. I agonised over these blue forms for some days, and then sent them back – empty. Enormous relief! I felt I had narrowly escaped walking into a cage. (I believe that the CMS scrapped the forms later and has become more development and human rights orientated.)

Then, walking down Tottenham Court Road one day in the spring holidays of 1943, I had bumped into Kurt Ostberg, a Jewish refugee acquaintance, whose parents had perished in Hitler's gas chambers. The British had sent him with many others like him to be interned in Australia (fearing them as a possible "fifth column"!), and he had just came back. Kurt had been a student at UCL where we had had mutual friends; but at that time did not know each other very well. However he recognised me; we had a meal together and exchanged news.

On hearing that I wanted to work in India, but felt I could not go under the auspices of the CMS, Kurt had said, "I think the Quakers sometimes take on non-Quakers to work abroad. Why not try them?" So I did. I was given an interview at Friends' House with Margaret

Backhouse, chairman of the Friends' Service Council. She said, "My dear, if you want to work with Friends, hadn't you better find out more about them first?" So she took me down to the Book Centre and gave me two little books: *Christian Life, Faith and Thought in the Society of Friends* and *Christian Practice*. I read them on the train back to Northampton. What a revelation, what a liberation! Here was a religious body without dogma, without paid priests or ministers; believing that every person – man, woman, child – has "that of God" – the Inner Light – within, so that each, in a way, can be looked upon as a priest. Clearly men and women were treated equally. There was worship without ritual, based on silence; much stress on simple living; on truth and honesty in all one's dealings; on kindness; and on practical help to those in need. Moreover, the Society had *a testimony against war*. In 1660 British Quakers had written to Charles II: "We utterly deny all outward wars and strife and fightings with outward weapons, for any end or under any pretence whatsoever. And this is our testimony to the whole world." (Quakers still hold to this testimony. In 1990 Friends' Meetings up and down the country received a letter from Friends House reminding them of it, because of the crisis in the Gulf.)

According to the custom, two Friends had been appointed to talk with me before I could be accepted into membership. One of them was Elizabeth Fox Howard, distinguished for her work on behalf of Jews in Germany. She therefore understood my position at that time: though deeply tormented by the war, I still could not wholeheartedly be a pacifist, for if ever there was an embodiment of evil, it was surely Hitler.

In the summer of 1944, therefore, at a loss what to do, or where to go, I thought of another Quaker organisation: the Friends' Relief Service. It had been helping people in bombed areas in the UK and would be sending relief workers into Europe as soon as the war ended. Supposing I could do work like that, really useful, which would be urgently needed? And England, after five years without the possibility of travel abroad, felt claustrophobic. For many years before the war I had been accustomed to spend some time in France. I do not think my motives were wholly altruistic.

Another interview at Friends' House. There was one vacancy left at the training centre for volunteer overseas relief workers, I was told. I was accepted for it! The next course began the following Monday, and I must be there the previous evening, Sunday, 17th September.

Basil McTaggart, a teacher from another school with whom I had made friends while at Wanstead, had already left teaching and joined the Save the Children Fund, then still a small and relatively little known organisation. I told him I had a place at "Mount Waltham" the FRS training centre in Hampstead. He already knew it. Some SCF workers were trained there; he had visited it several times. He also knew the Warden, who organised the courses. "You'll like Michael Aitken," he said.

---

1   William Douglas-Home, *Half-Term Report*, Longmans Green, 1954, p 179.

2   *Op cit* p 109.

CHAPTER FOUR

Work with Quakers in London and Le Havre

In the evening of 17th September 1944 I duly presented myself at Mount Waltham, 47 Netherhall Gardens. It was a large old house approached by a circular driveway with a monkey-puzzle tree in the middle. Opposite the house was a coach-house, always open, with two rooms above.

The Warden was welcoming new recruits in his office to the left of the spacious entrance hall. He was young (twenty-nine, I learnt later), and had a kind, reassuring manner. He took me up to one of the rooms over the coach-house, which I was to share with two other girls. My few possessions were already there, apart from my books, which were in store.

The next day, lectures began – on fascism (given by Professor Norman Baynes from UCL, whom I knew slightly: he had been an old school friend of my father's); on First Aid; on various infections and how they are spread; on Quakerism (the trainees were not all Friends, though all were COs). Every day began with a short silent meeting for worship. There were language classes: it was expected that we would be sent to Germany, France, Italy, Holland, or Greece. "Why Germany," I asked a fellow trainee, "when one knows what the Germans have done? Shouldn't we help those to whom they have caused so much suffering?"

"I think," she answered, "that the person who puts out someone's eyes is more to be pitied than the one who loses his sight." In the event, the first team sent to Europe found themselves in Germany caring for survivors at Belsen concentration camp.

There was practical work too. We learnt how to filter the dirty water in the rain tub and make it drinkable, and ate what we had cooked on a field kitchen we had had to set up. We learnt – in theory – how to deliver babies. One of the young men walked out on a film showing childbirth, unable to take it.

Michael Aitken would sometimes come up to me during morning break, when we all foregathered for a mug of tea and chunks of bread with peanut butter. He would ask my opinion about the language classes,

34

or in some other way open a conversation. I was puzzled and flattered by this attention.

The Quakers among us used to go to Hampstead Meeting on Sundays. One windy autumn Sunday as I sat in the silence, gazing out of the window at branches of trees tossing to and fro, a poem about the meeting took shape in my mind. By the end of the meeting it was complete. I quickly pencilled it down on returning to Mount Waltham. Avrilia Vlachou, a Greek who took some of the language classes, got hold of the poem somehow and showed it to Michael. This is what I had written:

Quaker meeting

> The silent square of worshippers,
> The ticking clock, and on the table flowers in a vase.
> Without, trees swaying in the wind;
> Massed branches tossed; the flickering of leaves.
> So come we here, each separate:
> Turned, lifted, twirled about, in self's perplexities;
> And as a body, pressed and buffeted
> In cross-movements of opinion
> Sweeping on (their origin unknown)
> Through closest foliage to far beyond.
> Yet stay we still, and feel the strands that subtly tie
> The leaf to twigs and other leaves;
> And branches firmly pass into the trunk,
> Where finally we meet,
> And draw the sap from calm strong depths of quietness.
> Nothing apparent, but the silent square,
> The flowers, and the ticking of the clock:
> Yet know we now, not only, "Thou, God; and I",
> But in a secret, wordless sense,
> "I, we, and Thou".

A day or two later Michael and I both happened to be looking at the notice-board on the stairs at the same time. He suddenly turned to me and asked if I would go out to lunch with him the following Sunday. We went to a Russian restaurant near Piccadilly, the "Troika". We talked and talked.

After lunch I went on down to Morden to see my mother and pick up my bike to cycle back on. That evening Michael asked if I would marry him. This time, I had no doubts whatever, and knew that even if my family objected, because he was a CO, I would stand firm. However, my mother liked him very much, and his being a Quaker helped. She had always admired Quakers! What attracted her in Quakers was the emphasis they placed on simplicity and honesty. She had taught me very firmly as a child that to tell a lie is a grave sin; that a person who lies is not to be trusted. I have never forgotten her words. Soon I learnt more about the moral courage it takes to be a male CO in time of war: the courage to face opprobrium and insult for the sake of what you believe to be right; and living close to Michael I began to understand more fully the basis of Quaker pacifism. If there is "That of God" in every human being, what right has one to take human life?

More than that, I learnt from him that one must actively look for the good in people – "that of God" – however much there may be in them to discourage the search; and one should try to encourage it to grow, as one encourages a feeble candle flame to grow bigger and brighter. And there was something else about Quakers[1], the Society of Friends, which I learnt: that they are not, or should not be, a body of inward-looking people, just friends among themselves. They are Friends of Truth, which means seeking the truth within ourselves as well as others; and loyalty to the truth, which means never knowingly telling a lie. If obliged to tell a hard truth, one should try not to hurt unnecessarily, but "speak the truth in love". It is very difficult. All too often, I think, we Quakers are too much on the side of the "softly softly" approach, so that hard truths, which should be told, are by-passed in our anxiety not to offend. Nowhere has this happened more disastrously than in the Israel-Palestine conflict, especially in the early years; less so now, in Britain at least. To allow lies to go unchallenged can surely be as mischievous as to tell them oneself. "All that is needed for evil to flourish is that good men say nothing".[2]

A friend said Michael was a good-looking man; but what mattered most to me was the kind look in his blue-grey eyes, and the confidence he inspired: something I needed very much. He was a "builder-up" of people and could put himself in another person's shoes, sympathise, and make allowances for failings. At the same time he was very wise in his opinions and his advice was always sound – qualities which made him eventually a very good Probation Officer. He had been a particularly competent relief worker in bombed areas – Bethnal Green and Liverpool; and for these reasons, I think, had been appointed to organise the training courses for relief work abroad. At Mount Waltham he was loved and respected, for he was gentle and humble and his sense of humour oiled the wheels of community life. It was a tradition there for him to read Thurber aloud after Sunday supper. Early in October – three weeks after we first met – he announced one supper-time that we were engaged to be married.

In the FRS office at Friends' House there seemed to be, though I could not account for it, some displeasure that I was going to marry Michael. I was sent for a time after the course came to an end to work in the students' hostel of the London Hospital. It had been lent to the FAU (Friends' Ambulance Unit). There I mopped floors, prepared vegetables, and mended linen. It felt like a punishment. Making arrangements for the wedding was rather difficult. The person in FRS responsible for my banishment to Whitechapel was herself married not long after and said to me, "I didn't realise what a lot there is to do for a wedding!"

We had a Quaker wedding – marrying each other – in the "small" meeting-house at Friends' House, Euston Road, on 16th December 1944. In the course of the silence, a Friend rose and said, "Know one another in the things that are eternal." Since then, I have thought much about those well-known words. They contain a truth more important than anything else in any relationship, I think, whether or not "the eternal" is acknowledged. I am pretty sure that even in the best marriages there may be difficult, agonising patches when the marriage nearly falls apart. If one is bound together with love rooted "in the eternal", one can come through. It was so with us anyway.

Michael was an immensely forgiving person. I wish more of his loving-kindness had rubbed off on me. But now he has died, he is still close, ready to help in times of perplexity *if I ask and listen.* This I know.

We stayed at Mount Waltham while Michael ran one more course, during which I had a training in case-work under Emmy Sachs, who was caring for Jewish refugees. Her office was in a Bloomsbury hotel which had been given over to refugee agencies. Then we made preparations for working abroad: we were measured for our uniforms, and we collected the necessary equipment.

Early in the summer of 1945 we were sent to Le Havre.

In September 1944, the RAF had bombed the town of Le Havre with thousands of tons of high explosive and incendiaries. Destruction in the bombed area was total. According to William Douglas-Home[3], about twelve thousand French civilians – our allies – were killed, though there were hardly any German soldiers there at the time.

The Quakers decided to send a team of relief workers to Le Havre, as a gesture of penitence and atonement. The team was made up of British, Americans, and French. The needs of survivors and the possibilities for meeting those needs had to be assessed. It was discovered that some houses on the fringes of the devastation could be repaired by good amateurs; clothes and food were needed and could be distributed; money too where appropriate and the need was most urgent. The team had already been at work for a few months when we arrived. John Kay, a French teacher, was its leader. When he had to return to his school, Michael was appointed to replace him; and I was to go as housekeeper to the team, which disappointed me. There turned out to be a local French one, Madame Aubel, and I thankfully took part in the relief work itself: not that housekeeping for a dozen people in a French town, where food was scarce after occupation and war, was an easy option, but what did I know then about housekeeping? And how relatively dull it would have been!

We lived in a small house, "l'Abimée" (the glass had gone from the windows), in a large garden, in the suburb of Sanvic, up on the escarpment to the north of the town. Dr Duclos and his family occupied the main house, and we soon needed his services. Only a few days after our arrival Michael went down with a severe attack of dysentery and was very ill. The bombing had destroyed sewage and water pipes, and everything was mixed up. There was a joke current that, if you turned on a tap, toilet paper would emerge. For a time I exercised authority as "housekeeper" and was fiercely strict over hygiene. Mercifully, no one else in the team fell ill. (To be honest, I do not think they had before.) It took Michael weeks to recover his strength. We went for a short time for him to convalesce to the Normandy countryside. Not far from Le Havre, at Héricourt, was a "preventorium" for children in the early stages of TB or in danger of developing it. Severe malnutrition was widespread in Europe after the war, and consequently there was much TB. Streptomycin had not yet been discovered as a cure. Quakers and other foreign relief workers had a link with the preventorium, having provided clothes and food for the children. There was a small house in the grounds, where visitors could stay, and we were warmly welcomed.

In spite of the misery all round, it was a strangely happy year. We were *doing* something – and that little something seemed enormously appreciated. It amazes me how resilient and how magnanimous people can be after suffering cruelly and unjustly. It was so, in the main, with the French of Le Havre. The relief team was a friendly one and made up of dedicated people, with enterprising ideas for how to help – ideas which they put into practice.

One day a goods train came into Le Havre station packed with men – deportees from Eastern Europe, mainly Baltic countries – whom the Nazis had brought to Germany as slave labour or press-ganged into their army. When the doors opened, emaciated creatures rushed out to find food – from rubbish tips, anywhere. They were starving. The local population did what they could. The worst cases were taken into one of the hospitals which still stood. Joan, one of the women volunteers, visited them. Soon she learnt that the French authorities were sending truckloads of these men somewhere else. Where to? The trucks left at dawn. Joan decided to get on board one and see. The men were taken to a camp near Dieppe. They needed clothes, blankets, and "extras", which were gradually provided.

Then there was "l'Hôtel Armstrong". John Armstrong discovered the shell of a house down in the devastated area which still had floors, and was unoccupied. Men were coming back from deportation and from German POW (Prisoner of War) camps to find they had no homes to go to, no one to welcome them. John decided that at least some would have shelter for a time and the best welcome he could give. He scrounged mattresses, blankets, utensils, food.

The team's work was centred in a few hutments in a yard on the way down to town from Sanvic, at the foot of one of the long flights of steps that connect the town with the escarpment. Michael had to spend most of his time there. Those who needed clothes or food or other help had, inevitably, to be "registered" and fill in forms; French officials liaised with and visitors welcomed; local French workers dealing with the distribution helped if problems arose. On Christmas Day he and I delivered boxes of goodies to impoverished families. Their surprise and delight made Michael say it was the happiest Christmas he had ever spent.

Two of the men, Bill (Wilfred) Brown and Peter Walsh, repaired roofs and windows. (Peter, in civilian life was an artist; and Bill a singer with a beautiful tenor voice.)

Four of us women took on *parrainages*. This meant visiting needy families and old people who needed financial relief and extra food or clothing. We worked separately, cycling along pot-holed roads. (On these cycling forays I had now cause to be thankful for the long woollen stockings my mother had knitted – grey this time. The FAU [Friends' Ambulance Unit] working with the Forces was obliged to wear khaki. We too had to wear army-style uniform, but as we worked with civilians we were allowed to have it in the traditional Quaker grey.) We went into some of the poorest homes. I found a family of five, three children, mother, and father with TB, occupying what had been a small henhouse. There was just room for a communal bed and a cooking stove in the corner. It was stifling. I besieged the town health officer for their transfer as soon as possible to one of the new one-storey concrete buildings that were rapidly going up. One day I got a joyful message from the mother asking me to visit her in her new home. It was bleak and bare, but it had three rooms and her TB husband could sleep separately. Elderly widows lived alone in attics without any mod con whatsoever: the loo and a cold water tap were down several flights of stairs in the yard. Madame Mouette was one such. Her room was at the top of stairs so badly damaged that it was like climbing a ladder: the middle part of each stair was gone. She was touchingly grateful for help, and insisted on doing something for me in return. She had been a seamstress. Had I any mending she could do? I had; and never have I seen such fine darning as that done by Mme Mouette. Madame Féron's tiny attic walls were *lépreux* – blotchy with damp, and the rain came in. She liked to talk of happier times with her husband and of their visit to Brussels. When we left Le Havre she gave me as a parting gift a little brass bell which her husband had bought there as a souvenir. It has a tiny replica of the famous statue of the little prince on top, making his *jet d'eau*... Monsieur Ducret I met in a queue at "Prixunic" (the French Woolworths). He was having a photo done for some official form. Tall, grey-haired, gaunt, and very shabbily dressed, he spoke with old world courtesy when addressed. There was something dignified and inexpressibly poignant in his appearance and manner. I asked if I might visit him. I found he rented a room in a house owned by singularly unfriendly people. It was without any means of heating whatever, and freezing cold. He said he did not mind. A cast-off American army sleeping bag lay on the bed. "Je me glisse là-dedans, et j'ai assez chaud," he assured me. The bag was brown, and the sheets underneath it, white originally, were shiny brown too, never having been washed; and the scrupulously tidy room was thickly dusty. M. Ducret liked to read, and had kept some old school books. He became a kind of *parrainage* and a faithful friend, corresponding with me after we left Le Havre in neat copper-plate writing. He had been a clerk. Dear Maurice Ducret. He even sent me a little book – a history of France's relations with Germany – which he wrote himself for me, all in that careful handwriting.

A friendship lasting till now has been with Anna, from the Ukraine. The Nazis had taken her from her home when she was only fifteen, for slave labour in Germany. There she met an emigré Russian from France who had fought in the French Army and become a POW. They married and came to live in his home town, Le Havre – and had then been bombed out. Anna needed shoes and came to Secours Quaker. She could speak no French, only Russian, so I was called on. We could find no shoes to fit her in the *vestiaire* (clothes store). However, a pair of mine did, perfectly. Anna was touchingly happy not just with the shoes but to have found someone she could talk with. Her emigré husband left her for another woman, and then she lived alone. When we made a return visit to Le Havre six years later she was happy again. One of the Baltic deportees who had arrived starving in the goods train had settled in Le Havre. Anton, a Lithuanian, became her second husband.

Anna, after about ten years of separation from her family in the Ukraine with no communication possible, found them again thanks to a Soviet Russian girl, Raya, who visited us in Cambridge. She too lived in the Ukraine. I gave her Anna's family's address, and also Anna's, in Le Havre. Raya did something that none of the other more prominent Soviet citizens I had asked had bothered to do. Anna and Anton have since made a couple of trips to the Ukraine. She wrote that her mother had died during the war, but her brother and sister were there to welcome them. And they have also been to Lithuania.

One day when I was at the *Magasin,* the distribution centre for clothes and food, a consignment of a different sort arrived. It was a case full of little sewing kits: needles, thread, scissors – all the basic equipment to "make do and mend" – just what was needed. Looking into one of the kits I discovered a message: "A nos amis français, avec les meilleurs voeux des élèves de Northampton High School for Girls"! And they did not know (as I later discovered) where exactly in France their kits would go, or where their old French teacher was. On our return to England, Miss Marsden asked me to give a talk to the school. I was able to tell those who had put the kits together that their gifts had arrived safely and to whom they had been given.

A couple of "waifs" lived for a time with the team. Gérard, a French boy in his teens, had no family left. He used to help in various ways and was handy with electrical repairs. Inge, a German girl, had somehow survived the RAF blanket bombing of Dresden – an even greater crime and tragedy than that of Le Havre. With all her family and friends dead, she had wandered westwards like a lost soul, somehow ending up in Sanvic. She devoted herself to a stray dog, which also lived with us. I can still hear her calling lovingly, "Meine Cora, meine Cora!" That little terrier, in default of all her near and dear, was something for Inge to love.

The full horror of the bombing of Le Havre was not generally known till forty-five years later. A British war crime, it had been conveniently swept under the carpet and forgotten. Then, in October, 1989, BBC 2 showed a film – *The Tragedy of Le Havre.*

Very moving information was given at the end of the film. William Douglas-Home, who had become an officer in the British Army, had distinguished himself by an unusual act of courage. Wildemut, the German Commander of the fortifications on the escarpment to the north of Le Havre (near where we had lived), had been asked to surrender. He requested time to evacuate civilians before negotiations began. The request was refused. He made a second offer – to evacuate to the town below all French civilians living in the fortified area, promising that he would send no German troops there if the British would give an equal undertaking not to bomb the town. That offer was also rejected. The Commander's son was interviewed in the programme. It is clear that Wildemut was known as a humane man. Former French Resistance leaders, also interviewed for the film, maintained that they had informed the British that there were very few German soldiers in the town, and only at certain points.

William Douglas-Home was ordered to be liaison officer for the combined attack of army and airforce on Le Havre. His reaction to the order was the logical and practical sequel to long, anxious thinking about the war, his campaign against "unconditional surrender", and then revulsion at what he saw in Normandy.

There were still three whole days, when William Douglas-Home received the order, before the battle was due to begin: ample time for the Le Havre civilians to have been evacuated. He refused to obey. He was court-martialled, cashiered, and sentenced to a year's imprisonment. Le Havre was bombed; but no attempt was made to bomb the German fortifications. Twelve thousand French civilians died needlessly; but not a single German or British soldier was killed or wounded.

His brave protest – which mercifully he made public by a letter to the press or it might have been hushed up – had one beneficial effect. The German commander of Calais was allowed to evacuate the French inhabitants before the bombing began there, so civilian casualties were few.

After the film I rang Mr Home. I am grateful to have had the chance to speak to this remarkable person; and since then to have read some of his books – in which an underlying seriousness is clothed in his special brand of delicious wit and humour.

Two years later, in 1991, another film was shown on BBC television – just after William Douglas-Home's appeal against the humiliating verdict of the military court had been turned down. It showed even more clearly the atrocity committed by the British, and the rightness of his stand. How lopsided things are! Nazi criminals were severely punished at the Nuremberg trials for *not* having disobeyed cruel and immoral orders; but one of our own people we punish and humiliate for having done just this. Is not the basic crime – war itself, for which politicians are mainly responsible?

By the summer of 1946 the energetic citizens of Le Havre were well enough on the way to rebuilding the city and its services to dispense with the modest help of foreign relief workers. It was time for us to go. We were all invited to a formal meeting at the *mairie* and treated to a *vin d'honneur* and speeches. Then came the sad personal goodbyes.

Before we left France Michael and I were offered the joint wardenship of the Friends' International Centre in London, then at

32 Tavistock Square. We accepted; but were able first to visit friends and Friends (French Quakers) in Burgundy and the south, make a short visit to Switzerland, and from there cross the border into Germany, so that Michael could meet once more the German friend with whom he had stayed to learn German in pre-university days. She lived in Freiburg im Breisgau. From Lausanne we went by train and then tram to the border with Germany; and then we had to walk.

As we stepped onto German soil some small boys appeared and appealed to us to let them carry our rucksacks on their home-made trolleys. They were barefoot and very thin, for there was little food in post-war Germany. We were grateful for their help, and though we had no German currency, it was clear how we should reward them. Arrived at the railway station we found some sandwiches in our rucksacks, which we began to distribute in the waiting-room. A little girl sitting opposite was watching anxiously. When we beckoned to her, she ran to us. To see those famished children enjoying food was very moving.

Michael remembered how to find his friend's house in Freiburg. It was in a pretty suburb apparently untouched by war. But when we got up the following morning we learnt our hostess had been out at first light to find bread for our breakfast. That day we went for a walk in the Black Forest. Before leaving, however, Michael and I decided we should see more of the town. Gretl preferred not to accompany us – and it was soon clear why. There was just a vast expanse of rubble; and over it a dead silence. This too was the handiwork of the allies. To me, it was even more horrifying than Le Havre, which, by the time we arrived, had been tidied up a little, so that the worst bombed area was largely empty.

While Michael and I were in Europe little news of the outside world reached us, and we were absorbed in what we were doing and the tragic sights we saw. It is hard now to realise how oblivious I was then to events in Palestine. On 22nd July 1946, Zionist terrorists of the Irgun under Menachen Begin (later to become Israeli Prime Minister), blew up the King David Hotel in Jerusalem. It housed the administrative offices of the British Mandate Government. Ninety-two British, Jewish, and Arab employees were killed. It was the start of a terrorist campaign on the part of the Zionists to drive the British out of Palestine. They eventually succeeded; and were then able to concentrate their attention on driving out the Palestinians, the indigenous people of the country.

The Friends' International Centre was, as the name implies, a place for people of different nationalities to meet. For some months we found it interesting and enjoyable to work there. It was partly residential: there were a few rooms for foreign visitors, mainly Friends; and there were frequent social gatherings during which one became quite adept at introducing people to each other without knowing their names beforehand. We also organised courses of lectures on specific countries: India and the Soviet Union, for example. In London there were experts to come and talk on various aspects of the countries chosen, and Michael was very good at making the right contacts.

We had our own little flat near the top of the house, but found it more and more difficult to spend time in it together. By now I was pregnant and longed for a home of our own. Since we had known each other we had lived a community life: at Mount Waltham, in Le Havre, and now at FIC. Michael spent an unconscionable time downstairs in the evenings with a girl who also lived and worked in the Centre; I was jealous and unhappy. However, a change was to come sooner than expected. Michael fell ill with viral hepatitis, and was recommended a long convalescence.

Agatha Harrison, a very kind and much respected Quaker with Indian connections – she had been a friend of Gandhi – came to our rescue. An acquaintance of hers had a studio in Porlock, Somerset, which she did not want to leave empty while she was abroad for six months. In those days it could have been requisitioned. Would we like it? We jumped at the offer.

Those six months – October 1947 to March 1948 – were some of the happiest and most peaceful we ever spent. Porlock was still a genuine, unprettified village with, in the main, local Somerset inhabitants. The "Studio" had a little steep garden and a view over a lovely valley. Exmoor was just up the lane. Michael now had time to think what to do for a permanent job. There was no thought of his going back to the FIC or being the industrial chemist he was before the war; and he was in no way a careerist. For him it was a question of doing something that was really needed by people in the post-war world. We now had a baby, Martin; and the chore of nappy-washing made Michael consider, briefly, the laundry business. But two things seemed to us at that time more important than anything else: the maintenance of peace and the production of food.

Michael decided he would try fruit farming. He was offered an apprenticeship with an apple-grower in Suffolk, and went off to house-hunt.

Before we left Porlock we made a very good friend from a prisoner of war camp in the neighbourhood. Remembering how we had had three German POWs to Christmas dinner at the International Centre and how much we had all appreciated it, I persuaded Michael to contact the commandant to find out if we could do the same thing again. It was decided that two men would come to us on Boxing Day: Hans and Werner. Every Christmas till his death more than thirty years later Hans used to recall that first meeting. The two came for lunch on Sundays for the rest of our time at the Studio. Weather permitting, we all set out for a routine walk with the pram in the afternoon. In the spring they both returned to Germany and married. We soon lost touch with Werner, but Hans corresponded regularly. He had been a Nazi adherent and an army officer; but was completely disillusioned, and was also trying to think out how he should lead his life and what work he would do in post-war Germany. He found a useful job connected with building – of which there was much to do.

When Hans's daughter, Christina, was school age they all came to stay with us; and later we all stayed with them in Ludwigsburg. Christina came for a while to Cambridge to attend a School of English; when she married she returned with her husband, to show him Cambridge and England. Hans's widow, Alwyne, does not know English; and now Michael has died there is no one in the family to write to her in German. It seemed the long contact had petered out, when we heard from Christina that she, her husband and daughter would spend their 1992 summer holiday in England and would visit Cambridge.

They came; and in the mysterious way children have, eleven-year-old Hannah and nine-year-old Sushila, my granddaughter, soon made friends, playing together in the garden all the afternoon almost without language – for Hannah knew only a few words of English, and Sushila no German at all.

1 The term "Quakers" was an early nickname, probably meant to be derogatory, given to the Society of Friends, based on the physical shaking that some showed before rising to speak in Meeting. The phenomenon is rare nowadays, but I have seen it happen.

2 A saying attributed to Edmund Burke. (1729-97).

3 William Douglas-Home, *Half-Term Report*, p 185.

CHAPTER FIVE

"Back to the Land";
CND, Russian, Russians, and Russia

Early in March 1948, when Martin was ten months old, we moved to Bramfield, a tiny village in Suffolk. "Apple Trees", the eighteenth century cottage Michael bought for just £1000 was built of lath and plaster, with a corrugated iron roof over thatch. It stood alone in about three-quarters of an acre of rough garden, surrounded by fields. Our water supply came from a well in the garden, into which a bucket was lowered by rope. For sanitation there was an earth closet in an outside shed. We had baths in a zinc tub by the kitchen fire, the water heated in kettles. However, there was one modern asset: mains electricity, so an electric pump eventually brought water to the house for us.

There followed three years of hard but enjoyable physical work. Friends and acquaintances of various nationalities came to visit us, and sometimes relatives. We were asked to have Fritz, a former German soldier, for a while – "to introduce him to democratic values". It must still have been a very hungry time in Germany, for he enjoyed my indifferent cooking, and rationing was still in force in England. He sadly missed the girl whom he had temporarily left behind; but would say with great feeling, "Wenn ich esse, vergesse ich beinahe meine Ilse!" ("When I eat, I almost forget my Ilse!") He helped Michael dig a ditch and build a septic tank. We soon had a bathroom and a flush toilet; but what this taught Fritz about democratic values I am not sure.

As I was weeding our vegetable plot one day about a month after our arrival, I puzzled painfully over news we had heard on the wireless. For some time there had been violence and counter-violence in Palestine; and now a terrible massacre of Arabs had taken place in a village near Jerusalem.[1] The killers had been Jews. This was the massacre of Deir Yassin on 9th April 1948; and it was to become a byword for barbaric cruelty. I did not learn the details till years later; now I was just confused.

How could *Jews* do such things? Feeling ignorant and bewildered, I thrust it all from my mind. Just then, Michael and I were bogged down trying to establish our own lives. What could we do about events in far-off Palestine, anyway?

Every day Michael cycled several miles to work with the apple grower. After about two years he decided to start up himself. The best root stock was ordered from Holland, and a thousand of these were planted out in our plot of land. Michael busied himself with pots of black sticky stuff and grafted different kinds of apple onto the root stock. It was tedious work and took a long time. The following spring it was apparent that out of a thousand grafts only *two* had "taken"! He also planted tomatoes: outside, as we had no greenhouse. There was a magnificent crop. One evening, very early in October, it suddenly felt extremely cold. Michael went out to look at his tomatoes. I did not see him for some time, until he re-appeared carrying a large dish piled high with round, black objects. The exceptionally early frost had been so severe it had destroyed the entire tomato crop. It seemed we were not cut out for earning a living from the land.

For a few months we were tided over by a grant from a Quaker trust, so that Michael could do some research into early Friends – many of whom were persecuted and imprisoned for their convictions. One, Thomas Ellwood, was locked in his bedroom by his father for a whole winter to make him recant. As he looked from his window he wrote a touching little poem:

> The winter tree
> Resembles me.
> Its sap is in the root.
> When Spring draws nigh
> As it, so I
> Will bud again and shoot.

It "spoke to our condition", as Friends say.

Janet was born in September 1949. We were very happy to have another baby. However, Martin, just over two, was so upset at her arrival, that he cried every night for months in spite of all our efforts to comfort him. At times domestic chores seemed altogether too much – washing – so many nappies! – cooking, washing up. Our only labour-saving device was an electric iron. No car, no telephone, no neighbours close by, and public transport minimal: so, in spite of lovely surroundings, fresh garden produce, eggs from our own hens, and the song of nightingales in spring, it was lonely; and I began to feel very much the captive wife and mother.

Michael bought me a Russian Linguaphone, and for a time that saved my sanity. But endless disturbed nights tired one out. For neither of us had the "back to the land" experiment worked out very well. Michael decided to become a Probation Officer. After all, he cared much more for people than for things, even growing things.

In June 1951 we moved to Bromsgrove, near Birmingham, where he took up his first appointment.

The little jerry-built villa in a strip of ribbon development for which we had exchanged our old cottage took some getting used to; but from our bedroom window we could see across fields to Bredon Hill, which meant a great deal to Michael. He loved the musical settings of Housman's *A Shropshire Lad* by Vaughan Williams and Butterworth. His probation work took him round the Warwickshire and Worcestershire countryside.

For a time I felt as frustrated as at "Apple Trees"; then, thanks largely to a kind woman who lived only two doors away and said she could come and help with Janet (now three) and the housework, avenues to freedom began to open up. Martin was already going to school. One morning I was grizzling to myself over the kitchen sink. Was my training and work as a teacher to end in *this*? On impulse I went to the telephone and rang the local Grammar School. "Do you by any chance need someone to give French coaching?" I asked the secretary.

"No, I don't think so," she answered doubtfully. "We have a full complement of staff." Then, suddenly, "Wait a minute, I'll go and get the headmaster."

He came to the phone. "Are you qualified to teach French?"

"Yes." It was Friday morning.

"Come and see me this afternoon," he said. When I saw him, he asked me to start on Monday. It turned out that he was in a fix. The school was to have a complete Government inspection the whole of that week; and his senior French teacher had suddenly to go into hospital. What a plunge! I had a full time-table. It included taking with the Upper VI a long Balzac novel which I had not read before; and I had not taught for seven years. I sat up till all hours.

We "blew" my three weeks' earnings on a weekend by the sea for us all to recover from the strain.

Thereafter I taught part-time at the Grammar School and part-time at Martin's little school, until we left Bromsgrove. And one evening a week, while Michael looked after the children, I drove into Birmingham for Russian classes. By then we had a car: a necessity for Michael's work. I was able to link up with the SCR (Society for Cultural Relations with the Soviet Union) and the BSFS (British-Soviet Friendship Society). Michael and I went to concerts and heard Khatchaturian conduct his own music and Emile Gilels play.

The idea of working towards mutual understanding and peace through personal contacts with Russians began to take root in the peace movement. The "Cold War" was developing fast and had to be counteracted in every way possible. To be able to communicate with Russians in their own language, and read their literature in the original, seemed quite a sensible first step. I soon discovered that the language itself, rich, musical, expressive, casts its own peculiar spell on the learner.

After three years at Bromsgrove, a vacancy came up in the Cambridge Probation Office. Michael applied and was accepted. We thought, rather naively, that Cambridge would be a good place for the children to be educated. They started at the Morley Memorial Primary School.

Almost immediately we were drawn into the anti-nuclear movement. Attlee's government announced the development of the H-bomb. I canvassed for signatures to a petition against this new horror. One woman with a son in the RAF said calmly, "If he is told to drop it, he will. It will be his duty." Similar chilling reactions were not infrequent. Then CND (the Campaign for Nuclear Disarmament) organised the Aldermaston marches. We all took part, year after year. The influence of those demonstrations has stayed with Martin and Janet. Each of them has continued the struggle against war and the nuclear threat; Janet in one way, Martin in another.

Over the years Michael often used verse to express his feelings about war and nuclear arms[2]. He encouraged me to continue with Russian seriously. Both Martin and Janet were now at school during the day, so it was possible to go to lectures and classes in the university. I enrolled at Girton College as an "affiliated" student and was able to take a CCK (Certificate of Competent Knowledge) – the equivalent of Part I of a language tripos.

Just as I started the course, a request came from the BSFS for me to act as interpreter for a group of Soviet artists who would be touring Britain. They turned out to be a very mixed group. There was a gifted and dedicated violinist, Valentin Zhuk, who remained somewhat apart from the others. (He has since achieved an international reputation.) There were also two married couples: a pair of ballet dancers, a pair of conjurors-cum-jugglers; a pianist; a miner from Siberia, head of his trade union; and of course the leader of the group, the Party man.

In Coalville, I accompanied the Siberian miner down a mine. We crawled in the darkness along a narrow passage, the roof only four feet above us, to the coal face. There my knowledge of Russian gave out. A crouching Pole who was chipping away came to the rescue: he spoke

Russian and knew mining technical terms. Down that mine there was a spirit of cheerful friendliness, similar to that which I found later in prison – another place where people are drawn into solidarity, strength coming from facing a hard situation together. I was thankful for a pit-head bath; but could not remove what looked like mascara round my eyes.

I began to teach Russian on a voluntary basis to a class of volunteer pupils (which included one member of staff) at Saffron Walden Friends' School; and personal contact with Russians grew. Quakers organised exchange visits, and when Soviet guests came to Cambridge we had them to stay; first of all a group of three – a young woman called Oksana Ulrich, Victor Khmara (a journalist attached to *Komsomolskaya Pravda*), and a historian whose name I forget. All of course were Party members. Oksana was charming; Victor too; but he wrote a very derogatory article about his visit to England on his return home. He had picked on anything he could possibly find fault with, and exaggerated it. But before I read that article, I had met Victor again – in Moscow.

My old friend, Auntie Periwinkle, died; and in the summer of 1955 I received £100 left to me in her will. Michael saw in *The Times* an advertisement for a tourist trip to Russia being organised by Progressive Tours, a left-wing outfit. It would cost just £100. Ordinary tourists, not "delegations", were at last being allowed in by the Soviet authorities: Stalin had died two years earlier.

We flew via Stockholm and Helsinki to Leningrad. On arrival at Leningrad airport, a member of our group met her son after a long separation. They were Jewish. Hitler and fate had driven one of them to the West, the other to the East. On the tarmac Mrs Sanderling was once again able to embrace her son, Kurt – who had become chief conductor of the Leningrad Philharmonic Orchestra.

The Soviet world, as far as one was able to see it in just over a week, seemed like Looking Glass Land. What westerners considered "good" was here "bad" and vice versa. One thing was clear: poetry in the Soviet Union had immense popular appeal. In Moscow, quite close to the National Hotel where we stayed, was a large bookshop. *Dyen' Poeta* (Poet's Day) was being celebrated there, as in all the other Moscow bookshops. Poets came to read their works to the public; and people arrived in droves, armed with the appropriate book to be autographed. I joined the scrum trying to get in to hear the poet in this particular shop. Unfortunately, I got stuck in the doorway, with my left arm behind me and could not pull it free. I felt something happen to my wrist. There were shouts of *Otdai chassi!* ("Give back the watch!") Freed at last, I looked down. The mechanism of the watch had dropped from its case onto the pavement, and the front of my dress was wet with blood: an unlucky outcome both for the thief and for me. He lost the watch, and in slicing the leather watch strap had cut into a vein. I had to go back to the hotel to have my wrist bound up, and so missed the poetry reading.

Watches – as so much else – were then very scarce in the Soviet Union. Our group included a lawyer, who shared my wish to attend a "People's Court". We discovered one, and were lucky to find it in session. The trial had just begun, but we were allowed in, and I whispered a rough translation of the proceedings to my companion. A young man was being tried by a magistrate with an "assessor" sitting on each side of him. The accused was a student. Having heard that watches were on sale at "GUM", the big department store on Red Square, he had joined the queue and eventually was lucky enough to buy one. As he came out, someone further back in the queue offered him a higher price for it than he had paid. He yielded to the temptation; and was denounced – for speculation. The sentence was two years in prison. The young man's university career was in ruins. When it was all over we were surrounded by others in the room. "What do you think?" "Isn't it a cruel sentence?" they asked. We could not but agree.

Victor Khmara came to meet me one evening at the hotel, carrying a bouquet of gladioli and a large book with photographs of Leningrad. He suggested taking me out to see Moscow by night. We went to Gorky Park: "The Park of Culture and Rest" – something like Battersea Park during the Festival of Britain, but on a grander scale. There was everything for leisure activities and fun: a hall for chess, a puppet theatre, basketball courts etc. We went up in the Big Wheel and had a wonderful view over the sparkling lamp-lit city. Then we walked round some more. I longed to sit in one of the inviting open-air cafés and have a drink; but clearly it would not do for Victor to be seen sitting with a foreign woman. On we went, in spite of my hints. We walked and walked. Having already spent the whole day sight-seeing, my legs were aching and I was ready to drop. Brazenly I took Victor's arm. He was too polite to object; but I could sense his embarrassment. I am afraid I was past caring. I cared even less in retrospect after reading the article he wrote about his visit to England. And though he was a Ukrainian and had said it would be easy to trace the family of our friend, Anna, in Le Havre he never did so. For all that, he was a charming man!

Oksana had given me her private address, but without her phone number. I decided to try and visit her. I did not realise that this was something one should not do at that time. I found my way to her flat on the outskirts of Moscow, near the university on the Lenin Hills. She was out, but her mother was at home and made me very welcome. She talked to me about the Revolution and the hard times that followed:

how she had had to sell everything she had in order to buy food. Oksana, who was married, had told me her husband was a teacher. I learned from her mother that he was an Army Officer. Oksana came in while I was still there, and seemed a little dismayed. Speaking in English, she explained that her mother was getting old and her memory was not what it was. The telephone rang. Oksana apologised for not being able to do something for the caller, as there was an unexpected visitor in the flat. She continued in an undertone and I heard no more.

Our Intourist guide arranged for us to have glimpses of Russian culture: the four Kremlin cathedrals and the Kremlin museum in Moscow, and the Hermitage in Leningrad – treasure houses of the ancient and beautiful in the past of Russia, and in the case of the Hermitage, of other countries also. In the Kremlin museum the sight of Ivan the Terrible's Bible, studded with jewels, gave a clue to the persecution of the Church after the Revolution. We were taken to the ballet, where we saw Prokofiev's *Romeo and Juliet* at the Bolshoi Theatre, with the famous Ulanova as Juliet. There we stumbled on a State occasion. In the former Tsarist box sat Khrushchev, Malenkov, Bulganin and Chancellor Adenauer from West Germany, a row of unsmiling faces.

One evening, tired with sightseeing, I decided to stay in the hotel while the rest of the group went out again. I soon realised my mistake. What a waste of time it would be! The Bolshoi was quite near, and so I set out. I arrived to find the doors closed, but managed to find a way in. I had no ticket, no roubles, and the performance had begun. Mustering up what Russian I could, I asked to be let in nevertheless: some cheek. I was taken upstairs and ushered into a box! Tourists then had a rarity value. Borodin's opera, *Prince Igor*, was in progress, and I was in time for the Polovtsian dances.

We returned to England by sea. In the Baltic there was a terrific storm. As the ship pitched and tossed for thirty-six hours, passengers lay prone in their bunks, listening to crockery and other objects crashing overhead. When it was over and we were once again in a state to go to the restaurant, I noticed a striking young Russian enter and join his companions. I was soon to see him again.

On my return home I began to think how personal contacts with Soviet citizens could be developed. There were usually a few studying in Cambridge, sponsored by the British Council in fulfilment of the cultural agreement between our government and that of the USSR. We started to invite them to our house. One of the most frequent of these visitors was an historian, Victor Israelyan, whom I had met in the tea-room at the University Library: a very good place for making the acquaintance of interesting people. Then it occurred to me that there might be many others in this country who would also enjoy meeting

Russians, and that Soviet visitors might welcome a broader acquaintance with British people. Through the ATR (Association of Teachers of Russian) I met Mr Gregory who shared this view, and through the Jesus Lane Friends' (Quaker) Meeting – David Blamires, a PhD student who lit up at the idea of creating a network of friends of all kinds who would be ready to host visitors from the USSR, and in this way forge links which might increase mutual East-West understanding.

We formed a committee, of course, and called our new organisation "Anglo-Russian Contacts" – ARC. It grew, and for a short time flourished. We found willing hosts all over the country, and were quite often able to fix them up with the appropriate Soviet visitors – for a meal, for a day, or for a weekend. There was also a memorable occasion when we invited a group of Georgian dancers to Cambridge. I had seen the Georgian State Dance Company perform in London and been enchanted. Going backstage, I met their manager and asked if any of the dancers would like to visit Cambridge. He assented with alacrity, and a car-full arrived a day or two later. Among them was the beautiful and charming chief woman dancer, Rusudan Enukidze. David Blamires, some students of Russian from the university, and I gave them lunch and showed them the colleges. I met them again on my second visit to the Soviet Union in August 1961 in Tbilisi, and was given a warm welcome.

ARC, however, lasted only four years, from about 1957 to late 1961. David left Cambridge. Mr Gregory said he had no more time. We had moved temporarily to Letchworth in Hertfordshire, and I was disheartened. Hitherto all Soviet visitors for whom we had catered had come to Britain through other organisations. I tried when in Moscow in 1961 to develop more possibilities for such contacts; but even the Russians who had stayed with us and had the power, as I discovered – one was the head of a cultural organisation for young people – were, back on their home ground, cool and unhelpful. Barriers were put up. ARC was probably neither official enough, nor strongly enough Left politically.

However, difficulties were not only on one side. In the spring of 1956 we had had for the weekend two guests from the Soviet Embassy, Vladimir and Gennady – more familiarly, Volodya and Gena. Some weeks earlier I had met Volodya at a reception at the Soviet Embassy, and found he was none other than the young man I had noticed on board ship in the Baltic. We had a party on the Saturday evening, so that Cambridge friends could have a chance to meet them. As I was already teaching Russian then at Saffron Walden Friends' School, I invited Joan, the English teacher in my class, to come with her husband. The next day I was rung up by the headmaster. He had been visited by the police, who wanted to know what a member of his staff had been up to – meeting Soviet Embassy officials. Police had watched our house all the previous evening, and Joan and Robin had been followed home when they left. It was annoying. I made an appointment to see the police superintendent. He said, "Since you have come to see me, I think I can trust you"!

Volodya came again a year later. By then he had married, and he brought his bride to see us. They enjoyed the singing in King's College Chapel. Whether our guests have been Soviet Communists or Muslim Palestinians, we have always tried to take them to Evensong at King's and it has always been appreciated. After the service, Volodya, Olga, Michael and I walked in the sunshine on "the Backs". In the avenue leading up to Trinity, the cherry trees on each side were white with blossom and underneath were red tulips, narcissi and forget-me-nots. "We'll never forget this time," said Olga.

In 1956 two manifestations of brute force took place almost simultaneously; one, in Europe: the Soviet invasion of Hungary, to crush the emerging democratic movement there; and one in the Middle East: the invasion of Egyptian territory by Israel, Britain and France, in an attempt to reach the Suez Canal. On the way there the Israeli army occupied the Gaza Strip. The British public was split down the middle on the Suez issue. Some people ardently supported the Government (as did my mother, who found it difficult to speak to me for weeks afterwards); others protested vehemently against Britain's involvement in aggression. I took part in a protest rally on Parker's Piece, the spacious green in the centre of Cambridge. As the Vicar of Great St Mary's (the university church) was speaking, a voice behind me shouted accusingly, *"He's been to Russia!"* and a toilet roll was hurled at the vicar, the paper draping itself on the way over shoulders in the crowd.

The invaders of Egyptian territory were obliged to withdraw as a result of the combined pressures of the UN and President Eisenhower – the only American president to date with the courage to stand up to Israel and the American Zionist lobby. Anthony Eden, the British Prime Minister, had ignominiously to resign.

It should be recorded that three massacres of Palestinians by Israel are associated with the 1956 adventure. At Kufr Kassem, a village in Israel near the border with Jordan, forty-seven men, women and children were shot dead as they returned from work in the fields, unaware that a curfew had been slapped on the village. Thirteen others survived by feigning death as they lay wounded. At Khan Younis in the Gaza Strip 275 were killed during house-to-house searches; and at Rafah in the extreme south of the Strip, when the Israelis had collected a large number of men together for interrogation, they shot and killed 100 for no apparent reason. A mass grave near the spot was discovered some years later.

In 1961 I was in Moscow on a month's course for teachers of Russian. Victor Israelyan, with whom I had become acquainted in Cambridge, came to see me at the hotel where we teachers were staying, and offered to take three of us in his car to visit an old monastery in a forest some way out of Moscow. It was an interesting trip. On our way back, as we were driving in the city along the embankment of the Moscow River, Victor pointed to a block of flats. "That's where I live," he said. "Now you can tell your friends in England that one Soviet citizen actually had the courage to show you the *outside* of his home!"

In Moscow in 1969 (again on a month's course for teachers of Russian), I made some new friends. In the Tretyakov Gallery of Russian painting I met an elderly man with a great love of poetry. We corresponded afterwards for a long time and he would always enclose a poem, usually by Esenin, a favourite of both of us. Then there were the young black marketeers who foregathered in the "Ivoushka", a café in Kuznetsky Most – one of the main Moscow streets. I met them there quite often and we talked a great deal; although I did not do business with them, they were extremely friendly. One of them, Boris, was himself something of a poet and he too wrote to me afterwards, always enclosing poems of his own.

It was in Letchworth (where we lived from 1959-63), at St Christopher School, that I started to teach Russian professionally. Martin was among my pupils, and passed his O-level in it. Janet I also taught later; and she went on to do Russian Studies at Sussex University.

Russian was beginning to flourish in schools and universities. It was because of this that the Association of Teachers of Russian had been formed. At one of its annual conferences I met Bal Faden, who was setting up a firm, Bradda Books, to publish Russian texts for students. "Would you like to edit a book of Russian poetry for beginners?" he asked me. I said I would love to and spent all my spare time reading Russian poetry to find simple poems that I liked.

The little book sold quite well; and was followed by another, for more advanced students. My appetite for editing was whetted.

Years earlier a friend who had lived in Russia before the Revolution had suggested we read together Tolstoy's *War and Peace* in the original. "When you've finished it, you'll know Russian quite well," she remarked. She had had to give up the sessions quite soon; but the story had gripped me and I plodded on to the end. It is a marvellous book. I vowed to myself that thereafter I would always read Russian literature in the original – so much is usually lost in translation; and that if ever I was in a position to teach Russian I would make sure my pupils did the same. I became particularly interested in Tolstoy, both in his art as a writer and in the philosophy he developed in his later years, which seemed to me to contain ideas appropriate for our contemporary materialistic and violent society. For Tolstoy, who as an officer in the Russian army had fought in the Caucasus and in the Crimean War (then written *Tales of Sebastopol*), had not only become a pacifist but had come to believe that we should return to a simpler way of life; and that it is only through loving and serving others that one can find inner peace. Mahatma Gandhi owed much to his influence. (Tolstoy's views, through Gandhi, have kindled a spark in Palestine; Gandhi's complete works are in the office of the Palestinian Centre for the Study of Non-violence in Jerusalem.[3]) Back in Cambridge, I decided to edit for students one of Tolstoy's last stories, *Master and Man*, about two men lost in a snowstorm, and the effect on one of them – a grasping merchant – of nearness to death. When it was done, I sent it, hopefully, to the Cambridge University Press. To my delight it was accepted.

I was then teaching at St Mary's Convent: sixth-form pupils who would take 'A' level in two years, starting from scratch. It was exhilarating, and hard work for all of us. But the girls did well, both in the language and the literature papers, for they read the set books in Russian, not in translation. My new book, like the others, was of course dealt with in out-of-school hours; and I tried always to put the family first. I could not have managed without a friendly "daily" who came in the mornings – above all without Michael. For a month he took over the cooking while I sat surrounded by huge dictionaries, compiling the vocabulary and notes for *Master and Man*.

The academic year 1965-6 was even harder work. I had been persuaded to complete a degree in Russian. The Senate in its wisdom decided I must take Part II of the Tripos in one year, and that very year, or I would never be accepted as a student. That meant, in practical terms, I would have eight months, as it was already October and the finals would be in May. (Part II usually takes two years.) "It is several years since you took Part I, you may have read a great deal in that time," I was told. Fair enough. Or was it fair – to be penalised for possibly having *read*? The BA is not a *competitive* examination as far as I know. "And it cannot be an Honours degree: you will have no grade." That was even harder to accept; but what, after all, did a label matter? The work itself would be interesting: and there would be the stimulus of lectures, and of fellow students. I enrolled again at Girton College. Dr

Nikolai Andreyev was an inspiring lecturer, and I was fortunate in having him for a supervisor. He told me later, on the side, that judging by my papers I should have been awarded a First. Nice to know! Long after I graduated, I used to attend whenever possible his lectures on the history of Russian thought, not only for their content, but to hear his beautiful Russian.

With the approach of finals, I had worried. How could I teach, cook for the family, and make the effort necessary in the last few weeks before the exams? The ideal solution came up. I found a friend in Larissa Haskell, a Soviet Russian married to the art historian, Francis Haskell (who soon afterwards became Professor of History of Art in Oxford). Larissa herself was also a distinguished art historian – she had been curator of the Italian paintings in the Hermitage Museum, Leningrad. Newly arrived in Cambridge, she was temporarily without a job and wanted something to do. She agreed to take my classes at the Convent for four weeks. A delightful person, she went down well with the nuns. I did not tell them that she had been, in Russia, a member of the Communist Party! As soon as the university exams were over I returned to school. 'O' and 'A' levels were still looming there.

---

1   *Deir Yassin*, 9th April, 1948. See Chapter Ten.

2   Some of it was published later in *Mishmash* – Brentham Press, 1987 and 1988.

3   See Chapter Seventeen, *Intifada*, p 193.

CHAPTER SIX

Two similar demos with different consequences:
Algeria; prison

One evening in 1960, Martin, Janet and I watched a favourite TV programme – *Tonight*. It featured on this occasion work being done on the edge of the Sahara by Wendy Campbell-Purdie, perhaps one of the earliest pioneers of tree planting to halt the spread of desert.[1]

The next day was a Saturday, and a demonstration had been organised in London by Bertrand Russell's "Committee of 100", which advocated non-violent civil disobedience in protest against the development of nuclear weapons. I went for the first time.

Like many other people I was becoming impatient at the apparent lack of effect on governments of all previous protests against the immorality and folly of developing – at huge cost too – weapons of indiscriminate mass destruction. (The close connection of this development with nuclear power "for peaceful purposes" and the enormous danger of that as well, both now and for the future, had not yet been generally understood[2].) We gathered that Saturday in Trafalgar Square; and when the speeches were over and the crowd prepared to move off to stage a "sit down" outside the Ministry of Defence, I noticed a woman standing alone, leaning against the pedestal of one of the lions. Her face seemed familiar. I went closer. Yes, it was Wendy! We spent the rest of the day together; and as we sat on the pavement she talked about the importance of trees – for the retention of the soil, for the development of a micro-climate which would increase rainfall, how it is, in fact, on trees that depends the well-being of humans and of all living things. She invited all the family to stay with her in the tree-planting season (mid-winter) to give her a hand. At that time she was creating a plantation in Tunisia; but it was not until eight years later, in 1968, that we were able to take up her invitation. By then she had moved to Algeria, and was working in Bou Saada, an oasis town in the extreme south of the inhabited part of the country. It was our first experience of the Arab world.

The journey there was not without adventure. We had decided to go by train and boat – cheaper and much more interesting than by plane; and were able to stop for a few hours in Dijon, to see my old Burgundian friends. It was with a couple of their friends – then *colons* in Algeria – that the memorable excursion over the Col de la Seigne had been made thirty years before. The Leuvrais recalled how they had visited these friends in the days when Algeria was still attached to France. They had even been to Bou Saada and were afraid it must have changed for the worse, being no longer under French rule. We went on to Marseilles, where a fierce *mistral* was blowing: an ill-omen for the long crossing to Algiers.

We were travelling "economy", and were shown into a tiny cabin with four berths. The ceiling came down low, and there was barely room to move. The crossing was very stormy and must have taken about twenty-four hours. It was nightmarish. As I lay feeling very sick with the ceiling pressing down, I kept thinking of the slave ships crossing the Atlantic 300 years before. A mere fraction of the torment others have gone through certainly helps one to sympathise as nothing else does. When we emerged to go to the communal loos, we had to step over piles of sand covering the result of other people's sickness.

Wendy had sent a car from Bou Saada to meet us, with a couple of Algerian drivers. We pleaded with them to let us stay overnight in Algiers to let us recover. But it was New Year's Eve; and what was more important to them, New Year's Day that year coincided with the Eid Al-Fitr, the Muslim feast that marks the end of Ramadan. It was absolutely essential that they spend it with their families. We drove on through the darkness and torrential rain. Part of the way was apparently through the Atlas mountains and then desert; but we could see nothing.

Wendy was still up when we arrived, with some supper for us and a wood fire in a corner of the room. When we woke the next morning, it was to see palm trees waving their fronds outside the window, and to hear the joyful shouts of children and the bangs that seem to be the necessary accompaniment of celebrations the world over. When we went out into the street little girls ran to greet us and show us the palms of their hands, stained with henna in honour of the occasion. One of them was the daughter of Aissa (Arabic for "Jesus") – Wendy's right-hand man, whom we were to get to know well.

As part of the celebrations and to feast us as guests we were treated to *méchoui*: a sheep was slaughtered and roasted whole – head and all. We sat round a low circular table and picked the meat off with our fingers. It was delicately flavoured with herbs; but, somehow, with our English squeamishness, we did not feel hungry: the eyes of the sheep stared blankly at us. Years later, in Nablus, I was again to partake of *méchoui*, and found myself sitting unhappily right next to the sheep's head. When one thinks about it, though, the Arab way seems more honest. We eat nicely presented and packaged meat; the animal has been killed for us out of sight. And, apart from chicken, the meat which Arabs usually eat is from sheep and goats which have led a healthy outdoor life.

Although we could be in Bou Saada for only ten days (Martin and Janet had to return to university and Michael and I to our jobs), the fact that we were working there gave us a glimpse into the lives of the people that we could not have had as tourists. We did indeed once ride camels, and once made an expedition by car; but most of the time was spent at the plantation or visiting the homes of Wendy's Arab fellow-workers, or seeing something of her other work. There was great poverty, with ninety per cent of the menfolk unemployed; and it was very cold, in spite of bright sunshine during the day. Symptoms of malnutrition were evident: the ill-clad barefoot children all had runny noses. Wendy had organised a centre for clothes distribution. The barren land provided little sustenance: sheep grazed on stony slopes with hardly a blade of grass visible.

We could not but be shocked by what we saw of the position of women in Bou Saada. It was mostly men whom one saw about. They worked in the little shops wide open to the street, or sat in the cafés, drank coffee and played backgammon. Janet and I boldly rode bicycles to the plantation, which was at some distance. The first time, men and boys stood on the pavements on each side of the road and accompanied us with laughter all the way. The few women one saw in public were shrouded in white from head to foot, the face veiled apart from just one eye. They would hold the cloth in place with their teeth, to leave one hand free for a child and the other for a basket. In one home we visited (and it was a great honour for us all – the two men included – to be invited in), the fifteen-year-old wife of a man in his late forties displayed inside the house a gaily coloured dress and a brightly painted face. She was already pregnant. But she seemed happy, and clearly respected her husband. I gradually learnt in later years that many Arab women feel that their traditional family arrangements, involving their extended families, give them a security unknown to Western women, which they would not exchange for our "freedom". In spite of that, I remain convinced by what I have seen of Arab society that it is, generally speaking, all too much a man's world. But it certainly does not hold the monopoly there.

I was invited to give a talk at the *lycée*. French was still widely spoken, and French institutions remained. I cannot remember what my subject was supposed to be; but the discussion came round to the position of women. I was in front of a class of boys. Though it was a mixed school for reasons of economy, the sexes were kept separate. How could half the population, I asked, be kept prisoner and prevented from using their gifts in the service of the community? Had not Algerian women played an important part in the struggle for liberation from the French *colons*? Would not Algeria have much to gain if women were now allowed more freedom? Only one boy out of the forty or so said, "Yes"! It was explained to me that women are the tempters of men, and the source of evil. They must be covered, or stay at home, so that men are not tempted, and the purity of society is preserved. A similar attitude can be found in other Arab countries, as I was to discover later; but apart from the occasional rare exception in the Gaza Strip, cut off for so long from the rest of the world, I have never seen a Palestinian woman with her *face* wholly covered.

One of Wendy's Algerian friends, a rich sheikh, owned a large Citroën, and took us through the desert to a celebrated mosque perched on the top of a hill. From this height we could see, far below, the road by which we had come. As I looked down, the tiny figures of two men in flowing robes approached each other. They met, flung their arms round each other and embraced. How much warmer seeming is this friendly Arab greeting between members of the same sex than the formal British hand-shake! We drove back as the sun was setting.

On this first visit to a Muslim Arab country I saw life in a remote oasis town very much from a Western viewpoint; but the memories of Algeria that I treasure most are the friendliness of the people, the awesome grandeur of the desert, and the flaming red glory of the evening sky above it.

The next Committee of 100 demo that year ended very differently from the one which eventually took us to Algeria; but for me the effects were even more far-reaching; for my family too.

This time the aim was to protest against the proposed test in the atmosphere of a Soviet hydrogen bomb. We were to sit down en masse in front of the Soviet Embassy. And indeed a large crowd of us proceeded in a very orderly fashion towards it down Bayswater Road. However, just before we reached the turning into Kensington Palace Gardens we were stopped by the police. There was nothing for it but to sit down where we were. We sat in rows, four abreast, leaving room for single-lane traffic on our right. Police vehicles drove along this lane, ordering us through loud hailers to move. Most of us stayed put. Then, a row at a time, we were arrested, made to get into police vans and driven to a police station. There, our names and addresses were taken down. Three weeks later I received a summons to attend Marylebone police court, and took my turn in the dock. I refused to swear (Quakers do not swear, for it would imply two standards of truth) and was allowed to make an "affirmation". I was found guilty of obstruction and offered the choice of a fine or a week in prison. I chose the latter; for what was the point of giving money to a government whose nuclear policy one disapproved of? That day, to my disappointment, no other nuclear disarmer in court felt able to make the same choice. I was then conducted "backstage" to a room where a posse of police were gathered. There I noticed a telephone. I asked if I might phone my husband. One of the policemen got the number of Michael's office and, discovering he was a probation officer, asked reproachfully, "Whatever *will* he think of you?"!

Then I was taken down to the cells, and put into a small room where a metal grille was locked behind me. Presently a young prostitute was pushed in. Her washing facilities at home – if she had a home – must have been woefully inadequate, for she was extremely smelly, poor girl. The grille clanged shut; but soon opened again for another prostitute, older and smartly dressed. She tried to wheedle something out of the policeman as he locked the grille on the outside once more. He answered with a strangely offensive smile. Then I was taken to another cell, with a solid door, and left alone. When this door was locked on me and I realised I had no way of communicating with anyone, I really began to feel what imprisonment can mean.

Eventually I was put into a "Black Maria": barely room to sit in a tiny compartment; the window closed and blackened. The previous unpleasant smell came from nearby. Our destination turned out to be Holloway jail. The routine for new arrivals was a bath, then prison clothes to put on – a green cotton dress (though it was late October), much-darned lisle stockings, shoes that were too big, and misshapen through other people's wear. I was conducted to a room in which women prison officers sat round a large table, and had to stand while one of them emptied out my handbag and read aloud a list of its contents. It was somehow embarrassing. I was handed a receipt, then taken to the second floor and my cell. It was one of many opening onto a gallery which ran round a gloomy interior like that of a cathedral, but bereft of colour. Slung across from one side to the other of the first floor was a vast wire netting. "To catch the suicides," a fellow prisoner informed me the following day as I gazed down on it.

My cell was vaulted, with a barred window, an iron bedstead (the mattress smelt of urine), a table and chair, and an old-fashioned washstand with a potty underneath. In a corner I found a sheet describing how I would be re-educated and rehabilitated during my stay. But on my bed was a book with a lurid cover – obviously sex and violence inside. "Is this to be my reading?" I asked in dismay. The officer who accompanied me quickly took up the book. "This isn't for you," she answered; "I'll get you something else." She explained that outside my cell door there was a notice to say that I was in for a week, and that that was the usual sentence for "drunk and disorderly". The librarian must have had a sense of humour, for the officer returned with Joyce Carey's *Prisoner of Grace*. I enjoyed that novel, and read it in the evenings standing on the chair to be as near as possible to the dim bulb in the vaulted ceiling. During the night there were yells from nearby – "I want a man! I – want – a – MAN!"

The day started with "slopping out". The first morning, I stood in the queue with my pot of pee in front of a middle-aged woman who was smoking a minuscule cigarette. (By way of economy, prisoners unrolled cigarettes they bought at the canteen out of their meagre earnings and rolled up portions of the tobacco separately.) She was very friendly. Holding out the cigarette, she offered, "'Ave a pull, dearie?"

There was a real camaraderie among the prisoners, similar to what I had found down the mine. On this floor we were "Star" prisoners, first offenders, (more accurately, offenders caught for the first time), a mixed assembly: prostitutes, one murderer (a lesbian who had killed her partner), thieves, nuclear disarmers, and others. Only a few women regretted what they'd done, but those that did, did so bitterly. There was a thief who (I am ashamed to admit it) kept us in fits of laughter by the way she recounted her exploits when we were in the common room. One of the prostitutes was a beautiful woman, with the *bouffant* hair style then fashionable, so that in profile she looked like Nefertiti. She understood the reference: others, she said, had told her the same thing.

"Nefertiti" explained to me that the quickest way to accumulate capital to start the shop for "separates" which she and her friend had set their hearts on was to earn it through prostitution. Occasionally there would be a police raid on their flat; once she related, laughing, how she managed to burn some money in the geyser in the nick of time as they were coming in. (Have men who use prostitutes ever been persecuted in the same way that the women are?)

Cynthia had been a teacher in a prep school. She was a sad little grey-haired woman, shocked at the place and the company she found herself in, and ashamed of something she had done. I did not like to ask what. "I was very silly," was all she said. I cannot think her offence warranted six months in jail. It certainly did her great harm: on her release she was in a mental hospital for a long time. We corresponded for many years, until her letters stopped. I think she must have died.

Catherine was in for an offence related to drugs. She had been happily married and had two children, but her husband developed a serious mental disorder and became violent. Told she must choose between him and her children, as the children would be in danger if he lived with them, she chose her husband and the children were adopted. Then her husband died; she went to pieces, was prescribed a drug on which she became dependent, and the amount prescribed became inadequate. After various ruses to have the prescription repeated before time, she tried adding a couple of noughts to a figure, was caught, and sentenced to six months in prison.

Then there was Barbara, a woman on remand. Like so many women at the menopause, she had behaved out of character, and had shoplifted a tiny Christmas item from Woolworth's for her small daughter. "I can't think what possessed me," she said. "It wasn't as though I couldn't have afforded it. Now we'll have to move. My husband and I will never be able to hold our heads up again in our neighbourhood." It is shockingly cruel in my opinion to send prisoners on remand before they have even been tried, to a closed prison for convicts.

For work, we sewed by hand blue airmail bags. Whether it was because we were women, or "star" prisoners, I don't know; but these bags were lighter and easier to sew than the other sort. "Exercise" was a dreary walk round and round a dreary yard, and a chilly business. We had cardigans to wear over the cotton dresses and a very short cloak was issued for outdoors. Food was adequate in quantity, but almost entirely lacking in vitamins (one tomato in a week) and most unappetising – served in indented tin trays from a table by kitchen staff (also prisoners) wearing aprons memorable for their filthiness.

I could not discover any attempts at "rehabilitation". On the contrary the whole experience seemed designed to humiliate and degrade, and to undermine self-respect. It took me a long time to shake off that feeling of degradation; and it was not because of the kind of companions I had had: I could not stop thinking of them and wishing they were free. After twenty-five years of work with offenders, including eight years as welfare officer in Wandsworth jail, Michael wrote:

> This system is a monstrous crime,
> But it's been with us such a time
> That we are blind and cannot see
> Its absolute iniquity,
> Ignoring totally, no less
> Its costly ineffectiveness.[3]

In the following months a number of us, men and women, who had been imprisoned for nuclear disarmament activities, met in London at frequent intervals to pool our experiences and opinions of prison. We had all been shocked. The outcome of our deliberations was a pamphlet, *Inside Story*[4]. It suggested reforms which could be carried out immediately and at very little cost, and was sent to the Home Office and circulated as widely as possible. I believe it had some effect. Soon, we learnt, women in Holloway were allowed to wear their own clothes. But what a long way there is to go! The prison population increases; there are no doubt some dangerous psychopaths for whom there seems no alternative, yet many prisoners have been no more than inadequate to cope with the jungle that society has become – ruthless competitiveness in every field; stores with goods displayed purposely to tempt and easy to take; a government that makes the pursuit of money and profit the prime object of life; broken homes; a growing callousness: tolerance of, and even glorification of violence emanating from millions of TV screens, blunting sensitivity; above all, unemployment. There is too the government example that, through the arms trade, turns killing into a profitable business.

Inside Story was to have an unexpected repercussion for me fourteen years later.

But my week in prison was a major turning point in my life.

I had not long been out of prison when an article of great significance appeared in *The Observer*. A lawyer, Peter Benenson, and some friends of his had founded Amnesty, later to become Amnesty International. One learnt that people were imprisoned, not for doing anything wrong – not even for impeding the traffic flow as I had been – and imprisoned for cruelly long periods, sometimes tortured, just for daring to express opinions unacceptable to their governments: prisoners of conscience. This was intolerable. It was suggested what one should do. Through local "Threes" groups one could bring pressure by various means on the relevant authorities and persuade them to release a prisoner, or, at least, reduce his sentence and improve his conditions; and one could assist prisoners' families. The aim was absolute impartiality – hence "Threes": one had to "adopt" one prisoner from the Western (capitalist) bloc, one from the Eastern (Communist) bloc, and one from a non-aligned country. I talked with my friends in Letchworth, where we were temporarily living, and we started a group.

We were asked to work on behalf of a prisoner in South Africa, a Soviet citizen, and a Greek. We shared out work for the prisoners among ourselves. "My" prisoner was Oksana, a Ukrainian, sentenced to many years in a Soviet labour camp for her nationalist activities. I wrote her letters and once a month sent her a food parcel. A receipt for it would duly arrive from the camp commandant. Two or three years later, news came in a roundabout way that Oksana had received a food parcel from England. So one at least got through to her. The Greek was Christos Dimtsas. At nineteen, in the aftermath of the civil war in Greece which followed World War II, he had been sentenced for life. He was said to be a Communist. We studied the historical and political background of such imprisonments, and, most crucially, consulted a small but very effective organisation based in London, the League for Democracy in Greece, devoted to the restoration of civil rights and liberties in Greece. The LDG had its own Relief Committee, a registered charity, for Greek political prisoners and their families. The dedicated secretary, Diana Pym, had made it her life's work to campaign on their behalf. After about two years, "our" prisoner, Christos, was released.

---

1   Wendy Cambell-Purdie and Fenner Brockway, *Woman against the Desert*, Gollancz, 1967.

2   See Chapter Seventeen, p 197.

3   *Mishmash*, Brentham Press, 1988, p 28.

4   Published for the Prison Reform Council by Housmans, London, 1962.

CHAPTER SEVEN

Greece and Greek prisoners

The following year, 1964, I went to Greece for the first time. My first port of call in Athens was the office of the Prisoners' Families' Association, to which I had been directed by Diana Pym. While waiting to speak to the secretary, Thetis Kotsaki, I got into conversation with a young man who knew English well. Glancing down on his desk, I noticed a letter in familiar neat handwriting. "Could you be George Zis?" I asked. He was. George was a student in England during the academic year and had translated our letters to Christos and to the Greek authorities. He and Thetis proved invaluable helpers – advising, guiding and interpreting for me when necessary that summer.

George took me to see Christos. It was a festive occasion. Christos had just married someone who had waited for about fifteen years for him to come out of prison. There was a delicious meal with a variety of Greek dishes. His wife was not only loyal and beautiful, but an excellent cook.

Thetis told me there were many more prisoners anxiously waiting for release, among them her husband and brother-in-law – both sick with TB in a prison sanatorium. So when I returned to England, our group wrote to Peter Benenson and asked for another Greek to be assigned to us. "No," was the answer. "We have it on the best authority that the remaining prisoners are spies." Espionage and violence rule out, for Amnesty, the adoption of a prisoner. However, we were not satisfied. We had learnt a thing or two about the background to these imprisonments, and persisted. "All right, Eleanor," said Peter, "if you feel so strongly about it, go to Greece yourself to investigate. If you bring a report to the Amnesty International AGM in Holland in September, we will consider it." – So in the summer of 1965 I went to Greece again.

Thetis advised me where to go, whom to see. Being neither a lawyer nor a journalist, I very much needed guidance. I had been given a list of prisoners from Diana before I left. Now I visited office after office. I shall never forget those hot Athens streets: one learns to pick every bit of shade to walk in. The people I consulted were lawyers and MPs for the most part. One of the MPs was Spiros Mercouris, an Independent, and father of the actress, Melina Mercouri, of *Never on Sunday* fame, who in later years became Minister of Culture. All, without exception, explained to me that these were men who, after the defeat of the Communist side in the Greek Civil War which followed World War II, had fled for safety to countries in the Eastern bloc. Homesick and separated from their families, they had eventually made their way back to Greece; but had been caught and sentenced without proper evidence to long periods of imprisonment as agents of the Soviet Union, Bulgaria, or wherever it was they came from. I was unable to visit any prisoners apart from those in the Athens prison sanatorium. There I was taken by Dimitris Loules, Thetis's nephew, who was visiting his imprisoned father, as well as Thetis's husband. It was a moving experience. Prisoners and visitors stood out in the open, a high wire fence separating them. There was no privacy; but at the same time guards stayed at a distance and did not interfere.

After a few weeks I was extremely depressed and tired, and felt the need for a few days' rest before returning home – and a longing to swim in the blue Aegean. So I went to the island of Aegina – the nearest island to Athens – and after a night there took a boat to Moni, a tiny island off Aegina, where I stayed for three or four days. I expect a hotel has been built there now; but at that time it was totally unspoilt – there were just a few tents for holiday-makers to rent. It was unutterably beautiful and peaceful. From Moni one could gaze across the sea to the distant mountains of mainland Greece. At night one could sleep under the stars.

Scheveningen on the Dutch coast was the venue for the Amnesty International AGM. There were two or three days for it; but, as often happens on such occasions when there is a great deal of business and people have a lot to say, it was not long before we were running over time. My piece was to come near the end. I had been allotted half an hour; but at lunch-time Peter Benenson (joint chairman with Sean McBride) told me I could have only seven minutes. I was nearly in despair. Mercifully, I had brought fifty copies of my report with me. I was to speak first after lunch and so was able to place a copy on each chair before the meeting began. People had a chance to glance through it. I spoke fast, trying to emphasise the main points, and sat down. Sean McBride rose and said, "I think we must postpone a decision till we have more evidence." I felt the tears rolling down my cheeks. Then someone stood up.

"We have enough evidence!" he almost shouted. "Now we must act!" One after another members of the audience rose in support. The platform had to give way. Amnesty adopted most of the prisoners on the list. In a few months all those adopted were free.

In the summer of 1966 I went to Greece for the third time, to meet some of the released prisoners who had become my friends. There were joyful celebrations. But there were still some prisoners inside. Thetis urged me to have an interview with the Minister of Justice, Stefanopoulos. He was not a hard right-winger and had a reputation for humanity, she said; but he had not been long in office and his position was not totally secure. Greek politics at that time were in turmoil. The Prime Minister, George Papandreou, had resigned. There were noisy demonstrations on his behalf in Constitution Square, close to the Greek parliament building, with youths shouting, "Papandreou! Papandreou!" No one knew what would happen next.

Just before I went to see the Minister, Thetis said, "Please ask him to release Eleni Voulgari, who has just been arrested. She is totally innocent of anything. All they have against her is that she gave shelter to her left-wing fiancé. He has been imprisoned too."

I come now to an episode of which I am ashamed and that I bitterly regret. I talked with the Minister about the prisoners on my list. He appeared sympathetic. For some reason Eleni Voulgari's name had not been written down. And was I overawed in the presence of the Minister? The awful fact is that *I forgot to mention her*. If I remember rightly, the other prisoners were released; but, however that was, Eleni and her fiancé were not.

I think if I had known then what I heard later, I *could* not, possibly, have forgotten her.

I learnt enough Greek to be able to write simple letters to Eleni, (I have one from her which I treasure) and tried to make up for my dreadful lapse by strenuous efforts on her behalf, but in vain. It is no doubt over-presumptuous to think that any pleading with Stefanopoulos on my part would have had any effect, but I cannot help feeling this bitter remorse.

Twenty-four years after these events, in 1990, in the sitting-room of St George's hostel in Jerusalem, this tragic story came vividly back. A grey-haired man who had just arrived from England came in, and we began a conversation. I learnt his name, and he mine. We remembered each other. He was the writer on international affairs, Keith Kyle, and had followed after me to Greece, where he *had* pleaded the case of Eleni Voulgari with the Minister of Justice. "There was something that puzzled me about that case," he said. "I sensed that something, something important, was being kept from me – it took me a long time to find out what it was. Eleni was pregnant, and as she was not yet married, her relatives did not want it to be known. Having learnt this,

I was able to tell the Minister, and plead her case more strongly. But two days later he was no longer in office. The colonels' coup had taken place." (Eleni's son, Miltos, was born in prison and stayed there for two years before he was taken away from her. Her mother, who had also been imprisoned at the time of the coup, was released in 1968 and able to take him. Eleni was in prison till 1974.)

It was in April 1967 that the great shock had come. Tanks rolled into the centre of Athens. The government was overturned. The King hesitated, then acted too late, and was forced to flee the country with his family. Fascists were now in power. A rumour had it (well-founded, so Andreas Papandreou wrote in an article published later in England) that the CIA was behind the coup.

All the prisoners for whom we had worked were inside once more; this time their wives were imprisoned too, and many, many others, including MPs and Ministers. Reports came of widespread and dreadful torture. Some of the prisoners, including women – Thetis among them – were deported to the remote waterless island of Youra, where conditions were like those of a concentration camp. Amalia Fleming, the Greek widow of Sir Alexander Fleming (celebrated as the discoverer of penicillin) with whom she had worked in London, was imprisoned also.

I saw in my mind the faces of people for whom I had grown to have both affection and respect, and could hardly bear it – and I felt helpless.

In the tea-room of the University Library, I met by chance an old friend – Ruth Feinstein. We knew each other from earlier CND days, when our family and hers had been on the Aldermaston marches; and we had worked together on protests against the war in Vietnam. I unburdened myself to her.

"We must do something about this," she said. We both had academic friends connected with Greece through their work in the university, who took an enlightened interest in the affairs of contemporary Greece.

We collected together a small group and started the Cambridge Greek Appeal. It never became a registered charity, so we were not handicapped by any "no politics" ruling. We organised public meetings, and distributed leaflets. Some of these were handed out at the doors of cinemas, then showing the film "Z" (the name of the Greek letter Z is "zeeta" – by which the film is known in Greece. It is also taken to stand for "zee" meaning "he lives"). The film told the story of the murder of the Greek Independent MP, Gregory Lambrakis, by agents of the right-wing government in power before the colonels' coup. Lambrakis had distinguished himself not only as a surgeon and athlete (Balkans Olympics gold medallist) but as a vigorous opponent of nuclear arms and American bases. *The story of "Z" is true* was the title of our leaflet, which related the facts of the murder and the attempted cover-up after it.

And we collected money to assist some of the families made destitute by the coup.

The first public meeting of the Cambridge Greek Appeal, held in the Cambridge Union, was memorable. The speakers represented Greek political parties opposed to each other in normal times but united in their opposition to the colonels' junta. Nevertheless, I felt a little nervous when I went to meet them at the station with our mini. Crammed into it were Helen Vlachou, editor of the respected Conservative daily, *Kathemerini*, and two noted politicians of whose names I have no record – one a Communist, the other from the Centre. It was the rush-hour, so they were in close proximity for about half an hour before we reached the restaurant appointed for dinner. But all was harmony.

The Union was packed. The speeches were excellent. At the end we had a bumper collection for the Cambridge Greek Appeal.

In 1967 Cambridge students were, I think, more politically conscious and active than most of them have been since. A powerful movement grew among them for a return to democracy in Greece. They invited Andreas Papandreou, son of the former Prime Minister (and later Prime Minister himself), to speak. They organised demonstrations, one of which became notorious as the "Garden House Hotel Riot". As luck would have it, I had flu and could not take part – perhaps just as well. Part of the junta's policy was to boost tourism and so win friends. (Some of the hotels which have disfigured the Greek coast were built then.) Cambridge tourist agencies, not loath to cash in on the situation, organised a big promotion dinner at the hotel. A crowd of students made their presence felt. I believe windows were broken; the police used hoses. Arrests were made and some of the student leaders imprisoned, one for as long as a year. Soon afterwards, a large part of the hotel was burned down. Some of us saw it as a judgement. (But a new, even plushier hotel is now in its place.)

The question arose – how to get our Appeal money to the Greek families in need? Diana Pym at the League had good contacts, so we sent it to her.

But I felt we should spread the net wider and draw in more people to support the oppressed Greeks. Being a Friend, I turned to the Society. There is a procedure to follow if a Friend wants the Society to take up his/her personal concern. First you must win over the "Preparative" Meeting you belong to. In my case this was Jesus Lane Meeting, Cambridge. This Meeting then decides if your concern should go further – to the Monthly Meeting, which includes several Preparative

Meetings in the area. In those days it had then to be passed on to Quarterly Meeting – even bigger – before reaching the "Meeting for Sufferings" in London, which is nation-wide in its representation and the ultimate decision-making body on such matters.

In due course a letter arrived from the Clerk of Sufferings inviting me to speak in Friends' House, London. It was the first time I had ever addressed such a huge gathering, and I was nervous. The clerk smiled encouragingly as I stood up, but after I had said my piece, there was a long silence. Then a young man stood up in the middle of the hall: it was my old friend, David Blamires, who had worked with me in ARC! "Why is everyone so silent?" he demanded. "This is something we should take up!" From here and there in the great hall agreement came and with it the necessary consensus for action. There was no dissent at all. The question simply arose, "How to set about it?"

The matter was handed to the FSC (Friends' Service Council), which then dealt with Quaker work abroad. Meetings all over the country were circulated. There grew up a network of Quaker families willing to "adopt" a Greek family. But how to find the Greek families to be adopted? The Society is a religious one, and non-political, so it prefers to work as independently as possible. I believe there was friendly communication between Diana Pym and the responsible person at Friends' House, in order to avoid overlap, but no more than that. A Friend must be found, capable of finding the right families in Greece.

She was found in Cambridge, in my own Meeting – Jesus Lane. Joy Jones was fluent in Greek. She and her husband, Noel, had run for years a Quaker boarding school in northern Greece after the war to train village girls in skills which would enable them to earn a living. In that police state which Greece had become Joy found the families in need; help and friendship came to them from British Quaker families.

The Cambridge Greek Appeal still had some money in the kitty. Diana Pym suggested that we should use it in a particular way. Among the many prisoners of the junta there were some who were very ill, mostly women. Could we find a person of standing, who would be recognised as such by the Colonels, who would be willing to go out to Athens and plead personally with Papadopoulos, the most powerful among them, for the release of these prisoners?

I went to consult the UNA (United Nations Association) Regional Officer for East Anglia, Basil Hembry. We had become acquainted when Martin was secretary and then Janet, chairman of Cambridge Youth UNA. Basil suggested Sir Robert Birley. Sir Robert was a distinguished educationalist, both historian and German scholar; had been headmaster of Charterhouse, then Eton; visiting professor at Witwatersrand University (from which he returned even more strongly anti-apartheid than he had been before); and then Professor at the City University. He was always deeply concerned for human rights, and accepted our proposal. There was enough money for his wife, Elinor, to go too. Before they left, I visited them at their home in Somerton, Somerset, to brief them. In the spring of 1969 the Birleys set out for Athens. We heard later that the conditions of the sick prisoners had improved – but they were not released.

Just two months after the colonels' coup in Greece, in June 1967, an event of even more catastrophic proportions took place in Palestine: the "six day war" which enabled Israel to seize territories it had not hitherto conquered, the "West Bank", the Gaza Strip, the Golan in Syria, and East Jerusalem. Not till five years later did I begin to learn something about the suffering that that has caused for the indigenous people of Palestine.

CHAPTER EIGHT

Soviet prisoners; first Middle Eastern journey

In 1969 Michael had a change of job which inevitably affected what I did. He always wanted to help those most in need and in the most effective way possible. For some time he had felt increasing frustration at the hours spent in the courts waiting for cases to come up; and saddened by what he felt unfair and unnecessary committals to prison. He decided to go where offenders most needed friendship and advice. (The official brief for Probation Officers was an enlightened one: "To advise, assist, and befriend.") The Probation Service had recently taken over the Welfare Service in prisons, so he took a post as Welfare Officer in Wandsworth: a jail for recidivists. An additional motive for taking this post was, I am sure, the need he felt at that time to put more distance between himself and me.

> Let there be spaces in your togetherness
> And let the winds of the heavens dance between you.
> Love one another, but make not a bond of love...

So wrote the Lebanese poet, Kahlil Gibran. Paradoxically, by keeping spaces between us we each became the other's closest friend; each "doing our own thing", but lending a hand in the other's work as appropriate. Over the years several of Michael's "clients" on probation stayed with us when they needed a roof over their heads; and Michael encouraged and helped me in my various endeavours.

Wandsworth is on the far side of London from Cambridge. At first we both thought we should move to live nearer the prison; and as there was a scarcity of teachers of Russian, I gave in my notice at St Mary's Convent, the school where I had been teaching for six years, so that they would have plenty of time to appoint my successor. Then I went house-hunting in Wandsworth.

Being country-bred I have never liked big towns – London least of all, in spite of its many advantages. And Wandsworth, after Cambridge! The whole area seemed grey and depressing. Luckily, Michael was not

sure if he would be able to stand working in the prison indefinitely –
we had better not give up the Cambridge house, he thought. So he
lived for eight years in a bed-sit near the prison during the week, coming
home at weekends. He enjoyed the complete change, he assured me,
with gardening and walks in the country. During the week Wandsworth
Common and concerts at the Festival Hall revived his spirits; and an
outlet for his feelings about the prison system was provided by his gift
for writing verse, just as it had for what he felt about nuclear arms. An
only child, he was always something of a loner, needing space around
him as well as companionship. And he was never fussy about living
conditions. The arrangement worked quite well for some years till a
tragedy occurred.

To help discharged prisoners, for whom it is very difficult to find
jobs, especially if "of no fixed address", Michael bought "Hill House"
in Wandsworth: it was going unusually cheap. It was to be a half-way
hostel. We all, Martin, Janet and I, together with friends of theirs, re-
decorated and prepared it for the first residents – who soon moved in
with a warden.

It was Easter weekend, and we were sitting in the garden, when the
phone rang. Michael returned from answering it, looking shaken and
pale. Half of Hill House had been burned down, and one of the men
had died in the fire. It appeared he had fallen asleep while smoking in
bed. He may have been drunk; and his door was locked, apparently on
the inside. For Michael this blow was indescribably painful and bitter.
A year or two later he took early retirement. He was a very tired sixty-
two.

Alone in Cambridge during the week without a job I had had to
find something to do. Sadly, in Greece the political situation seemed
set and unchangeable for the time being, and by 1970 many people
were giving humanitarian aid. I was in the fortunate position then of
not needing paid work. Both Michael's parents had died; and as he was
the sole legatee we were now reasonably well off. (That, indeed, was
how he had been able to buy Hill House.) My Russian was good after
having completed a degree in it in 1966 in Cambridge, and having
practised it for many years, so I decided to try and use it on behalf of
Soviet political prisoners. My third visit to the Soviet Union in 1969
had been particularly depressing; and back in Cambridge I had read a
book which had greatly affected me. It was Marchenko's *My Testimony*,
in which he describes in horrifying detail life in Soviet prisons and
labour-camps.

I consulted Peter Reddaway, a Cambridge acquaintance lecturing
in Soviet Politics at the London School of Economics, with whom I had
become acquainted when, as a postgraduate student in Russian Studies

he had been expelled from Russia at the same time that I had been turned back from a Dutch airport. (I had gone to Holland to take part in an international women's demonstration against nuclear arms outside the building where a NATO conference was being held. For a few hours only, the Dutch authorities banned foreign demonstrators from entering the country. I was unlucky enough to arrive during the ban, of which I was unaware. It is a sickening experience being put back on a plane and it helps one to understand the torture that asylum seekers and stateless refugees have to endure when shuttled to and fro between inhospitable countries.)

Peter said there was something even worse going on in the Soviet Union than labour camps and prisons: it was the abuse of psychiatry to put dissidents in both ordinary mental hospitals and prison mental hospitals. There they were being given drugs which could destroy their personalities. David Markham, an actor who had been in the Soviet Union, was particularly concerned about one such victim whom he had met, Vladimir Bukovsky. Peter suggested that the three of us join together and start a group to work on behalf of these unfortunate people. He was receiving papers smuggled out – case histories of victims, *samizdat* articles – i.e. typed and circulated clandestinely (*samizdat* means "self-publishing") – and so on. So my voluntary work was handed me.

During the next eighteen months I was glued to my desk translating these papers. I also wrote a pamphlet on the subject (*The Internment of Dissenters in Mental Hospitals* printed by John Arliss, Cambridge, and distributed by our group), a letter to *The Times* signed by VIPs (Very Important Psychiatrists), and acting as the group's secretary, maintained a growing correspondence with psychiatrists in various quarters of the globe, to whom I sent the translated papers. Our group grew in size, meeting regularly in London at the LSE. Finally, I was asked to edit a book.

One weekend early in 1972, I was stuck in the translation of a particularly turgid piece of Russian prose by a dissident called Valery Chalidze. I broke off and went down into the garden, where Michael was digging. "Have a break," he advised. "Do something quite different. What about a holiday?"

I thought I might recharge the batteries by meeting some of the victims of this psychiatric abuse. Not keen at that time to return to the Soviet Union, it occurred to me I might visit the Soviet Jews who had been allowed to emigrate to Israel, and of whom I felt I knew a little, having translated their case papers. Peter, I thought, would tell me how to contact them. He advised me to seek help from an acquaintance of his in West Jerusalem, an American Jew on sabbatical leave there for a year, who had become involved in the same campaign.

A visit to Israel seemed a good opportunity also to look into that other matter which had been bugging me for years – the question of the Palestinian refugees. How were they living? Why were they still in camps? I knew then very little about travelling in the Middle East apart from the fact that if one wanted to visit Arab countries and Israel one should go to the former first, and Israel afterwards, as Arab countries refused admittance to travellers with an Israeli stamp in their passports. I wrote for advice to UNRWA – United Nations Relief and Works Agency for Palestine Refugees.

In 1969 UNRWA had issued an urgent appeal world-wide. It was for money to build shelters for the thousands of Palestinians who had fled or been driven from their homes in the West Bank and Gaza Strip in the "six day war" of June 1967, and had not been allowed back by Israel. Many of them were refugees for the second time, living in tents on the barren hillsides of Jordan: suffering from the heat in summer, but even more from the torrential rain and bitter cold in the winter. First their tents collapsed in the rain, then came snow. UNRWA had decided to put up shelters which would provide more protection. For as long as they could, the refugees held out against this. They were afraid that more permanent dwellings than tents would diminish their chances of returning home (their natural right according to the UN Declaration of Human Rights). But small children and old people were suffering too much: they gave in. However, they would not accept solidly built shelters – the walls were to be only of asbestos or zinc. UNRWA in its appeal gave the price of such a shelter. That year, 1969, Michael and I would celebrate our silver wedding: we decided that two shelters would be our presents to each other. The decision had far-reaching consequences for us both.

The Commissioner-General of UNRWA, Sir John Rennie, had sent a very friendly "thank you" letter and more information about the Agency's work. At that time UNRWA ran a sponsorship scheme: contributors, when they paid the cost of a student in vocational training or of a child at school, were put in touch with the student or school pupil in question. Michael and I decided to "sponsor" a girl in the UNRWA VTC (Vocational Training Centre) at Ramallah, "West Bank". Her home was in Deir el Balah Camp, Gaza Strip. It seemed to me, if I was going to the Middle East, that UNRWA might be the organisation to turn to for help and advice. I looked forward to seeing more of its work both in Jordan, where the new shelters had been put up, and in the Gaza Strip. Now our student's training was finished, and she was teaching English at a school in her camp. It would be interesting to meet her. We would be able to talk, I thought, although I knew no Arabic.

When I wrote to the Contributions Officer at the UNRWA HQ, then in Beirut, about my plan, I was kindly offered help in making a comprehensive tour. I would go first to Lebanon, then Jordan, and then the Occupied Territories in Palestine: the "West Bank" and Gaza Strip. I set out in early June, 1972.

At that time Lebanon was relatively calm; but I could not like Beirut. Never before had I seen such a glaring, obscene contrast between wealth and extreme poverty. Cheek by jowl with blocks of luxury flats were some of the most pitiful refugee camps where Palestinians lived. Under the arches of bridges were huddled destitute families of other nationalities. Not till I returned to India and saw Calcutta, Madras and Bombay did I see anything like it again. (Some of these Palestinian refugee camps were soon to be destroyed, and thousands of their inhabitants slaughtered: Tal al Zaatar in 1976; Sabra and Shatila in 1982; then Bourj Barajneh.)

An UNRWA official, Madame Vidal, took me to see some of the camps in Beirut and South Lebanon: those in the south were poor and overcrowded, but what I saw of them gave me the impression of relatively settled small towns. (They were soon to suffer: battered by massive Israeli air-raids in 1974, when I was next in Beirut; continuously struck in a similar way ever since, and some almost totally destroyed during the Israeli invasion in 1982 – to be painfully rebuilt and then battered again and again.)

Madame Vidal also showed me what UNRWA was doing for the refugees. I was taken to clinics and schools. The schools, of course, interested me most. I was struck, as all privileged westerners are, by the contrast between the desperate keenness of the pupils to learn and the absence of so much that our children, less keen, are able to enjoy: libraries; playing fields; pictures and maps on the walls; gymnasiums; music; drama; sport; and educational toys for the little ones. There was none of this. It was all cramped and spartan: old-fashioned fixed desks for two, usually occupied by three children; two schools using the same building in shifts.

For a few days I stayed in Brummana, a beautiful resort high up in the pine-covered mountains above Beirut – at the Quaker boarding school there. How different it all was! I could not help appreciating the good education that was being provided there for Arabs of various nationalities – from Lebanon itself and the Gulf (there were even a few well-to-do Palestinians) as well as for the children of some European and American expatriates; but the contrast with the UNRWA schools down below was painful.

I was taken from Beirut by UNRWA transport through the mountains down into the Syrian plain and across it to Amman, Jordan. There Ann

Foley, one of the two Quaker volunteers responsible for kindergartens in Jerash and Baqa'a (two of the new 1967 refugee camps), rescued me from a rather scruffy hotel, put me in the YWCA, and took me under her wing.

The kindergarten walls at Jerash camp were pock-marked with bullet holes, as were other buildings – traces of the fighting in September 1970, when the Jordanian army, on King Hussein's orders, drove the Palestinian guerrillas out of the country, killing thousands of civilians as well as guerrillas in the process. I admired Ann's work with the children and their as yet untrained teachers. Here was a little oasis for the little ones to escape to from their tiny box-like refugee shelters: a place where there were toys and games and books; and their mothers could have a little relief, knowing their offspring were being cared for and set on the right path for learning.

Ann did a great deal for my education on the Palestine question. She described what had happened to these people in 1967: how one little girl she knew, escaping with her parents across the Allenby Bridge over the Jordan River, had been terribly burned with napalm and was still suffering. Napalm – the hideous weapon that shocked the world when the Americans used it in Vietnam! Did anyone know that this is what Israelis had used on Palestinians and Jordanians, I wondered. Then there was Ralph Halabi, a Palestinian refugee who grew roses in the Jordan valley, on the eastern, Jordanian side. Questioned by a Western journalist as to why he once gave hospitality to a guerrilla, he answered, "I would give food and drink, even to an enemy, in this heat." (The Jordan valley, 1,400ft below sea-level, is tropical.) Shortly after this remark was made public, Ralph Halabi went at Christmas time to pick some of his roses. He was seen by an Israeli sniper on the other side of the river and shot dead.

At the YWCA I made friends with two Palestinian ladies who were living there. They both came from Nablus, in the "West Bank". One of them had been deported for organising assistance for the families of men who had been killed or imprisoned in the wake of the 1967 war. The other was an artist, responsible for the art teaching in all UNRWA schools – in Lebanon, Syria, Jordan, West Bank, and Gaza Strip. With minimal resources, she was having a hard job.

UNRWA showed me round the "established" camps, dating from the 1948 exodus, as well as the 1967 ones, then still called "emergency camps". The city of Amman had grown round the old ones in the same way as Beirut had grown round the camps there. The new camps were raw and bleak. Baqa'a, for example, is situated some distance from Amman on a particularly barren hillside, windswept in winter, and exposed to the baking sun in summer. (In a few years, however, trees

79

planted by the refugees provided some greenery and shade.) The clinics and schools I saw told me a similar story to those in Lebanon.

Gradually the Palestinian tragedy began to unfold in a living way before my eyes: I saw that thousands upon thousands of people had been forced to flee their country, and had not been allowed by their country's new foreign rulers to return to their homes. (About 750,000 Palestinians were driven out in 1948; about 400,000 in 1967 – and, of course, their numbers had increased with the birth of children and grandchildren.) Why had it happened? And how was it that they were still living in camps? In England, it was said, "They are kept there by Arab governments to be used as political pawns against Israel." In Jordan, it looks quite different. Jordan was (and basically still is) a poor country, largely desert. It was helped economically after the establishment of OPEC in 1963, by Saudi Arabia. How could such a country be expected to absorb a vast and sudden influx of destitute refugees, mainly peasants, with no other skill beyond that of producing food from the soil? There was no cultivable land available for them in Jordan! A few found casual labouring jobs – but Jordan had its own unemployment problem. Before World War II, affluent, industrial Britain had demanded £100 guarantee (equals £2,900 in 1998) for every single refugee trying to escape from Hitler's gas chambers, and many of them had qualifications, moreover, which could have been put to good use in Britain. It seems incredibly presumptuous and cruel to criticise hospitable poor countries which open their frontiers to numberless masses fleeing for their lives.

Moreover, ever since its establishment in 1948, Israel has ignored repeated UN Resolutions insisting that the refugees be allowed to return; ignored too its own assurance, made one can only suppose in order to be accepted into membership of the UN, that it *would* allow them back. Never has anything been done by the international community to oblige Israel to obey the resolutions. How different from the treatment of Iraq!

An Israeli friend has said to me, "We took their country – their land, and everything they had, and turned them into refugees; and we have the nerve to say, 'Their Arab brothers should look after them.' To me, it stinks."

I was taken down into the valley of the River Jordan which marks the eastern frontier of Palestine with the Kingdom of Jordan. And there I saw Karameh.

CHAPTER NINE

Westwards to Jerusalem

Karameh…acres and acres of broken mud huts, the most pathetic ruins I had ever seen: sadder, more pitiful, than bombed Le Havre, or the rubble of Freiburg; more distressing than any destruction I had seen in blitzed London: for here had lived 40,000 refugees driven from their homes in Palestine in 1948, who had lost everything they possessed; and had then, through great toil and hardship, built their lives anew in a hot, barren land. They had found water underground, dug wells, and irrigated the soil. Once again they had been able to grow the citrus fruit for which they had made the name "Jaffa" famous, and in addition – thanks to the tropical heat in the Jordan valley – bananas and papayas. They had built for themselves those humble homes, and UNRWA had provided a school and a clinic.

Here and there among the ruins I saw washing hanging out and children playing: a few refugee families had crept back and were rebuilding. It was June 1972: five years since the "six-day war" and four years, three months since the Battle of Karameh in March 1968.

After the "six-day war" and the establishment of military occupation in the West Bank, young men had set out from Karameh on guerrilla raids westwards across the narrow river. As always, massive retribution followed. The Israelis mounted a major offensive, crossing the river into Jordan with tanks, and supported by bombers. They were repulsed by the Jordanian army and Palestinian guerrillas fighting together; but Karameh lay in ruins. The inhabitants had fled from the fighting; some were killed or wounded as they fled; and some were on the move for the fourth time: first it had been to the West Bank in 1948, when the Zionists in Palestine, during their "War of Independence" had had the chance to empty the land of its Palestinian inhabitants and thereby create a Jewish State of Israel; in 1967 to the tented camps near Amman; driven down by cold and torrential rain to Karameh, January 1968; and then away again, two months later, by the fighting. A few had ventured back to look after their crops; but were shot from across the river, as Ralph Halabi had been.

We crossed the short wooden bridge over the River Jordan – by special bus. No cars or "service" (communal) taxis are allowed across this "frontier". On the western side of the bridge a young Arab woman, heavily pregnant, was turned back by an Israeli border guard. (Refugees might then, if they could afford the permit – and otherwise qualify – obtain permission to cross from Jordan to visit relatives in the occupied West Bank for one month in the summer between 1st June and 30th September.) She had, apparently, come a week too early. Perhaps she could not read the permit document, written in Hebrew, with dates in western numerals? The bus left her at the roadside, crying.

And then followed hours of waiting in the intense heat, with interrogation and minute examination of every article I had in my luggage; even my toothpaste was squeezed from the tube. When the guard came to a box of Lebanese chocolates that I was bringing as a present for a friend and began to tip the chocolates out, I lost patience and stopped him. I could get away with it because I was European. It would not do for a Palestinian to protest. Many a time in the years which followed I heard Palestinian friends relate what had been done to them at the "Bridge". When I next crossed it, I found that tourists and pilgrims, privileged Westerners for the most part, went through a different channel from the indigenous inhabitants of Palestine. The tourists have preferential treatment, and cannot see what is being done to the Palestinians. One Palestinian friend has told me how a beautiful picture of King's College, Cambridge, which I had given her, was taken and not returned; another, over seventy years of age and one of the most respected citizens of Jerusalem, how she was forced to undress and open her legs so that a woman soldier could look up between them with a torch. And another how she had had a new dress returned to her torn and soiled; and so on and so on: the process taking hours.

We drove on to Jericho, through the town and then a flat plain past a large refugee camp on the right – Aqabat Jaber – and then up a winding road through the wilderness; from below sea level and the tropical heat to the relative cool of the hills. As we drove past Bethany and round the Mount of Olives, a view of Jerusalem opened out on the left, with the golden dome of the "Mosque of Omar" conspicuous in the foreground. But straight ahead, along the crest of the hill to the north of the city, rose serried ranks of eight-storey buildings with slit windows. My heart sank. I knew what they were: new blocks of fortress-style flats built for Israeli Jews on land confiscated since 1967 from Palestinians.

We arrived at the Shepherd Hotel – no longer a hotel now – situated on a bend of the road going north to Nablus, on the slope of the hill at the top of which those new flats stood. Bulldozers and cranes were at work close by, for more such buildings to go up.

After lunch and a short siesta, I went out. All I had seen weighed heavily on me: the huge refugee camps in Jordan, the destruction of Karameh, the occupation by foreign newcomers of the land on the edge of Arab Jerusalem near the hotel. Tears were always near the surface with me and I found myself crying in the street. I turned to hide my face and looked through some railings at a bed of brightly-coloured flowers in someone's garden. A voice asked, "Why are you crying?"

I looked up and there was an elderly gentleman wearing a red tarbush standing the other side of the railings, a watering-can in his hand. "It's because of all I have seen," I answered. "This morning I crossed the Bridge from Amman."

He invited me into his garden, asked me to sit down, and made some coffee in his garden hut. It was my first experience of the ready hospitality and friendliness which Palestinians show a stranger. We drank the strong sweet Turkish coffee out of tiny cups, had a chat, and I felt calmer. My host's family name was Husseini. His red tarbush was the traditional head covering for a Palestinian "notable".

Then I went for a walk in the field which sloped down opposite the hotel towards the Old City. A young man was walking up and down deep in a book. Some boys were playing ball. They threw it to me, I caught it and joined in their game; and then, suddenly, it was stones coming at me! The young man came to my rescue and told the boys off. He was a student of history at the Arab University of Beirut, he said, Nabil by name, and he was preparing for an exam by learning the text-book off by heart (!). As we walked back, I noticed a man sitting by an onion bed. Nabil remarked, "He lives there."

"Lives there?" I asked incredulously. I could see no building at all. We went down, closer. Nabil spoke to the man, who showed us that there was a cave in the hillside. We were invited in. There were three beds in it and a paraffin stove for cooking. The entrance to the cave had been built up and a door made in it. It was very dark inside. I was introduced to the man's wife and daughter, and Nabil and I were invited to drink coffee. A stool was brought for me to sit on and I learnt this family's story.

The husband had owned a large citrus orchard to the west of Jerusalem, and employed four workmen. They were comfortably off. "And then, in 1948, the Jews came, and there was shelling and bombs. My two brothers were killed, so we left quickly. We found this cave and are still here. We have not been allowed back. When we left, I had just had a big operation, so I could not work, and I hadn't enough money to buy a house. It is better in the cave than in a refugee camp, for we can look out over Jerusalem. I've planted some vegetables and a few fruit trees. My daughter works as a servant. I don't like that. But we have to eat. Yes, in winter it is very cold and damp in the cave. But what can we do?"

That night I could not sleep; but writhed with anger and indignation at all I had seen and learnt. It was not the last of such nights.

(Some years later I again visited the family in the cave. The old man was very sick and in rags. There are other caves in that hillside, also inhabited by refugees, but I have not been into them. Will the people be evicted to make room for new buildings for Jewish immigrants from the Soviet Union? It is happening not far from this spot. If so, where will the homeless people go?)

Mr Jarallah, the UNRWA Information Officer for the West Bank, took charge of my visits to some of the refugee camps in the area. There are *twenty* in the West Bank! Several are round Jerusalem and Bethlehem – places where tourists and Christian pilgrims go. How often do such visitors notice the camps, I wondered, and think about the people who live in them, ask where they came from, why they left their homes, why they are still in the camps, and what kind of existence they lead – twenty-four years on? (Now, in 1998, fifty years on?) Certainly, one or two, such as Kalandia, north of Jerusalem, or Jalazone, north of Ramallah, about ten miles from Jerusalem, look to the casual observer much like villages, though the little houses are crammed together more than is normal, and are not built so solidly as those of Palestinian villages. Dheisheh, just south of Bethlehem, was hewn in 1948 out of a rocky hillside, and its inhabitants have needed all the guts that that endeavour showed to stand up to the special persecution they have suffered since 1967.

We drove down again into the heat of the Jordan valley, to visit the camps spread out round Jericho, below the Mount of Christ's Temptation: Aqabat Jaber, Ein el Sultan, and Nuweimeh. Nuweimeh was a ghost camp. Its entire population fled into Jordan in 1967, terrified by the approach of the Israeli army and the shooting. Prickly weeds were growing in the sandy alleys. In the compounds of the little mud houses was still evidence of hasty departure – an overturned flowerpot, a sandal or a sock sinking into the sand. Inside, strewn on the floors: old letters, UNRWA exercise books, a tattered copy of *David Copperfield* abridged and simplified. I picked up a bullet with Hebrew letters on it. Clothes, furniture, utensils, all the possessions which the inhabitants could not take in their headlong flight had gone – looted by Israeli soldiers, I was told. It was hot and very quiet. A few people had stayed in Ein el Sultan and Aqabat Jaber. For economy's sake, boys and girls from the two camps were attending one primary school: the first UNRWA co-educational establishment. Teachers and pupils alike seemed to be enjoying the experience. *A quelquechose malheur est bon!* Only a tenth of the thousands of inhabitants of the three camps had remained to look after the orchards and fields which, as on the other side of the river, they had created. And bit by bit the land was being taken away from them for new Israeli settlements, and the water supply drained from the land they were left, by the deep wells which only new Israeli settlers are allowed to bore.

Antranig Bakerjian, for more than thirty years an UNRWA official, has described to me how the refugees fled from these camps:

> On the Monday when the war began the Israelis had dropped napalm on the two Jordanian military camps north and south of Jericho. The effect on the Jericho people was terrible. They were called upon, on an emergency basis, to help take the victims of the napalm out of the army camps to hospital. All available transport – military and civilian – had to be used. For the first time, the people saw the effect of napalm on the human body, and understood what war was. The convoys of victims passed by the refugee camps. When they saw the Jordanian army retreating, they tried to escape with it.

> The Israeli soldiers arrived on 7th June and it was, of course, extremely hot. The harvest was ripe all over the flat fields around Jericho. The Israelis cleverly dropped incendiary bombs on them – the whole area was set on fire. Can you imagine the scene? Convoys of soldiers with thousands and thousands of refugees sandwiched between the military vehicles, being strafed from the air, streaming in terror along the road with fields aflame on every side. It took the Jericho refugees from about 10.30 a.m. to 7 p.m. on that day to leave the town. By 6 p.m. most of the people had left. The Israelis then blew up the Allenby Bridge across the river. Just the broken bridge – a cat-walk – was left for the remaining refugees to cross over by. The Israelis stormed at high speed through all the streets of the town, in tanks and armoured cars shooting wildly on every side, sirens hooting. A curfew was declared, loudspeakers announcing that anyone outside their house would be shot on sight.

I did not forget the other purpose of this trip to the Middle East, and telephoned the contact in Jewish West Jerusalem whose name Peter Reddaway had given me. An American voice answered, "Sure, come along!" I asked for directions. "Aw, get a taxi!" he replied. It would be expensive – a private taxi from one end of Jerusalem to the other, so I decided to find my way by bus. There were several changes, and I arrived a little late for the appointment, rather hot and bothered. A young man was before me, standing on the doorstep. We were ushered in together. The American suggested I should sit and drink a glass of lemonade while he dealt with the young man first. Waiting in the same room, I could not help overhearing their conversation, which was about the Soviet dissidents in mental hospitals. They were planning to publish the papers (including ones I had translated?) and make a business of it. Make a business out of the suffering of those unfortunate people?

My turn came. Yes, the American knew my name, and the work I had done. I asked if he would kindly give me the phone number of Ilya Rips and other Soviet Jews who had come to Israel, and whose cases had become familiar to me; I would really like to make the personal acquaintance of those whom I knew only through their written histories. "No," he answered, "I don't think it is necessary for you to meet them." I was surprised and disappointed; but did not question or protest. (After my return, a Jewish friend in the Working Group, Ellen de Kadt, said to me, "You really are simple, Eleanor! Didn't you see that he looked on you as a rival, and that is why he didn't want you to meet those people?") The heat and physical weariness had something to do with my passive acceptance I think; but even more the other subject that was occupying my mind: Palestinian refugees – forgotten, it seemed, by the Western world: despairing after twenty-four years, or five years as the case might be, of living in wretched camps, with UN resolutions in their favour ignored; for Israel did not want them back, and had a powerful ally in the Security Council: America.

I made one more effort to see a new Jewish immigrant from the USSR. I had brought with me the phone number of Professor Boris Zuckerman. I found he lived with his family in a new flat in one of the great blocks beginning to encircle Arab Jerusalem, in Ramat Eshkol. He had not been incarcerated in a mental hospital in the Soviet Union, but I understood he might have been. It was not clear whether he was happy or not with his new life. There was a melancholy about him, but he said very little. I continued to struggle mentally with the dilemma I was in.

It had been relatively easy to persuade Western psychiatrists and the public of the English speaking world, all round the globe, of something unhealthy going on in the Soviet Union. Letters were accepted by *The Times* without question. Soviet abuse of psychiatry had quickly become common knowledge. There were protests at conferences – a campaign was already well under way. Had I made my contribution? Was there something else I should put my mind to? I resolved to try, when I returned to England, to do what I had promised – draft a book on the Soviet subject; but at the same time think what could be done about this other problem, more desperate, more deep-rooted, and concerning a far larger number of people, which included children; but most of all because I had begun to suspect that a smoke-screen had deliberately been spread for years over the facts. *More people had to know the truth,* I thought.

A day or two later we went on to the Gaza Strip. There is a military check-point at the entrance to it, which over recent years has become more and more complex and forbidding. Quite soon beyond it there was then and for some years later a herd of camels in a field on the left – gone now. Further on, on each side of the road, all the way to Gaza town, there are orange groves. In winter, which can be grey, cold and wet even here, the masses of golden fruit among the dark green leaves gladden the eye; and at blossom time there is a delicious scent. After World War II we could buy, in England, oranges stamped "Gaza"; but not since 1967. Any Gaza oranges are lumped in with those marked "Jaffa" – which is now in Israel. There are vineyards growing out of the sand too, also planted by Palestinians.

On arrival in Gaza town it is not only the sights you see that are depressing; but the smell. There are pleasant quarters, near the sea: wide streets with abundant greenery – palms, and fruit and flowering trees. But much of the town is littered with garbage, and some of the garbage is of a very insanitary kind: rotting vegetable matter, loo paper, the occasional used sanitary towel or dead animal. The whole of the Gaza Strip, barely twenty-five miles long by five miles wide, is sand; it lies at the coastal edge of the Negev desert. The sand gets everywhere, and makes cleanliness in the streets difficult, for all but the main streets are unpaved dirt tracks; but more important, military occupation has prevented any kind of organised self-help under pain of punishment, and the occupation authorities have never been concerned with the upkeep of any urban areas inhabited by Arabs. There is a twenty-five mile long beautiful sandy beach, (since the occupation with restricted access for Palestinians); and the glowing red sunsets reflected in the water of the Mediterranean can for a moment take the visitor's mind off the miseries on the land.

I was put by UNRWA into a comfortable private hotel, "Marna House", with a wide lawn, two trees with dense foliage which provide shade for a veranda, and flower beds bright with canna lilies and roses. It was not nearly as expensive in 1972 as it is now (for the cost of living has rocketed) and the proprietress, the late Mrs Nasser, as soon as she learnt on my next visit that I was trying to help the refugees, refused from then on to charge me for meals. Recently, there was a programme on TV about Marna House. The hotel has become quite famous – and, alas, too expensive for my pocket.

There are eight huge, particularly squalid and congested refugee camps in the Strip: Jabaliya in the north; Shati (or Beach) Camp adjacent to Gaza town; Deir el Balah (Shrine of the date palms) also by the sea, further south; in the centre of the Strip, Nuseirat, Mughazi, and Bureij; further south still, Khan Younis; and at the southernmost end, on the frontier with Egypt, Rafah. More refugees live crowded together in the slums of the main towns: Gaza, Khan Younis, and Rafah. The many thousands of refugees from what has become Israel outnumber the Gaza residents. The population density is one of the highest in the world: about 900,000 in an area less than twenty-five miles long and five miles wide. Between the camps and villages the Strip residents and the refugees have made the most of the land, growing fruit and vegetables and other crops. The people in the camps have not since 1967 been allowed to build homes for themselves outside the camp confines for their expanding numbers, unless they buy land on an expensive lease and destroy their original home. This does nothing to lessen overcrowding in the camps, of course. And one wonders what will happen to those who have moved when the lease expires.

Into this crowded area have come Israelis. Already in 1972 there were new settlements – surrounded by barbed wire, with watchtowers manned by armed soldiers. For the settlements are built on Palestinian land, and settlers mean there is not only less land, but less of the precious water for local people. As in the West Bank, the settlers are armed. By 1994 about forty per cent of the land of the Strip had been taken and a whole length of beach, which is for Israeli settlers and tourists only.

(In 1987 I was taken on a "settlement tour" in the Strip. One port of call I cannot forget. It was to a place for relaxation and enjoyment for Israelis. There was a pavilion with a well-stocked bar; stables, and a field with a track round it for horse riding. Just outside the fence we saw a man in Arab dress at work in a small vegetable plot. Our guide spoke to him in Arabic and translated for us. "He says all this used to be his land. When I asked if he was paid adequate compensation for it, he laughed and said, 'You must be joking!'")

UNRWA took me to its "installations" as it had done in Lebanon, Jordan and the West Bank: schools, clinics, and welfare centres where women do sewing and embroidery so they can earn something for their families. And of course I was taken to visit Tahrir El Ghazawi, whom Michael and I had "sponsored" for her teacher training in Ramallah. The UNRWA Information Officer for the Gaza Strip, Said Filfil, went with me.

Tahrir lived with her mother and father in Deir el Balah camp, quite near its northernmost end, and not far from the sea. Unusually for a Palestinian family, her parents had had only two children. There was an elder sister, much older than Tahrir, married, with a numerous family, who lived a few doors along in the same narrow alley.

Said Filfil and I had been invited to lunch. This meal was my first of many in Palestinian homes; and now, as always later, I felt overwhelmed by the generous hospitality. That day we ate stuffed pigeons, various salad dishes, and fruit. Sometimes one knows that the spread of delicious food has meant sacrificial inroads into the family income. (If one has had time to do so, it is good to say in advance if one is a vegetarian, for meat is very expensive; otherwise, if you are offered it, you should eat it, so as not to hurt your hosts, even if you are a vegetarian!) We sat in one of the two small rooms that comprised the Ghazawi home – the other was the kitchen. Tahrir's mother, who had done the cooking, did not sit with us. Being of the old school, she would not eat with a man not of the family. But, to my surprise, Tahrir needed Said Filfil as interpreter to be able to talk with me, although she was a teacher of English.

This set me thinking. Among their other deprivations, Palestinian refugees cannot normally travel. As a modern language teacher, I knew how valuable, how essential indeed, it is to live for a time in the country and among the people of the language one teaches. The refugees have not the means to do this; in addition, all Palestinians in the Gaza Strip, refugees and residents alike, are stateless people. They have no right to a passport: and every Palestinian under occupation must get a *laissez passer* from the Israeli military authorities, even when they are fortunate enough to travel on UNRWA business, when they may be issued with a temporary UN passport.

Tahrir could teach only from the text-book. How dull for her, I could not help thinking, and how dull for her pupils! In the Gaza Strip, native English speakers are more rare than in the West Bank, so there is little opportunity for practice. And there are still very few books in English – very few books of any kind. The Red Crescent Society has a small library in Gaza town; but to date, there is no public library in the whole of the Gaza Strip – population nearly a million.

CHAPTER TEN

Background history of the Israel-Palestine conflict; maps

If you want to go from Jerusalem to a West Bank village by bus, you go to the Arab bus station just outside the walls of the Old City. Behind the buses is the rocky slope of a small hill, in which are two large holes like eye sockets. This is believed by some to be the "place of the skull" at the summit of which the Crucifixion took place. If you turn right as you come out of the bus station and go round the corner into the Nablus Road, opposite the Damascus Gate, you will soon find on your right a little lane which leads to the entrance to the Garden Tomb. At the far end of the garden you are on the "place of the skull".

The garden is beautifully kept and a quiet place to sit, if there are not a crowd of tourists there. One day when I went in, a man was lecturing to a tourist group gathered in front of the Tomb, and I stopped to listen. He was extolling the achievements of the Israelis in Palestine, and knocking the Palestinians. Politics, and of such a kind in this holy place, and in Arab Jerusalem, illegally annexed by Israel after military conquest? Surprised, I asked at the little souvenir shop inside the entrance who the lecturer was. "He is Colonel Orde Dobbie, Chairman of the Friends of the Tomb Association." A few years later I found the name again on one of the leaflets published by the "International Christian Embassy of Jerusalem", and was shocked by what I read. It was political propaganda of the crudest kind; and the ICEJ Director was Johann Luckhoff, a pastor of the South African Dutch Reform Church, noted for its approval of apartheid. Israeli political leaders, such as Yitzhak Shamir, were prominent among the ICEJ's supporters.

When we lived in Seaton, a Major Dobbie used to run evangelical services on the beach during the summer holidays on behalf of the CSSM (Children's Special Service Mission). I had enjoyed those services for the singing and the competitions and sports associated with them. Major Dobbie had tremendous charisma and "a way with children". He later became Governor of Malta, and during World War II it was said that he wielded a sword in one hand and a Bible in the other. Was Colonel Dobbie of the ICEJ a relation? And why the unusual name "Orde"? Orde Wingate was a captain in the British army and a fanatical Zionist, who became notorious in the "Arab Revolt", 1935-9. An example of his ruthless methods is given in an account written by Leonard Mosley, a British journalist:

> Wingate had led one of the Special Night Squads to the edge of an Arab village. He himself went off into the darkness. And then, straight into the trap which Wingate had laid from them, came the Arabs. Dayan and Brenna, nearest the village, let the Arabs pass; they had instructions to hold their fire until the Arabs could be surrounded. Only when the Jews farthest away opened fire did Brenna and Dayan begin to pick off their victims. They killed five and captured four.

> Wingate came back, carrying a Turkish rifle over his shoulder. He looked calm and serene. "Good work. You are fine boys and will make good soldiers," he said.

> He went up to the four Arab prisoners. He said in Arabic: "You have arms in this village. Where have you hidden them?"

> The Arabs shook their heads, and protested ignorance. Wingate reached down and took sand and grit from the ground; he thrust it into the mouth of the first Arab and pushed it down his throat until he choked and puked.

> "Now," he said, "where have you hidden the arms?"

> Still they shook their heads.

> Wingate turned to one of the Jews and, pointing to the coughing and spluttering Arab, said, "Shoot this man."

> The Jew looked at him questioningly and hesitated.

> Wingate said, in a tense voice, "Did you hear? Shoot him."

> The Jew shot the Arab. The others stared for a moment, in stupefaction, at the dead body at their feet...

> "Now speak," said Wingate. They spoke.[1]

I felt I would like to meet Col Orde Dobbie; but first consulted a Palestinian friend as to the wisdom of such a move. "Go, and just listen to what he has to say," was the advice. I made an appointment to see Col Dobbie at his flat in West (now Jewish) Jerusalem. The rain was bucketing down as it can in Palestine in winter, and the streets were awash. My friend offered to take me in his car. "But I won't wait," he said. "You'll have to find your own way back." (Palestinians do not normally go now into West Jerusalem if they can help it.)

The door was opened by a tall, florid-faced man whom I would not have recognised as the lecturer at the Garden Tomb. There was a strong smell of alcohol. He did not recall my name or remember the appointment; but he welcomed me in. He was happy to talk about the ICEJ. Major Dobbie of the CSSM was, he told me, his cousin; and Orde Wingate his godfather, after whom he had been named.

Yes, indeed, the State of Israel was the fulfilment of Divine promise. It was Jews who had the best right to be in the country.[2] Col. Dobbie quoted the Old Testament a great deal; but in the course of the conversation he said with emphasis, "Jesus is my personal Saviour." I have never been able to see, myself, any connection between the life and teaching of Jesus with the theory and practice of political Zionism, the cause of which Col Dobbie had so earnestly espoused. In fact, that Christians can approve robbery, dispossession, and persecution I find highly offensive, as I do the distortion of the truth which makes such approval possible. His words in such a context seemed to me quite meaningless. I asked him if there was anything in the *New* Testament to support the idea of the present State of Israel. "Certainly," he replied, "um…um…" He could not quite put his finger on it and turned to his wife, who had joined us. "Can you help me, dear?" She thought for a time but drew a blank too. At last he said with relief, "There's a verse in the Epistle to the Hebrews…"

On my return to England after this interview, the thought began to nag that I had said nothing whatever to counteract what seemed to me the pernicious falsehoods which the ICEJ was spreading with apparent success. Thousands of simple-minded fundamentalist Christians, particularly "born again" Americans, were now flocking annually to Jerusalem at the invitation of the ICEJ to dance in the streets for the Festival of the Tabernacles, and were generously funding ICEJ activities. Rightly or wrongly, after a couple of months of hesitation I wrote a letter to the Dobbies, pointing out as plainly as possible how many of the ICEJ's statements bore no relation to the facts.

What has happened in Palestine has been presented to Westerners as "very complicated": an assertion that has formed part of the smoke-screen successfully hiding the truth for many years. The basic fact is quite simple: Palestine, the land of the Palestinians, has been taken over by Zionists in two main stages – 1948 and 1967. Most of the indigenous inhabitants of what is now Israel were driven out; those remaining have been discriminated against; and in the occupied West Bank and Gaza Strip, harshly kept down, their lives made so intolerable that some have chosen to leave, for the sake of their children. Many have been deported – from their own country. The Palestinians who took refuge in Lebanon and Jordan and elsewhere in the Arab world have not been allowed back nor even to re-build their lives peacefully outside Palestine. The Palestinians have become the persecuted Semites of today.

The rôle of Britain in the take-over has been inglorious, to put it mildly. The name of Arthur James Balfour, in particular, is associated with it. A politician apparently without moral scruples, compassion, or vision beyond national self-interest of a limited kind, he had, in the early years of this century, been instrumental in promoting the Aliens Act designed to prevent Russian Jews from finding a refuge in Britain when they were fleeing from Tsarist pogroms. (Politicians to this day seem to act on his example in relation to the persecuted who seek asylum here.)

In 1917, when Foreign Secretary, he wrote his notorious letter to Lord Rothschild – to be known later as the Balfour Declaration – in which he expressed the desire of the Government to see established in Palestine a national home for the Jewish people.[3] He hoped that our route to India through the Suez Canal would be protected by having grateful Europeans settled near its Eastern shore; and that the Allies would be supported in the war with Germany by German Jews. Leaflets were dropped over Germany and pamphlets circulated to Jewish soldiers in the armies of Germany and her Central European allies, announcing that, "The Allies are giving the Land of Israel to the people of Israel...Stop fighting the Allies who are fighting for you, for all the Jews...An Allied victory means the Jewish people's return to Zion".[4]

The Declaration clashed with two previous British commitments. In 1915, two years before, Britain had promised Sherif Hussein of Mecca, the leader of Arab Muslims, that certain regions in the West of Arabia, including Palestine, would become independent after the war, if the Arabs in them helped to defeat the Turks, our war-enemies and their overlords. The Arabs honoured their part of the deal.

On 9th December, 1917, General Allenby's forces captured Jerusalem. There he made a public proclamation: "The object of the war in the East on the part of Great Britain was the complete and final liberation of all peoples formerly oppressed by the Turks and the establishment of national governments and administrations in those countries deriving authority from the initiative and free will of the people themselves."

But in 1916 a secret pact had been made with France: the Sykes-Picot Agreement, whereby that very region would be divided into French and British spheres of influence. Lebanon and Syria would go to France; Transjordan and Iraq to Britain. Palestine's fate was left vague.

Britain had been guilty not merely of double-dealing, but triple dealing, so that Arab lives, including Palestinian lives, had been sacrificed in vain.

It is noteworthy that the one person in the British government who opposed the Balfour Declaration was a Jew – Edwin Montagu. (He was to protest again when a few years later Britain discriminated against the Arabs of Palestine in favour of the Jewish immigrants.)

In the post-World War I years, a central principle of the newly-formed League of Nations was the self-determination of peoples. In a secret memorandum to the Cabinet, Balfour wrote: "In Palestine we do not propose even to go through the form of consulting the wishes of the present inhabitants of the country...the Four Great Powers are committed to Zionism..." Moreover, in relation to official statements issued to allay Palestinian suspicions of Britain's intentions, he actually confessed: "So far as Palestine is concerned, the Powers have made no statement of fact which is not admittedly wrong, and no declaration of policy which, at least in the letter, they have not always intended to violate."[5]

The war ended, a Mandate was granted to Britain by the League to govern Palestine and Transjordan. Transjordan (the Jordan of today) was soon given independence; but not Palestine. The reason was clear. Into the Preamble of the Mandate was written the Balfour Declaration! How could it be expected that the people of Palestine, left to themselves, would welcome unlimited foreign immigration into their country – about the size of Wales? *Would we have?*

From 1920 onwards Jewish immigration increased, with the Zionists frequently buying land from absentee landlords. Landlords in Lebanon found it a convenient transaction: they were now under French rule, so the collection of rents had become difficult.

For the Palestinian tenant farmers the aftermath of the sale of the land was even more disastrous than the actual Jewish immigration. For the new landlords *evicted* them with the connivance of the British and often by force. (The film *To Live in Freedom*, made over twenty years ago by dissident Israelis, illustrates this from archive material.) Thousands lost not only their livelihoods, but the homes in which they and their families had lived for generations. They were suddenly made destitute. That was how the troubles began.

In other ways the British showed favour towards the Jewish community. In the Advisory Council for the High Commissioner (Herbert Samuel, himself a Zionist, was the first High Commissioner), the Arab Muslims were in a minority, though of the total population they constituted eighty per cent; and the Zionists were allowed to establish an Agency of their own – "an Administration within an Administration"; but the Palestinians had nothing comparable. Very significantly, only Jews were officially allowed to possess arms. There were demonstrations and riots as a result of all these injustices.

By 1935 immigration numbers had risen to nearly 70,000 a year, swollen by refugees from Hitler's Germany. But the Palestinians have seen no justice in being made to suffer for European crimes. Their great revolt, 1935-9, was put down by the British with extreme cruelty: 5,000 Palestinians were killed, 14,000 wounded. (If one considers population size, that would be the equivalent of 200,000 British killed and 600,000 wounded.) One hundred Palestinians were hanged.

There was a lull in the troubles in Palestine during World War II apart from some activities of *Lehi* (the Stern Gang), the Jewish terrorist group which, for example, murdered Lord Moyne in 1944. At the close of the war this group and a similar one, the *Irgun*, under Menachem Begin, came into their own. The Jews also had a well-trained and well-equipped army, the *Haganah*. The British had disarmed the Palestinians as far as possible.

At last the British, with Ernest Bevin as Foreign Secretary under the new post-war Labour Government, tried to be even-handed, and to ensure the establishment of an independent Palestine with the two peoples living on terms of equality and mutual respect (the initial dream of the PLO). Infuriated, the Zionists waged a terrorist war against the British in Palestine. The blowing-up of the King David Hotel in 1946[6] was followed by other incidents.

The war-weary British threw in the sponge, announcing they would hand over the problem to the infant United Nations and that they would quit their responsibilities in Palestine by 15th May, 1948. For Palestinians it seemed a betrayal; it was certainly a decision with catastrophic consequences for them.

The UN prepared a Partition Plan to be put before the Assembly in November, 1947. America stepped in. The Zionist lobby pressurised the US Administration, now headed by President Truman, who had, it has been reported, been greatly helped in his election campaign by $1,000,000 from a Zionist Jew.[7] In any case, he publicly stated that he had to consider the large number of Jewish voters in his constituency – there were no Arabs. The US Administration in its turn pressurised member countries of the UN – many fewer than now, as "Third World" countries were not yet members – especially those impoverished by the war. "No Marshall Aid for you, unless you vote for the UN Plan to partition Palestine," was the message conveyed.[8] A similar message had been conveyed previously to the British, in order to make them allow 100,000 new Jewish immigrants into tiny Palestine, far more proportionately than America herself was prepared to admit.[9]

The Partition Plan was passed in the Assembly by the minimum majority permissible according to the UN constitution. In after years when third world countries gained representation at the UN, the plan might well not have won a majority vote. Only Security Council Resolutions have legal force. But this Partition *Plan*, no more in fact than a recommendation, passed by the *Assembly*, has had similar powerful consequences to those of the equally illegitimate Balfour Declaration.

The Zionists of course were delighted; all Arabs were outraged; in particular, the people of Palestine, who had not even been consulted. Propaganda has it that "the Arabs" refused outright the Partition Plan (so are to blame for all that followed). The truth is more complex. Among Arabs other than Palestinians opinions were varied; some even advised acceptance. Among Palestinians there were some who urged that the matter be taken to the International Court at the Hague.

The Israeli writer and peace activist, Simha Flapan, has written in his book based on de-classified official Israeli documents, *The Birth of Israel: Myths and Realities*[10], "Israel's acceptance of the resolution remained its most important propaganda weapon, even as it violated one section of the document after another. Today...the myth lingers on, engraved in Israel's national consciousness and in its schoolbooks." In fact it was a strategic "acceptance" while Israel's hidden agenda was very different: to expand, and to ensure there were as few Arabs as possible in the new Jewish state. Flapan lists seven myths, which he proceeds to debunk:

Myth 1	Zionists accepted the UN Partition and planned for peace.
Myth 2	Arabs rejected the Partition and planned war.
Myth 3	Palestinians fled voluntarily, intending reconquest.
Myth 4	All the Arab states united to expel the Jews from Palestine.
Myth 5	The Arab invasion made war inevitable.
Myth 6	Defenceless Israel faced destruction by the Arab Goliath.
Myth 7	Israel has always sought peace, but no Arab leader has responded.

Norman Finkelstein, an American Jewish academic, in the Introduction to his book *Image and Reality of the Israel-Palestine Conflict*[1] has quoted the response of his mother, (a survivor of the Warsaw Ghetto and the Nazi death camps), when asked her opinion about the Middle East conflict. "What crime did the Palestinians commit, except to be born in Palestine?" she answered. Finkelstein goes on to comment, "That is the core reality lost in all the fabricated images of the Israel-Palestine conflict. The great offence of the Palestinians was that they refused to commit auto-dispossession; they balked at 'clearing out' for the Jews...One does not need more than a rudimentary [ethical] standard to measure that the people of Palestine have fallen victim to a colossal injustice. And I fail to see any redeeming virtue in 'connecting' with the perpetrators of that injustice as against the victims of it."

Not only had Palestine, a country promised independent sovereignty, been divided by foreigners – with the UN violating its own charter asserting the right of peoples to self-determination – but the terms of the Partition were outrageously unfair. Over half the country was to be given – in spite of all the immigration – to less than one third of the population, who owned by purchase only six per cent of the land. And the most fertile part, along the Mediterranean coast, with its Palestinian Arab citrus groves, its Palestinian Arab orchards and wheatfields, was to go to the Jewish State where the Palestinians were actually in the majority. The rocky hills were allotted to the indigenous people.

Jerusalem, home to many nationalities, sacred to three religions, Jewish, Christian, and Muslim, and built by Palestinian Arab hands, was to be a *corpus separatum* – an international city. The Zionists ignored *that* clause, and have tried to ensure that Western countries do so too.

In October 1991 the campaigning of the International Christian Embassy of Jerusalem reached Cambridge, where its representative addressed a meeting in a hall hired from the unsuspecting YMCA. The audience was to learn that after the news was announced of the UN Assembly's acceptance of the Partition Plan, and fighting broke out in Palestine, the Jews fought with their *bare hands* (*sic*) against armed Arabs! The majority in the hall appeared to swallow this amazing information.

Some months earlier, in January 1991, shortly before the Gulf war started, I had been invited to give "the Palestinian viewpoint" in a symposium organised to discuss aspects of the crisis. There is no *one* Palestinian viewpoint on any issue, any more than there is *one* British or *one* Israeli; but it was shocking to see, on television, Arafat embracing such a man as Saddam Hussein. That was not the first and has not been the last of Arafat's unstatesmanlike actions to cause harm to his people.

Then there were those crowds of refugees in Jordan and elsewhere demonstrating in Hussein's favour, holding aloft his portrait. Palestinians had suffered grievously through America's support for Israel: their homeland taken from them with America's connivance; their homes destroyed, their relatives and their children killed and wounded by American bombs and bullets. I showed the gas canister, brought from the West Bank, marked "Made in Pennsylvania".[12] A "plastic" bullet which I dropped on the table in front of me, had a distinctly metallic ring. And the American-led UN had never invoked force to expel the Israeli invader from Palestinian, Lebanese, or Syrian territory. The people in those crowds saw Hussein as the one Arab leader who had stood up to America. I tried to explain some of this to the audience.

Nevertheless, when I sat down, a man in the audience got up and exclaimed angrily, "I have never in my life heard such a biased talk! What about the cruelties Palestinians have inflicted on Israelis?" I asked "What cruelties?" He was silent, though unfortunately he could of course have given some examples. So I asked where he got his information from. After a slight hesitation, he replied, "From a book called *Exodus*"[13]. "Oh, a novel!" was all I could reply. I decided to re-read the book. By an American Jewish novelist, it is worth looking at quite closely, for it has had such a widespread and lasting influence. It is cleverly written.

Much of it is based on verifiable historical facts. The first part deals with the appalling sufferings of the Jews in Poland under the Nazis: the horrors of the Warsaw ghetto and the concentration camps. The suffering is personalised in the main characters of the story, and could not but be accurate – it has been related many times, and survivors are still amongst us. It is deeply moving. The description of a camp in Cyprus set up by the British as a temporary measure for would-be immigrants into Palestine also rings true. It was extremely frustrating for the refugees to be detained there, but conditions were not harsh; and the novel describes how young able-bodied Jews were trained there clandestinely by Zionist agents to fight with guns and knives. That, too, is no doubt accurate; and seen through the eyes of the novelist it appears an admirable achievement.

But the author does not describe the effective use to which such training was put.

On 9th April, 1948, there took place the notorious massacre of Deir Yassin.[14] The position of this village was strategically important to the Zionists, because it was situated on the Western outskirts of Jerusalem, the city they wanted to capture above all others. Deir Yassin had to be obliterated.

In a combined operation, the two terrorist groups, Irgun and Lehi (the Stern Gang) and the Palmach (the striking force of the Jewish army) attacked the sleeping village and slaughtered men, women and children; mutilated bodies were stuffed down a well. For a long time the number of victims was thought to be around 250; but research undertaken by Bir Zeit University suggests a more accurate figure would be 170. The village was one of many destined for destruction. Menachem Begin, later Israeli Prime Minister, referred to the massacre as a "victory", crucial to the foundation of the Jewish State. Skilfully used in Jewish broadcasts in Arabic, it was instrumental in emptying Palestine of many of its indigenous inhabitants. "Flee, or your fate will be that of Deir Yassin!" was the emphatic message.[15]

The representative of the International Red Cross, Jacques de Reynier, was on the scene at Deir Yassin very quickly. In his memoirs[16] de Reynier describes his first sight of the perpetrators of the deed:

All of them were young, some even adolescents, men and women, armed to the teeth: revolvers, machine-guns, hand grenades, and also cutlasses in their hands, most of them still blood-stained. A beautiful young girl, with criminal eyes, showed me hers, still dripping with blood; she displayed it like a trophy.

He went into a house piled with bodies and managed to rescue a little girl who was still breathing.

The massacre itself was witnessed by an Israeli soldier present, Meir Pa'il, who, however, refused to allow his description of it to be published till twenty-four years later. The inhabitants of many other villages were similarly treated[17], though no doubt Deir Yassin was the most notorious atrocity at that time.

In the novel *Exodus* the distortions of truth continue when the author writes about the Palestinian Arabs: then he stoops to scurrility. He is on safe ground, for few Europeans would know much about them, and even fewer Americans, who already wielded the most influence on the Israeli-Palestinian scene. Here is what he chooses to write about the Husseinis, one of the leading Palestinian clans:

The leader of the dreaded El Husseinis was the most vile, underhand schemer in a part of the world known for vile, underhand schemers. His name was Haj Amin el Husseini... El Husseini was backed by a clan of devils...(p 274)

The gentleman in the red tarbush who as so kind and hospitable on my first day in Palestine was a Husseini. And a young woman distinguished for her benevolent work in the 1940s was a Husseini.[18]

The novel *Exodus* portrays the Palestinians as dirty and lazy, as well as cruel and devious.

> The distant beauty of the village faded with each step they took nearer and was soon replaced by an overwhelming stench…(p 232)

The author then uses his vivid imagination to describe the unutterable squalor of an Arab village in Galilee, where the houses according to him were tumble-down mud hovels and the countryside neglected. Houses everywhere have been traditionally built with the materials available locally. In Galilee, it would not have been mud[19] except in mortar to bind the stones used. The land itself was carefully cultivated.[20]

It is of course a main plank of Zionist propaganda that the Jews "made the desert bloom". The desert area in Palestine is the Negev. Much of it, also, was cultivated: by Palestinian Bedouin, who grew not only most of the wheat and barley for Palestine but also fruit.

Mohammed Abu Mallouh is a friend with whose family I have several times enjoyed the traditional generous Arab hospitality. In his house one can drink big glasses of fresh orange or grapefruit juice. His family owns a small citrus orchard in the Gaza Strip. He told me:

> We are Bedouin, living in the southern part of Palestine. My father's family lived in the Gaza Strip, but my mother's lived near Beersheba. They used to come and visit us every summer till the invasion of the country in 1948. In the Negev they cultivated fruit – melons and water melons. They would bring their fruit and we would give them ours – grapes, figs – in exchange. All this has stopped now, of course.

The author of *Exodus* describes the heroic struggle by which Jewish settlers reclaimed marshland.

There was indeed unused marshland in Palestine. The first Jewish settlers who tried to reclaim it ignored the warning about malaria given by local people whom they regarded as "barbarians". For five years they struggled against sickness and death. It seemed they must abandon their efforts. But then Baron de Rothschild in Paris promised funds. Egyptian labourers were hired, who also "died in scores".[21] Eventually the necessary drainage was completed. So it was through Rothschild money, Arab labour and the sacrifice of Arab lives as well as Jewish, that the marshland was eventually reclaimed for agriculture and the creation of a prosperous Jewish town, Hadera.

It was not only through violence and terrorism that the Jewish forces took over Palestine and drove out the Palestinian Arabs. Deception was also used.

In his book, *Ha Sepher ha Palmach* (The Book of the Palmach), Yigal Allon, its commander (later an Israeli Cabinet minister), describes how and why he tricked thousands of Palestinians into fleeing.

15th May 1948 was the date by which the British were finally to have left. On that date the new Jewish State would be declared, its boundaries already defined by the UN Partition Plan. But the Zionists wanted even more; and they had a plan – *Plan Dalet* – to take more and to remove the existing inhabitants. In the months preceding 15th May the British hold on Palestine was becoming slack and weak: this gave the Zionists the opportunity to pursue their aim, which they did, quite ruthlessly. Allon writes:

> There were left before us only five days, before the threatening date, the 15th May. We saw a need to cleanse the inner Galilee and to create a Jewish territorial succession in the entire area of the upper Galilee. The long battles had weakened our forces...I gathered all of the Jewish *mukhtars*, [mayors] who have contact with Arabs in different villages, and asked them to whisper in the ears of some Arabs, that a great Jewish reinforcement has arrived in Galilee and that it is going to burn all of the villages of the Huleh. They should suggest to these Arabs, as their friends, to escape while there is still time. And the rumour spread in all the area of the Huleh that it is time to flee. The flight numbered myriads. The tactic reached its goal completely. The building of the police station at Halsa fell into our hands without a shot. Wide areas were cleansed...

*Cleansed...*It is clearly not only Nazis, like Americans and Australians before them, who have practised *ethnic cleansing*. *Ha Sepher ha Palmach* does not seem to have appeared in an English version. One can understand why. When I first read this extract, more than twenty years ago, I found it hard to take on board; so I got hold of the Hebrew original and asked an independent Hebrew scholar to translate it afresh. "Cleanse" was indeed the correct translation, the Hebrew word meaning ritual cleaning. All official Israeli and Zionist policy to this day indicates that the Palestinian Arabs are considered inferior beings – somehow unclean, a nuisance to be "transferred" as far as possible outside Israel's boundaries by one means or another, except those needed for menial work and essential work on the Sabbath, which Jews prefer not to do.[22]

And indeed, as early as November 1937 the Jewish Agency had formed a special committee: "The Population Transfer Committee" – the word "transfer" being euphemistic.

"Among ourselves it must be clear that there is no room for both peoples in this country. The only way is to transfer the Arabs from here to neighbouring countries. Not a single village or a single tribe must be left"[23], wrote Yosef Weitz of the "Population Transfer Committee" in his diary in December 1947. "We must expel the Arabs and take their places...and if we have to use force...then we have force at our disposal," wrote Ben Gurion in a letter to his son. The Zionist forces did indeed succeed in totally destroying most of the Palestinian villages: 395 out of 485, and in annihilating or expelling most of the Bedouin tribes.[24]

Violence, deception. There was, and is, a third effective means used and re-used in the service of Zionism: supremely sophisticated propaganda, full of distortions of the truth (but always with a grain of genuine truth in them, to make them more effective), and of the sort to move and convince the Western world, with the psychology of which Zionists have of course always been more familiar than Arabs could ever be. The novel *Exodus* is based on the story of a most successful, but also most cruel piece of propaganda enacted on 4,500 unfortunate Jewish refugees.

The Zionists purchased an old boat and secretly crammed it with as many refugees as possible including the young men and women they had been training in Cyprus in the use of arms, made sure that their enterprise would have journalistic cover, particularly photographic, and set out. They knew the British were now trying to enforce immigration controls, that there would be trouble, and that by depicting British harshness towards victims of Nazi persecution the sympathy of the American public, seeing the events in cinema newsreels, would be all for those in the boat – which would probably be turned back. This piece of propaganda, from which the refugees involved suffered greatly, was highly successful.[25]

At the close of World War II America, with its great open spaces and infinite capacity for making use of educated people, had admitted relatively few Jewish refugees: only a small proportion of the total of 300,000 Displaced Persons it finally agreed to take were Jewish; but 100,000 Jews were, America insisted, to go to tiny Palestine.

The armistice of 1949 left the Israelis in control of areas which had been assigned to the Arab State. However, it was not enough for them, as future events were to show.

In 1950 the Knesset passed the Law of Return, enabling Jews from anywhere in the world to come to Israel and claim citizenship. The new state was definitely not to be just a refuge for Jews suffering from persecution. Palestinian refugees were not included in the Law of Return, for though Semitic, they are not Jews. (Interestingly, some Palestinian refugees are now pointing out that there would be room for them to return to their homeland, even in what is now Israel, *without* displacing Israeli Jews.[26])

The following paragraphs are a concise outline of how Israel acquired more of the land of Palestine from 1966 onwards, besides territory outside its borders in Syria. How Israel occupied Lebanese territory is told in the chapter on Lebanon. To this day Israel has no internationally recognised *frontiers.*

As a prelude to a war which would provide the opportunity for extending the armistice boundaries, Israel provoked her neighbours. In November, 1966, Israeli forces with eighty tanks and twelve aircraft attacked and destroyed the Palestinian village of Samua, outside the armistice line, in Jordanian controlled territory. They killed both the Palestinian inhabitants and Jordanian soldiers who came to defend the village. The American representative at the UN Security Council condemned the Israeli attack as "a raid into Jordan, the nature of which and *whose consequences* far surpass the cumulative total of the various acts of terrorism conducted against the frontiers" (my italics). It was a prophetic statement.

The armistice line was drawn at the end of the fighting which broke out when the Partition Plan was announced. In some cases the line cut villages off from their fields and orchards. The villagers could see the crops they had cultivated, and on which their livelihoods depended, in the hands of others. Men ventured across the line to gather what they considered theirs. When caught, they were shot as "infiltrators". Understanding the danger, the Palestinians then went armed, and on occasions in their anger they took cruel revenge, with acts of terrorism. This was so in the case of Samua, when three Israelis had been killed by a grenade lobbed into what was now their house. This act was followed by the heavy reprisal described above. (Unfortunately a similar pattern persists to this day of terrorist acts followed by hugely magnified counter-terrorism).

A senior UNRWA official has told me that Samua was for them "the writing on the wall": Israel, obviously, was preparing to launch another war. Stocks of food and medicines were laid in for the refugee camps.

The following spring (1967), Israeli warplanes flew over Damascus and shot down six Syrian MIGs. Only after this did Nasser, the Egyptian leader, feel he had to make a gesture of support for Syria, with which he had the year before concluded a defence accord. He requested U Thant, the UN General Secretary, to withdraw partially the UN force stationed inside the Egyptian border. (Israel had refused to have any

UN force at all on its side.) U Thant's reply was that the whole force should be withdrawn, or none of it. So the whole force was withdrawn, and Nasser closed the Straits of Tiran so that strategic materials should not be supplied through them to Israel. Nevertheless, he indicated a willingness to negotiate a diplomatic settlement in relation to Tiran, and the Egyptian Vice-President prepared to leave for Washington. Two days before his arrival, however, Israeli bombers destroyed the entire Egyptian airforce on the ground. Israel's success in the ensuing "six-day war" was thus assured.

The Golan Heights in Syria, the West Bank, the Gaza Strip, and East Jerusalem, were seized; West Jerusalem had been in 1948. The Sinai peninsula was also captured, but given back to Egypt in 1978. (Peace with Egypt secured Israel's rear in the south so that she was free to undertake the invasion of Lebanon in the north, which took place not long afterwards.) All the other areas remained under Israeli military occupation. The West has not been quite so easily persuaded of Israel's right to these territories as it was of areas that had been allotted to the Palestinian State in 1948. No foreign embassy has been established even in West Jerusalem – yet. Only the "International Christian Embassy of Jerusalem" – neither international, nor Christian, nor an embassy, in any true sense of these words.

One of its most unchristian aspects is that its propagandists try to sow discord in the Palestinian community, by suggesting that in Palestine Islam is a threat to Christianity. This has not been so for a long time and is not so now. An indication of their mutual respect is that the key to the Church of the Holy Sepulchre in Jerusalem is entrusted to a member of a well-known Muslim family, lest rival claims to it from different Christian denominations should sour relations between themselves.

With the break-up of the Soviet Union and the re-emergence of old prejudices including anti-Semitism, Jews there are not unnaturally alarmed and looking for ways to emigrate. Until recently, Zionist sympathisers in Congress were pressing the US Administration to admit more Jews, complaining that restriction plans were anti-Jewish. But now, under the influence of urgent appeals from Israel, which has a "demographic crisis", the pressure has changed. Before long, Arabs might equal or even outnumber Jews – awful thought! – in Eretz Israel (Greater Israel, which includes the Occupied Territories).[27]

The ICEJ has been doing its bit to increase the flow of immigrants. At its meeting in Cambridge in October 1991, the audience was urged to donate money for its latest enterprise: the organisation of coaches into the disintegrating USSR with ICEJ representatives accompanying them to persuade yet more Jews to come than were flocking in already.

The money would also help to build them homes – no matter if illegally, in the West Bank. "The Bible does not say you will receive *half* of the land of Canaan. Yet all the world's governments want to give part of it away, and they are supported – would you believe it? – by many of the Jewish people. We are better Zionists than you Israelis."[28] Leaflets were available at the meeting. In one, entitled *Exodus Latest* (24th October 1991), its representative describes the journey in a coach filled with Jews collected from the Ukraine:

> I walked to the back of the bus and sat and talked awhile to a young man of twenty who was wearing a wedding-ring and sitting alone. I enquired, 'Why did you decide to go to Israel and not to America?' – 'You know ninety per cent of the people on this bus are going to Israel because they were not able to go to America. But I have friends in America. They say life is easier there, but the Mexicans are considered second-class citizens. I want to go where I can be a first-class citizen and get some education.'

> 'Do you have a family in Kiev?' I asked. 'Yes,' he said. "My mother and father. My wife and I divorced just recently so I could go to Israel. My wife's mother has relatives in America and they want to go there. But now it is very hard to go to America.'

Rather oddly, at the end of this piece, there was a photograph of a woman waving farewell to those departing in the coach – her face a picture of tragic grief. "Tearful goodbyes" are referred to more than once. What do these "Christians" think they are doing – deliberately splitting up families?

At the border, the leaflet relates how the ICEJ's skilful and persuasive guide triumphantly got the coach through, past *"560 other coaches (not to mention cars) that had been waiting for five or six days without toilet facilities, food or water"!* (my italics).

In another leaflet, frank acknowledgement is now made of the ICEJ's political character, and biblical justification found. St Paul can be brought to the rescue – if one tries hard enough:

"The spiritual did not come first, but the natural, and after that the spiritual" (I Cor 15, 16). The enemy realises only too clearly that natural Israel will ultimately become spiritual Israel and therefore invokes all the political forces of this world to destroy her…To stand with Israel politically and practically therefore has ultimate spiritual implications.

It is difficult to imagine how anyone could accept such a farrago of nonsense. But 400,000 American fundamentalist-evangelical Christians were expected, at the ICEJ's behest, to come in 1992 to Jerusalem to celebrate Israel's "Independence" Day.

The influence of these "born again" Christians on White House policy seems to be second only to that of the Jewish Zionist lobby. On 27th January 1992 its leaders placed a whole page advertisement in the *Washington Times*: "70 million Christians urge President Bush to approve loan guarantees for Israel." Clinton, the most pro-Zionist US President of all, has referred to a Christian minister who in his youth convinced him that his duty lay in wholehearted support for Israel. He has certainly followed this "Christian" injunction.

No doubt some of these Christians sincerely believe they are doing Jews a service (though many Jews would not agree). But their main concern, it would appear, arises from their eschatological doctrine: the second coming of Christ followed by the millennium must be preceded by the ingathering of the exiles to Zion. They are trying to hasten the process.

What a contrast to the devout orthodox Jews of Naturei Karta in the Mea Sharim quarter of Jerusalem! Early in January, 1993, they issued a communiqué concerning the 415 Palestinians deported to Lebanon: "We propose to welcome our Palestinian brothers into our autonomous sector – until the Palestinian State is born" – and they express the hope that those banished "will be able to overcome the Zionist barriers and return to their native land".[29]

Hind Husseini

One of the oldest houses in a large compound in East Jerusalem is part of the family home of a frail-looking elderly lady, Hind Husseini. In a corner of her sitting-room are cushions covered with her neat, gorgeously coloured cross-stitch embroidery in the traditional Palestinian designs. She does an hour's embroidery early every morning before the day's work begins. Other buildings in the compound provide a home for small children, a school for girls, and a college. The whole is known as Dar el Tifl, and it is her creation. Hind Husseini told me its story:

> At the beginning of April 1948, after the massacre of Deir Yassin, we were called for a meeting in the Old City – men and women. On my way to that meeting, I saw gatherings of little children here and there – near the Church of the Holy Sepulchre, and further on, too. I asked them, "What are you

sitting outside for? It's dangerous. There are shells falling, and bullets coming. Go home." They said nothing, but crouched closer to the walls. I repeated my question. Then one of the girls answered, "We have no home. We are children from Deir Yassin" – and she started crying. I went on to the meeting, troubled.

I asked permission to speak first. I said, "Deir Yassin children and other children are homeless in the streets of Jerusalem." The chairman said, "But, Hind, we are here to discuss how to raise money for such purposes." I said to them, "OK. You go on with your meeting, and I will go out and think what to do while you decide." I went straight to the place where some of us women had two rooms for a crèche for working mothers. At that time the crèche was closed – there was nobody to employ any mothers and so no children were coming; and I called at the house of Haneh Kasheh, a nurse who was running the crèche. I said, "Haneh, come and open the crèche. I want to bring some children. Are you ready to work with me? I am without the committee." "Of course", she said, "whatever you like, Sitt Hind."

The next day we started collecting the children. A man from the Social Welfare Department helped me – Adnan Tamimi. We had, that first week, fifty children and an expectant mother, whose husband had been killed while trying to escape from the village. Her first four children were with her: Farid and Farida, Zakid and Zakida. She gave birth to the baby; it was a boy, and we named him Usama.

Unfortunately, the troubles went on. We were expecting them to last only a few weeks. I had only about 148 Palestine pounds. We bought blankets and rugs for the floor. We had only twelve mattresses. But there were more incidents – and so more orphans.

That place in the Old City where we were became very dangerous, and I was obliged to move the children. We were given shelter in a corner of the convent of the Sisters of Zion ("Dames de Zion"). The Mother Superior at that time, Mère Godelaine, was so good – she said, "Come and choose the place you like." I chose a corner with an outside wall; it was called "Sitte Mariam" (Lady Mary). We could feel we were on our own. Moving there was quite funny, and sad at the same time. We went in procession. The older children carried our things; the little ones, as many as could, clung to my hands and my skirt. Later I went to see the old crèche where we had been. It was completely destroyed. We'd moved the children just in time. We stayed at the Zion Convent about six weeks.

When the cease-fire came we moved again, to this house – my grandfather's house. We occupied the whole of it. The little ones and the toddlers were downstairs, the older ones upstairs with me. Then we were able to have my mother's grandfather's house – also in this compound. Now, as you see, we occupy the whole compound, and we have new buildings in it too. There's the school; and the children's house, built with a gift from the German Lutheran Foundation. The basement of the school was the gift of Aramco. Then we built the college: it was started as an institute to train social workers and then we thought it would be better to develop it into a college for the arts. We have now, as well as the social work training, Namira for the teaching of Arabic and English. So we started with fifty-five little children. Now in 1990 we have 1,500 girls.

Recently I was in Amman and was recognised by some of the old Deir Yassin children. They waved – two now doctors, and a business man who said, "Sitt Husseini, if you need any help, tell me. I have a car and a driver. If you want to go anywhere, he will take you." I felt very proud and happy. But, sadly, they still remember Deir Yassin.

We have trouble with the Israeli soldiers. They harass our older girls when they are outside and they throw gas-bombs inside. An officer came in and wanted to know all about everything, what we did, where we got our money from, and so on. I said, "You can read our report. We have supporters all over the world." I asked him, "Do you want to see the buildings you have surrounded us with? The ugly blocks you have built, spoiling Jerusalem? You can see from my balcony. Come."

And Hind Husseini took me to where she had taken the officer, out onto her balcony.

1 Quoted by David Hirst, *The Gun and the Olive Branch, Roots of Violence in the Middle East,* Faber, 1977, pp 104-5.

2 An interesting explanation for the origin of the "promise" idea is suggested in *The Story of the Stories: the Chosen People and its God* by Dan Jacobson (Secker and Warburg, 1982), "Yahweh [Jehovah] enters their [the Israelites'] story with his revelation of himself to Moses, just when they were about to become engaged in a life-and-death struggle to drive another people out of the land which they wanted to occupy and enjoy. What could be more convenient for the newcomers to believe, than that they had been specially chosen, by divine decree, to perform the task of cleansing the land of its inhabitants?" (p 33).

3 See the Appendix for text of Balfour Declaration and notes on it.

4 Anthony Nutting: *Balfour and Palestine, a legacy of deceit,* pamphlet published by CAABU – Council for the Advancement of Arab–British Understanding, London.

5 Doreen Ingrams, *Palestine Papers* 1917-1922, Seeds of Conflict, John Murray, 1972, p 73.

6 See Chapter Four, p 43.

7 Preface by Gore Vidal to *Jewish History, Jewish Religion, The Weight of Three Thousand Years,* by Israel Shahak, Pluto Press 1994.

8 Margaret Arakie (former UN official): *The Broken Sword of Justice: America, Israel, and the Palestine Tragedy,* Quartet, 1973, pp 64–5.

9 Adams and Mayhew: *Publish it Not,* Longman, 1975, pp 18-19, and R Divine: American Immigration Policy, Yale University Press, 1957, pp 122-9.

10 Simha Flapan, *The Birth of Israel: Myths and Realities,* Croom Helm, 1987.

11 Norman Finkelstein, *Image and Reality of the Israel-Palestine Conflict,* Verso, 1995.

12 There is a tragic irony here. Pennsylvania, given its prefix "Penn" by Charles II in honour of Admiral Penn to whom he was much in debt, repaid this debt by granting the Admiral's son, William, a tract of land in America. William Penn was a leading Quaker and pacifist, and a close friend of George Fox, the founder of Quakerism. William Penn would not allow arms in the province, and envisaged it as a haven for the persecuted. In 1683 he made a famous peace treaty with the Indians there and was rewarded by their trust and friendship. He proved to be an enlightened statesman, and as long as he was in charge peace and contentment reigned in Pennsylvania.

13 Leon Uris, *Exodus,* Allan Wingate, London, 1959.

14 Referred to in Chapter Five on p 46.

15 David Hirst, *op cit* p 125.

16 de Reynier, *A Jerusalem un drapeau flottait sur la ligne de feu*, Editions de la Baconnière, Neuchâtel, 1950.

17 See the stories of Yahya Dabbagh and Elias Chacour, Chapter |Sixteen, pp 170-183; and Norman Finkelstein, *op cit*, p 76: "Consider the massacre at Ad Dawayima in late October. A soldier eyewitness described how the IDF, capturing the village 'without a fight' first 'killed about 80–100 [male] Arabs, women and children. The children they killed by breaking their heads with sticks. There was not a house without dead'. The remaining Arabs were then closed off in houses 'without food and water' as the village was systematically razed…'One soldier boasted he had raped a woman and then shot her. One woman, with a newborn baby in her arms, was employed to clear the courtyard where the soldiers ate. She worked a day or two. In the end they shot her and her baby…Cultured officers…had turned into base murderers and this not in the heat of battle…*but out of a system of expulsion and destruction.* The fewer Arabs remained – the better. This principle is the political motor for the expulsions and the atrocities'." (Emphasis added.)

18 See pp 100, 106-108

19 For a description of the way Palestinian village houses were built see Suad Amiry and Vera Tamari, *The Palestinian Village Home*, British Museum Publications Ltd, 1989.

20 For a description of Palestinian cultivation, see p 154 – a passage quoted from *We belong to the Land* by Elias Chacour, Marshall Pickering, 1990.

21 David Hirst: *op cit* pp 22-23.

22 Israel Shahak, *op cit* pp 45-47.

23 David Hirst, *op cit* p 130.

24 David Hirst, *op cit*, see also notes in Chapter Ten p 101, and map on p 220.

25 David Hirst, *op cit* p 115.

26 S H Abu-Sitta, *The Right of Return: Sacred, Legal, and Possible Too* (PhD thesis, 1996) and *The Return Review*, Palestinian Return Centre, London.

27 Article by Elfi Pallis in *Middle East International*, 11th October, 1991.

28 Van der Hoeven, ICEJ spokesman, quoted in the *Jerusalem Post* Magazine, 24th July 1984.

29 Reported by AFS (Agence France Presse) and quoted in *France-Pays Arabes*, February, 1993.

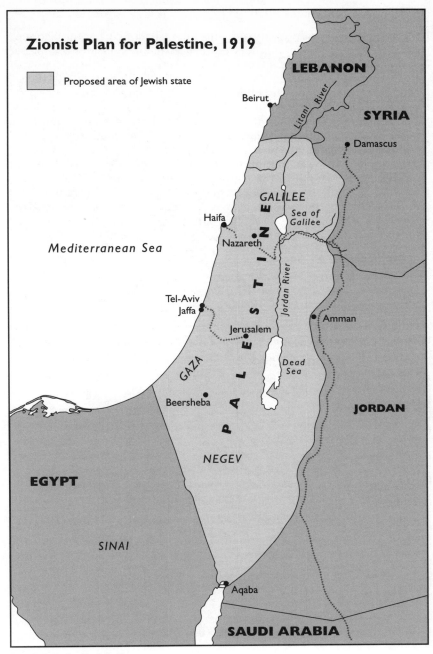

Zionist Plan for Palestine, 1919

Proposed area of Jewish state

LEBANON

Beirut

Litani River

SYRIA

Damascus

GALILEE

Haifa

Sea of Galilee

Nazareth

Mediterranean Sea

P A L E S T I N E

Jordan River

Tel-Aviv
Jaffa

Amman

Jerusalem

Dead Sea

GAZA

Beersheba

JORDAN

NEGEV

EGYPT

SINAI

Aqaba

SAUDI ARABIA

From *The Birth of Israel* by Simha Flapan

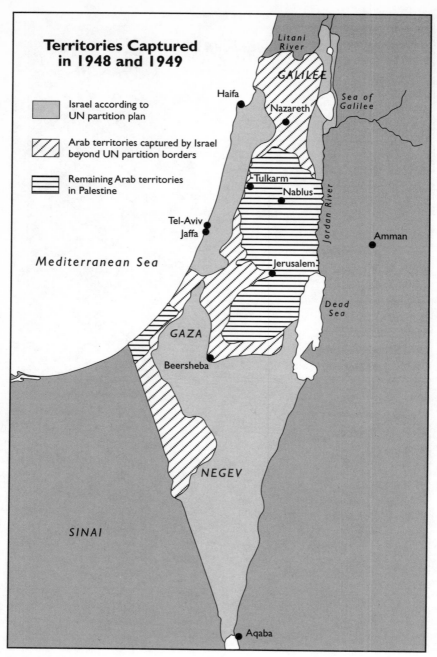

Territories Captured
in 1948 and 1949

Israel according to
UN partition plan

Arab territories captured by Israel
beyond UN partition borders

Remaining Arab territories
in Palestine

Litani River

GALILEE

Haifa

Sea of Galilee

Nazareth

Tulkarm

Nablus

Jordan River

Tel-Aviv
Jaffa

Amman

Mediterranean Sea

Jerusalem

Dead Sea

GAZA

Beersheba

NEGEV

SINAI

Aqaba

From The Birth of Israel by Simha Flapan

Based on: A Near East Studies Handbook, 570-1974, Jere L. Bacharach, 1974.

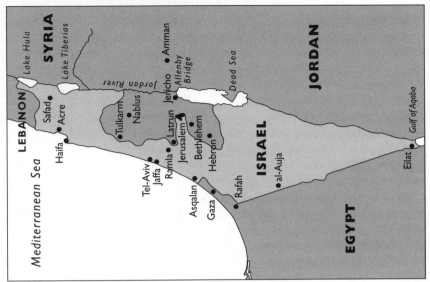

The Israel-Arab Armistice Lines, 1949

Based on: The Birth of the Palestinian Refugee Problem 1947-1949, Benny Morris, 1987.

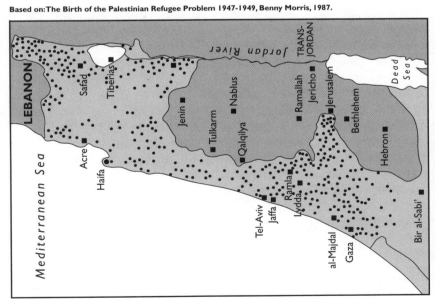

Villages Depopulated or Destroyed by Israel in 1948

From *Palestinians: Life Under Occupation* by Nancy Murray

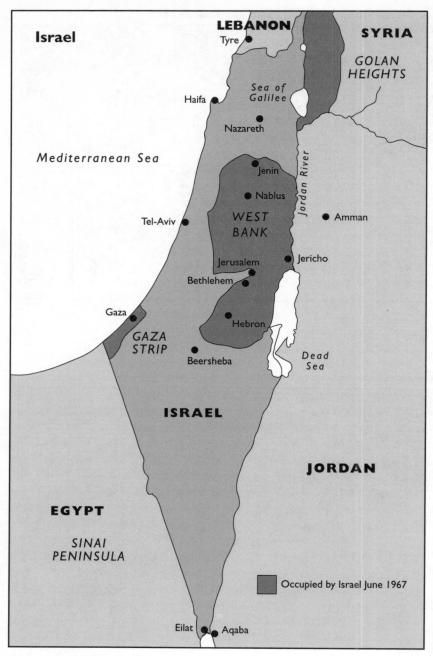

Israel

LEBANON

SYRIA

Tyre

GOLAN
HEIGHTS

Sea of
Galilee

Haifa

Mediterranean Sea

Nazareth

Jenin

Nablus

Jordan River

WEST
BANK

Amman

Tel-Aviv

Jerusalem

Jericho

Bethlehem

Gaza

GAZA
STRIP

Hebron

Dead
Sea

Beersheba

ISRAEL

JORDAN

EGYPT

SINAI
PENINSULA

Occupied by Israel June 1967

Eilat

Aqaba

From *Palestinians: Life Under Occupation* by Nancy Murray

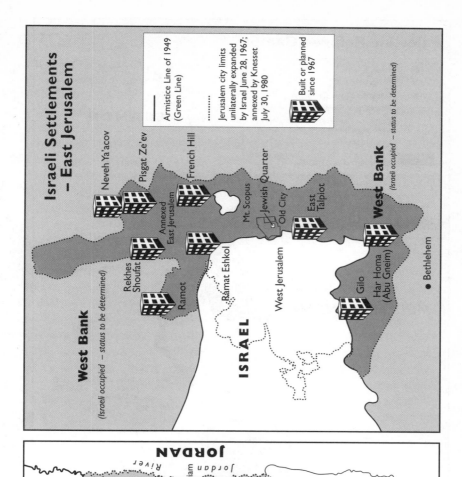

Israeli Settlements – East Jerusalem

West Bank
(Israeli occupied – status to be determined)

— Armistice Line of 1949 (Green Line)

········· Jerusalem city limits unilaterally expanded by Israel June 28, 1967; annexed by Knesset July 30, 1980

Built or planned since 1967

Neveh Ya'acov

Pisgat Ze'ev

French Hill

Mt. Scopus

Jewish Quarter

Old City

Annexed East Jerusalem

Rekhes Shoufat

Ramot

Ramat Eshkol

West Jerusalem

East Talpiot

Gilo

Har Homa (Abu Gneim)

• Bethlehem

West Bank
(Israeli occupied – status to be determined)

ISRAEL

West Bank

West Bank

Mediterranean Sea

JORDAN

Jordan River

Ma'ale Ephraim

• Jenin

Nablus

Immanuel

• Ariel

• Jericho

Alfe Menashe

Oranit

Elkana

Bet Arye

• Tel-Aviv

ISRAEL

▲ Ramallah
▲ Givat Ze'ev

Jerusalem

Ma'ale Adumim

Bethlehem
• Betar
▲ Efrat

Gush Etzion

Hebron
▲ Kiryat Arba

(Israeli occupied – status to be determined)

Jerusalem city limits unilaterally expanded by Israel June 28, 1967; annexed by Knesset, July 30, 1980.

D e a d   S e a

—— 1949 Armistice Line
········· 1967 Cease-fire Line
▲ Israeli Settlements

After Palestinians: Life Under Occupation *by Nancy Murray*

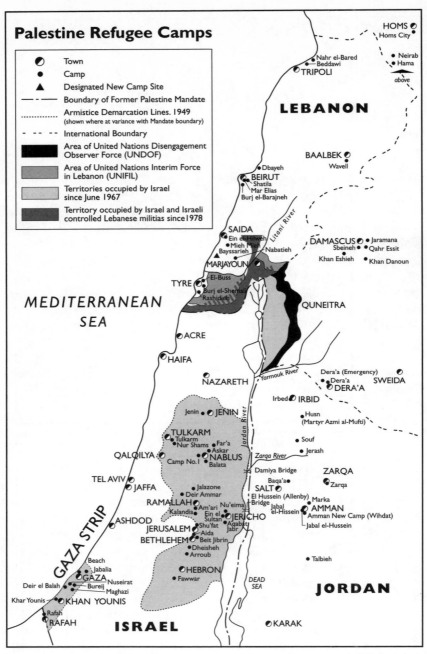

Palestine Refugee Camps

Legend:

- ⬤ Town
- ● Camp
- ▲ Designated New Camp Site
- —— Boundary of Former Palestine Mandate
- ·········· Armistice Demarcation Lines. 1949
  (shown where at variance with Mandate boundary)
- – – – International Boundary
- ▮ Area of United Nations Disengagement Observer Force (UNDOF)
- ▮ Area of United Nations Interim Force in Lebanon (UNIFIL)
- ▮ Territories occupied by Israel since June 1967
- ▮ Territory occupied by Israel and Israeli controlled Lebanese militias since1978

Map labels:

HOMS
Homs City
Neirab
Hama
Nahr el-Bared
Beddawi
TRIPOLI
above

LEBANON

BAALBEK
Wavell

Dbayeh
BEIRUT
Shatila
Mar Elias
Burj el-Barajneh

DAMASCUS
Jaramana
Sbeineh
Qahr Essit
Khan Eshieh
Khan Danoun

SAIDA
Ein el-Hilweh
Mieh Mieh
Bayssarieh
Nabatieh
MARJAYOUN

TYRE
El-Buss
Burj el-Shemali
Rashidieh

QUNEITRA

MEDITERRANEAN
SEA

ACRE

HAIFA

NAZARETH
Yarmouk River

Dera'a (Emergency)
Dera'a
DERA'A
SWEIDA

Irbed
IRBID

Husn
(Martyr Azmi al-Mufti)

Jenin
JENIN

TULKARM
Tulkarm
Nur Shams
Far'a
Askar
Camp No.1
NABLUS
Balata

Souf

Jerash

QALQILYA
Zarqa River

Damiya Bridge

ZARQA

Baqa'a
SALT
Zarqa

TEL AVIV
JAFFA

Jalazone
Deir Ammar
RAMALLAH
Am'ari
Nu'eima
Kalandia
Ein el-Sultan
Shu'fat
JERICHO
Aqabat
Jabr
JERUSALEM
Aida
BETHLEHEM
Beit Jibrin
Dheisheh
Arroub

El Hussein (Allenby)
Bridge
Jabal
el-Hissein
Marka
AMMAN
Amman New Camp (Wihdat)
Jabal el-Hussein

ASHDOD

GAZA STRIP

Beach
Jabalia
GAZA
Nuseirat
Deir el Balah
Bureij
Maghazi
Khar Younis
KHAN YOUNIS
Rafah
RAFAH

HEBRON
Fawwar

Talbieh

DEAD
SEA

JORDAN

ISRAEL

KARAK

Litani River

Jordan River

Based on UNRWA's map of Palestine Refugee Camps, 1993

CHAPTER ELEVEN

Which way now?

Back home in Cambridge my mind was still in the Middle East, after my first journey there. I had to talk and write about what I had seen and learnt. A letter in *The Guardian* earned me an appreciative response from Said Hammami, who was then PLO representative in London. For his vision, his moderation, and his articulateness he was assassinated some years later.[1] By the time of his death I had learnt to appreciate his outlook and his stature; but in 1972 "PLO" for me still meant violence – "terrorism" – and I was not particularly happy to hear from him. I had a great deal to learn.

When friends came to see me, I could not help unburdening myself. One of my first visitors was Ellen de Kadt from the "Working Group". We were good friends and had usually thought along the same lines. It was a sunny summer day and we were sitting in the garden. For the first time I heard the absurd but painful charge, often to be repeated in the years which followed. It was put to me kindly by Ellen, but with emphasis: "Be careful, Eleanor, you are becoming anti-Semitic!" How could such an intelligent woman so completely misunderstand? Not long afterwards I had a phone conversation with my old friend from student days – Irene, who had fled Hitler in 1938. What she said hurt even more: "You can't expect me to be interested in Palestinian refugees!" Irene had not greatly suffered from the Nazis; but she had obtained financial compensation from the German government "for interrupted education", and had been able to spend the money on a Mediterranean cruise with her husband. Palestinian refugees, who had everything taken from them, have received no compensation at all from Israel for their enormous losses, only continued persecution.

I began to see things were not going to be easy. In fact, I discovered quite soon that many people with an otherwise lively sense of social justice have a blind spot when it comes to Israel/Palestine. It seemed that it was taboo to criticise or even question Israel's actions because of what Europe did to the Jews. Strangely illogical.

But then Sir Robert Birley called. He was in Cambridge primarily, I think, to see one of his "old boys" from Charterhouse – Omar Pound, the son of Ezra Pound, the news of whose arrest by the American forces at the end of the war had exploded during Sir Robert's time as head and Omar's as a pupil. Sir Robert never forgot a former student, a friend, or a fellow worker, so he came to see me too.

I had to tell him all about the miseries of the Palestinians, about the colossal injustice committed against them. He had been a close colleague in our efforts on behalf of Greeks imprisoned for their left-wing views; and I knew that if he felt people were wronged, he would never be intimidated into suppressing his opinion, but would go out of his way to help. I had forgotten momentarily some of his background. After the war, being a German scholar as well as historian and distinguished educationalist, he had headed the Education section of the Control Commission which went to the British zone of Germany to help lead the country back towards democracy after the ravages of Nazism. It was natural that his first sympathies would be with Israel, as the refuge of persecuted Jews. I was walking up and down the sitting-room in agitation, talking. He sat listening. I stopped suddenly. What was I thinking of, haranguing this eminent man? "I am so sorry, Sir Robert," I said, "to be going on like this. The experience has got right under my collar."

"Yes, my dear," he answered quietly, "I can see that."

Some time later Sir Robert wrote an appreciative review of Fawzi Al-Asmar's book, *To be an Arab in Israel.* He had learnt from it, he said. Sir Robert was a man who till the end of his life never stopped learning. He had a wonderfully open, enquiring mind, and a very human heart. He became one of the first sponsors of the educational charity I was to start for Palestinians later that same year, and an invaluable ally.

I struggled on with the draft for the book on Soviet dissidents in mental hospitals; and when it was done, sent it to Peter Reddaway. I never heard a word. Probably it was not much good: my heart was elsewhere. When weeks had passed with no news, I decided to devote my time and energy to other work. It seemed I was no longer wanted for the Soviet dissidents. (Eventually the book, *Russia's Political Hospitals*, was written by Peter and Sidney Bloch, an Australian psychiatrist who had joined our group.)

In the Cambridge University Library I continued my education concerning the Palestine question – reading anything that promised to be informative. In those days there were few books on the subject which were not written from a Zionist viewpoint. This fact in itself probably explains in part how misconceptions have persisted so long. Mercifully, the position has greatly improved in the past twenty years.

But even at that time one could read *The Arabs in Israel* by Walter Schwartz, a Jewish journalist for some time attached to *The Guardian*; *The Evasive Peace* by John Davies, an American, formerly Commissioner-General of UNRWA – both books very enlightening; and *Bitter Harvest* by Sami Hadawi, a Palestinian professor, which was such painful reading I gave up before the end. I could scarcely believe some of what I read about Israeli atrocities. Sadly, I know better now than to doubt the truth of such accounts.

In spite of these doubts, my anger and indignation at the overall situation continued to grow. It seemed to me abundantly clear that an entire people had been robbed of its birthright. And like Esau, deprived of his by his brother Jacob (later called Israel) the people of Palestine had been robbed of theirs by clever deception – through which many people in Western nations, particularly fundamentalist Christians and Jews in Britain and America, had been hoodwinked into believing that the land had gone to its rightful heirs, just as Isaac believed he was giving his blessing to the rightful son. But the Israelis had used violence as well as deception to carry out their massive robbery. And it had been the people of Palestine, the Palestinians – the victims of the situation – who were being blamed (and are still being blamed) for its not being a satisfactory one: for causing trouble.[2] Most of the inhabitants were driven out by force and terrorism: that has now been conclusively shown by two Israelis; and that this was a deliberate policy, by an American Jewish academic.[3] Their villages (*395 out of 485*) were destroyed to obliterate traces of their presence, and prevent their return.[4] The UN Resolution in favour of their return or compensation (No 194) was ignored (it had been worded "return and compensation", but America insisted on the altered wording "to return *or* compensation" and this helped to prevent implementation – as most, if not all, of the refugees wanted to return to their homes and farms, *and* had been made destitute. The UN Mediator, Count Bernadotte, who advocated the speedy return of the refugees, was assassinated in September 1948 by the Stern Gang (Lehi), headed by Yitzhak Shamir, till recently Prime Minister of Israel.

The indigenous people of Palestine[5] have suffered many savage conquests by nations possessing superior force: by Hebrews, Romans, Byzantine Greeks, Crusaders, Arabs, Turks, British. Sometimes in the past their conquerors assimilated with them. They did not drive them from the country. It has taken Zionist Jews to do this!

Life is indeed a labyrinth, through which it is often difficult to find a way, and it seems that mere chance may decide the direction. But is it ever "mere" chance? There is also, surely, something inside oneself, a thread like Ariadne's – which helps one to accept the right chance, the one that is meant, that must not be ignored; Quakers would say, I think, that it is "the leading". Then part of the way through is traversed. So on one goes, round one corner after another, often stumbling, but holding onto the thread, the "leading". And as in the ancient Greek legend, one may find a monster in the centre of the labyrinth – but must not lose heart.

In the year following my return from the Middle East there were a number of developments pointing, on the one hand, to the possibility of involvement in some kind of work on behalf of Palestinians, and on the other confirming to me that I had no longer any rôle in "the Working Group on the Internment of Dissenters in Mental Hospitals".

Our friend Basil Hembry, who had given such helpful advice over Greeks, (it was he who had introduced me to Sir Robert Birley), combined farming in Essex with work as Regional Officer for the East Anglian branch of the United Nations Association (UNA), a post he filled for many years with great dedication. In 1972 the AGM for the branch was held in Cambridge, at Churchill College. Basil asked me to give a talk on my Middle East tour. It was the first of a number of talks in other towns and to various groups – societies, schools, churches, etc. – in the next three or four years, with my slide photographs supplemented by others from UNRWA.

When the university term began in the autumn I gave my first talk to a student group. It led to my acquaintance with Ian Black, a Jewish undergraduate (later to become Jerusalem Correspondent of *The Guardian*). He was sympathetic then towards the Palestinians, and together with a Lebanese friend had started a student "Anglo-Palestine Society".

Ian did much for my education in the political background of the Arab/Israeli conflict, introducing me to the publications of the self-exiled Israeli Left in London. In one of these I read a poem by Erich Fried, an Austrian Jewish refugee from the Nazis. With it was the photograph of an Egyptian soldier – his feet bandaged, exhaustion and agony in his face. After the defeat of the Egyptian army in the Six-Day War of June 1967, the media had reported, on information received from Israel, that the Egyptian soldiers had thrown off their boots so they could run away faster. At the time a distraught Egyptian academic had called to see Michael – then Christian Aid Secretary for the Cambridge area – to beg for relief to be sent them urgently: they were dying in the Sinai desert of thirst and sunstroke, scarcely able to move because of the blisters on their feet from the burning sand. Erich Fried tells how this really came about:

Hear O Israel

When we were the persecuted
I was one of you.
How can I remain one
when you become the persecutors?
Your longing was
to become like other nations
who murdered you.

Now you have become like them.
You have outlived
those who were cruel to you.
Does their cruelty live on in you now?
You ordered the defeated:
'Take off your boots'.

Like the scapegoat
you drove them into the wilderness
into the great mosque of death
whose sandals are of sand
but they did not take upon them the sin
you wished to lay on them.

The imprint of their naked feet
in the desert sand
outlasts the traces
of your bombs and your tanks.

Many years later, on BBC 2, in a series entitled *Exiles,* Erich Fried
recalled that episode: we saw a film sequence in black and white, clearly
contemporary, showing Egyptian soldiers lined up with their hands on
their heads, made in turn to take off their boots, which were then thrown
into a heap. The poem was read as this took place.

Early in September 1972, an international conference of "Christians
for Palestine" was held at the University of Kent, Canterbury, which I
attended. The Christians came from European countries, the Middle
East – Syrian and Egyptian Christians principally – and from Africa.
Two or three days before the conference began, Palestinian gunmen
had taken Israeli athletes hostage at the Munich Olympics. One hostage,
trying to escape, had been shot dead by them. Others died in the battle
with the German police, who had been ordered to rescue them. Most
of the Palestinians were killed too. They were members of "Black

September", (so named after the month in 1970 when the Jordanian army, on orders of King Hussein, drove the PLO from Jordan (an operation which caused an estimated 20,000 deaths, mainly civilian). The media gave full expression to the feelings of horror which swept the country. I do not remember anyone asking *why* it happened, or *why* "Black September". The shock of Munich was followed by that of Palestinian hijackings of aircraft. Palestinians had been waiting for all of twenty-four years, trusting that the international community, through the UN, would redress the injustice it had done them, but they had trusted in vain. Then, unfortunately, they remembered the success Zionist terrorism had had in its aim of driving both the British and their own people out of Palestine.

There was an extremely vocal contingent of Belgian Communists at the conference, openly and energetically advocating the use of violence in the manner of Munich in order to redress the injustice. Their views received, it seemed, a sympathetic response in the audience. That troubled me, and I ventured to make an "intervention". The microphone was thrust in front of me and I put in as urgent and eloquent a plea as I could that Palestinians should *not* repay Israeli violence with violence of their own. There was a shout of scornful laughter from the Belgians; and from then on I was cold-shouldered by a number of the conference participants. But after that session an Englishman present came up to me and endorsed what I had said. He was Kenneth Cragg, the Anglican Bishop for Egypt, Palestine, Jordan and Syria – a gentle, scholarly man, deeply sympathetic towards Palestinians, Muslim and Christian alike. His books on Islam are standard reading for those wishing to understand it better.[6] Present also at the conference were Lord Caradon (author of the celebrated UN Security Council Resolution 242) and Sir John and Lady Richmond. Sir John had been in turn Ambassador in Kuwait, Jordan, and Sudan, before taking up an academic post at the University of Durham. Both he and his wife, Diana, were Christians not merely in name. The Middle East experience and the support of all these four people were of immense value in the following years.

I returned home to Cambridge after the conference profoundly disturbed – horrified by more reports of Israeli atrocities which I had heard there: the seizure of land for settlements; the destruction of homes; imprisonments; deportations; massacres – and worried by the belligerency of many, if not most, of those "Christians for Palestine".

In one of the lunch breaks I had had the chance to talk with the Richmonds and Lord Caradon, as we were standing in a group together, and to discuss the possibilities of doing something practical to help Palestinians – perhaps in the field of education. They were very encouraging. At that time I did not know that many Palestinians felt that Caradon on one point had let them down with Resolution 242, which referred to "a just settlement of the refugee problem", but made no mention of the Palestinians' right, like that of the other peoples of the world, to self-determination. He told me some years later that he regretted that omission.

The huge contrast between educational opportunities for Palestinians and those for British young people kept nagging. I had been very fortunate in my own education; and I saw Cambridge, with its university, rich in libraries, laboratories, teachers, playing fields, gardens; a city also with its libraries, theatre, cinemas, sports facilities, swimming-pools, and its many well-equipped schools...And Palestinian children in crowded refugee camps, with nothing, nothing, nothing...And we British were the originators of their misery, through the Balfour Declaration of 1917[7] and the Mandate Government, 1922–48[8]! It was not to be borne.

One must *do* something!

First of all, I was told, I must find respectable, well-known people who would give their names as sponsors of a Fund designed to help those "terrorists".

In Cambridge, Professor Derek Bowett, then President of Queens' College, and an international lawyer of repute, had formerly been legal counsel to UNRWA in Beirut when its HQ was located there. He was our first sponsor, and became Chairman of the Trustees. The Dean of Trinity, Dr John Robinson, the former Bishop of Southwark who had scandalised churchpeople of narrow views with his book *Honest to God*, was known for his humanity and broadmindedness. He too agreed, and proved a strong support.

Then there was Sir Robert Birley, of course, the *doyen* of British education; I wrote to him and to Lord Caradon, the Richmonds, and Bishop Cragg. There was a "Yes" from them all.

And just after the Munich affair, I had read a penetrating and sensitive article in *The Listener* by Raymond Williams, radical writer, thinker and teacher, and Fellow of Jesus College. He too agreed to be a sponsor. Referring in his article to the TV coverage of those fateful Olympics, he had written:

> I looked round...at the national flags. I soon lost count of the number which represented states which had come into existence, or had been powerfully assisted, by acts of terrorism or armed revolt. Is this one of the effects of conventional, rule-contained competition: that every moment is a starting-point, with all previous history forgotten? Were there no

irregulars of a score of honoured revolutions, no Narodniki, Mau Mau, Stern Gang, and a thousand others, before Black September? I knew I could only mourn the seventeen dead if I remembered the history which had made them victims: a continuing history, without rules, which by the end of the week had greatly added to their number, and which as so often before had included women and children killed in their villages by attack from the air...One wrong doesn't excuse another wrong. I believe that is true and that it needs to be generally applied.

Gradually I came to know Cambridge people with first-hand knowledge of the Middle East and Palestine, and a committee was formed. It met at our house for fifteen years. It included Sue (Ann) Dearden, for many years on the staff of *The Guardian,* ME correspondent of the *Economist,* and author of what was for a long time the standard book on Jordan[9]; Cynthia Davison, born and brought up in Jerusalem; and, eventually, three university teachers. Margaret Deakin, a Quaker who had worked in Lebanon, was our honorary treasurer and accountant for eleven years. They all found time to attend meetings regularly. Our old friend, Basil Hembry, became chairman; and our first contributor, Helen Brock, honorary treasurer for the first year. A leaflet was printed; and in January 1973 a public meeting took place in the Friends' Meeting House, and Unipal (Universities' Educational Fund for Palestinian Refugees) was launched. (Now the sub-title is "Universities' Trust for Educational Exchange with Palestinians". It is felt that this expresses best the twofold aim of Unipal: *mutual* education). Quite a number of students attended as well as townspeople.

In the audience was Peter Crouch, the first in a long line of students to give active help. He became a volunteer in Gaza, one of the first four in the Occupied Territories, and then came onto the committee. We engaged a lawyer to draw up a Trust Deed and became a Recognised Charity, which meant that we were able to recover Income Tax on "covenanted" subscriptions, but had to be careful to avoid too much involvement in politics – something that becomes more and more difficult for charities working in countries where poverty, deprivation and oppression are often the direct result of a given political régime, and this becomes more and more obvious to an increasingly well-informed public.

In the Residents' List of Cambridge University the names were listed of over 4,000 senior members, with their colleges and private addresses. We decided to circulate them all. As we had no money, the envelopes were addressed by hand and delivered by hand to the colleges. It was a

124

labour, but worth it. The first cheque received in answer to the appeal, was £10 from a don at St John's. For years we also raised money by selling things on a stall in Cambridge market.

I ransacked the house for sellable articles, and stopped spending money on things I had thought important before – clothes, hair-do's. The family were unstintingly helpful. Gradually Palestine and the plight of its people took over my life, absorbing my thoughts, and all the energies I had previously channelled into other causes. The fate of the Palestinians, I felt profoundly, was an international scandal (as it still is). But the Western world, in particular the English speaking world, had either shut its eyes or looked the other way. Would the Middle East explode, perhaps to ignite a third world war, and this time a nuclear one, before Western politicians came to their senses?

More people should see and learn for themselves, I was convinced. Somehow intelligent young people, in the future no doubt to hold responsible positions, must be helped to go to Palestine. A prestigious university, with twelve thousand students, was on our doorstep.

In March 1973 we had our first "flag day" or street collection. At that time, not only did every charity need to obtain permission from the City Council to organise a flag day, but collectors were allowed to stand only at the entrance of a college or shop – on the bit of pavement forming part of the college or shop's property. So every single one of them had to be written to in advance.

Marks & Spencer gives huge sums of money to the State of Israel. In Cambridge the store occupies an excellent site in the City Centre. The first answer I received was from the manager of Cambridge M & S: "Yes, certainly; and our best wishes for a good collection." (A few shops refused.) Since then, I have not been able completely to boycott M & S, in spite of its record as a firm supporting an oppressive, militaristic state. I confess I do sometimes buy things from the Cambridge branch.

It was a bitterly cold flag day, with a driving icy wind, sleet, and snow. The collectors bringing back their tins to the Friends' Meeting House were chilled and wet, but cheerful. One I remember in particular, whose furry hat was sprinkled with snowflakes. He was a Christian Palestinian PhD student, Nabil Matar; his family originated in Nazareth; and he was writing a thesis on Thomas Traherne, the seventeenth century English poet and mystic. Ever since, he has been a faithful friend and supporter; and it was a great grief to learn a few years ago that he had been kidnapped in Beirut. By then he was a lecturer in English at the AUB (the American University of Beirut). After being held captive for five months he was released. Our media have usually remembered Western hostages; but have seemed to forget the hundreds of others, mostly Palestinian, many of whom just disappeared and have not been heard of again.

That flag day, twenty-five years ago, we collected £215. After that the amount increased year by year, till by 1987 it amounted to well over £1000. To begin with all the money we collected and all contributions were given to UNRWA – always short of funds. That was before we were advised by an UNRWA official to do our own thing and pay for that, instead of putting money into UNRWA's bottomless deficit. After Israel's invasion of Lebanon in 1982, when the refugee camps in the south were devastated by bombing, we earmarked the annual flag day money for a kindergarten in El Bass camp, not far from Tyre. There, small children find a haven where they can have fun with toys and games, of which there are none at home, and at the same time, under the guidance of trained teachers, have good foundations laid for their education. When possible they are given a midday meal. The kindergarten has been destroyed by Israeli bombing and rebuilt more than once.

Subsequent annual "flag days" provided an opportunity to publicise opportunities for voluntary work in Palestine, with photographs and excerpts of volunteers' reports on display. For this work we received a growing number of enquiries and applications from students who had helped us by rattling collecting tins in the street. From the first, I spoke frequently at meetings of various student societies. The word went round "on the grapevine"; and later we circulated the careers offices of all British universities. A proper system of selection had to be established, with an application form; references were obtained; finally there were interviewing sessions for the most promising candidates. The work acquired its own momentum, with returned volunteers taking part in interviewing, then in briefing of those selected. Eventually it was returned volunteers who shouldered much of the office work as paid staff – albeit on minimal wages.

In the winter of 1973 there occurred two incidents that finally quelled any lingering guilt feelings I had for switching my allegiance, as it were, from Soviet dissenters to Palestinians. Vladimir Bukovsky, for whom we had worked so hard, and who had come to England, had had "no time" to meet me, he said, after he had not turned up when I had invited him to lunch. He had been taken up by important right-wingers, such as Winston Churchill, MP, had a place at King's to continue his studies, and a room in the college with his private telephone. He had found his niche.

Valery Chalidze, whose article I had had difficulty in translating, also came to England. He gave a series of lectures at the LSE, the last one on the subject of the emigration of Jews from USSR. I went to it. The hall was full. After his lecture there were questions. Right at the end, I managed to get mine in. I asked, "Do the Jews emigrating to Israel understand what it involves for the indigenous people? Do they know how land is taken from Palestinians so that homes can be built on it for them, the newcomers?" Chalidze answered mockingly. He treated this as a big joke; and the audience burst out laughing. I was furious; and inevitably the tears rolled. However, everyone was leaving by then. On the way out I bumped into Larissa Haskell, the former Soviet citizen who had taken over my Russian classes at the Convent for a month before my final BA exams. She comforted me a little by saying, "It was an interesting question."

Sponsors for our new charity had been found, their names printed on our leaflet; a committee had been formed; a Trust Deed drawn up; there had been a successful flag day; and a back bedroom in our house had been turned into an office.

The next thing was to do something practical. My thoughts turned to Tahrir El Ghazawi, teaching English from a text-book, unable to converse in the language herself. I had known from experience how, with the best teachers at school and university, it was only through staying in France that I had learnt to speak French well; and realised how essential that was in order both to teach it with confidence and infect pupils with an interest in it, so that they wanted to learn. It is now taken for granted in Western affluent countries that teachers of modern languages must regularly spend time in the countries of the languages they teach.

The conviction that good English was important for Palestinians grew stronger on listening to the radio and comparing the English of Israeli and Zionist speakers with the sometimes stumbling English of Palestinians and other Arabs. English is for Israelis their first foreign language; for many Zionist Jews elsewhere their native language; and most have had excellent educational opportunities. We are, as a nation, very insular and prejudiced in our outlook, and poor linguists ourselves. We expect people of other nationalities to speak our language; and if they do so well they are considered civilised, "one of us"; if they do not, we tend to feel instinctively they are alien, uncivilised. It has been so in relation to Arabs, in spite of their ancient civilisation and their contributions to western culture in various fields, including mathematics, architecture, and medicine. Their traditional courtesy, hospitality, and, with Palestinians at least, their patient capacity for long-suffering are still models for us to admire and try to imitate.

Maybe, I thought, one could combine the teaching of English – an obvious way for native speakers of the language to give help – with the learning on our part of these more fundamental things. Surely there was room here for mutual education? And then, dispossessed of their land and therefore of their traditional livelihoods, education had become a life-line for the Palestinians. It was something which gave them hope for the future. We British, responsible for so much of their suffering, should try to do something, however small and insignificant, to alleviate it. And if able to communicate better in English, a language fast becoming the *lingua franca* of the world, I hoped that Palestinians might feel less tempted through sheer frustration to resort to violence – provided, of course, that more people were willing to *listen!*

A tiny start was made with one teacher of English – Tahrir el Ghazawi.

1   By Abu Nidal, *the* Palestinian terrorist. See Patrick Seale, *Abu Nidal: A Gun for Hire*, Hutchinson, 1992. See also Chapter Eighteen, p 215.

2   *Blaming the Victims. Spurious Scholarship and the Palestine Question*, Edward Saïd and Christopher Hitchens, Verso, 1988.

3   Simha Flapan, *The Birth of Israel: Myths and Realities*, Croom Helm, 1987. Benny Morris, *The Birth of the Palestinian Refugee Problem 1947-49*, CUP, 1987, and Norman Finkelstein, *Image and Reality of the Israel-Palestine Conflict*, Verso, 1995.

4   *Middle East International*, No. 442, 22nd January 1993, and *Publish It Not*, Michael Adams and Christopher Mayhew, Longman, 1975, pp 150–160. Mohammed Mehdi, *A Palestine Chronicle*, Alpha. Documents of the Israeli League for Human Rights, 1970 and 1972. Christopher Uehlinger, Palestinian localities destroyed after 1948, a documentary list, *Association pour Reconstruire Emmaüs*, Geneva, 1989.

5   The people of Palestine, the Palestinians, are the descendants of ancient peoples dating from well before 2000 BC: the Canaanites, Philistines and others, with an admixture of peoples who came later.

   The Canaanites, a Semitic people, had one of the oldest civilisations in the world, and were probably already living in Palestine in the tenth millennium BC. It was they who gave us, via the Greeks, the word *alphabet*, and they were the first to cultivate wheat from a species of wild grass, the *amer*.

   The Philistines also were a cultured and civilised people who, in the twelfth century BC, established five city states along the southern Levantine coast with Gaza as their capital. They were known for their tall stature. Palestine took its name from them. But they were given a bad reputation in the Old Testament. (See Gerald Butt, *Life at the Cross-roads, a History of Gaza*, Rimal-Scorpion Cavendish, 1995.)

6   e.g. *The Call of the Minaret*, OUP, 1964. Charis Waddy has also written a very readable, informative book – *The Muslim Mind*, Longman, 1976, and Grosvenor, 1990.

7   See Appendix.

8   cf Chapter Ten.

9   *Jordan*, Hale, 1958.

CHAPTER TWELVE

Palestine; Palestinians and Israelis; a terrible discovery

Tahrir came to England in the summer of 1973, and stayed with us in Cambridge for two months. As yet there was no network of kind and willing hosts to welcome Palestinian teachers into their homes. That was gradually built up. In the following years Palestinians coming to England for courses through Unipal were able to make friends all over the country – though, principally, of course, in the towns where they were studying – and the experience has indeed been one of mutual education, in some cases leading to permanent friendships.

Tahrir's visit was an eye-opener for us all. In some ways she was quite untypical of the Palestinian girl. She could not cook, nor it seemed, even make tea. Almost like an only child (one sister, much older), she was very intelligent and dedicated to her studies. Her mother, who was illiterate, and her father, like most Palestinian refugees, formerly a peasant farmer, had encouraged her to concentrate on them. Her mother had evidently not only not taught her the domestic arts but had positively discouraged her from spending time on them. Tahrir paid dearly for this lacuna in her education when she married, poor girl.

On the other hand, she was unusually enterprising for a young woman from Gaza, so long cut off from the rest of the world, where women normally lead very restricted, sheltered lives. She was ready to go out in the evening with friends she made at the language school; in fact she occasionally came in quite late. But she managed very well and her fluency in English increased dramatically. She became really talkative.

One day the conversation turned on the difference between Western and Arab attitudes to behaviour between the sexes. Tahrir mentioned, almost casually, that if an unmarried Palestinian girl in Gaza becomes pregnant her family has to kill her. I could hardly believe my ears. She continued, "Yes, it is the family duty. The men of the family must kill her, although it grieves them. She has soiled the family honour."

"And what about the man in the affair?"

"People disapprove of him, of course, but he is not punished."

Tahrir was so calm, accepted so readily this situation, I could have hit her. However, we had a good Palestinian friend in Cambridge, Mohammed, at that time like Nabil, working for his PhD in English. He befriended Tahrir, and while he showed her round the colleges they spoke of this subject. He convinced her, I believe, that such killing is even worse than the offence it is meant to punish. The practice has not completely died out but it is rare, according to a Gaza friend, who told me recently that the man may be punished too, if it is known who he is. The strictest propriety between men and women not of the same family is always *de rigueur*.

This Mohammed had become another friend thanks to the tea-room at the University Library. In July 1972, just after my return from the Middle East, I was reading at lunch there an illustrated book, *One in Three Million – the story of a Palestinian refugee.* A man sitting next to me suddenly asked, "What do you think of it?"

I looked at him. He could have been Jewish from his features, though he seemed unusually sunburnt. Not wishing to offend, I replied evasively, "It depends on one's attitude."

"I too am one of the three million," he said. And I learnt his story. He had been in Jordan studying when the "six day" war erupted in 1967; and he had not been allowed by the victors to return to his home. His mother still lived in a West Bank village, alone.

It was Mohammed who introduced us to Hassan, a Palestinian, and a Cambridge undergraduate. Hassan had been in England for about four years, and had somehow managed to earn enough money by hard manual work on building sites and on roads to get himself to Cambridge. In his third and final year the money had run out and he was in debt to his college. The authorities there were very harsh and were threatening to turn him out. Financial worries and the thought of having to leave without the degree which would mean so much for his future and for which he had worked so hard drove Hassan to despair. He tried to commit suicide. Whether such attempts are genuinely meant to end life or to draw attention to one's plight is often a matter of conjecture; at all events they indicate great emotional distress. Mohammed told me that Hassan was in Fulbourn – the mental hospital just outside Cambridge. I went to see him there. He was recovering. "Mohammed has told me you understand about the situation of my people," was the first thing Hassan said. I was struck that this was what he wanted to talk about. There was no self-pity; no request for help, even. I left the hospital determined to look into the matter. The sum of his debts turned out not to be enormous. The government measure was not yet thought of which was to oblige all foreign students to pay in full the cost of a university course, ensuring that only the rich or those with governments or firms to sponsor them can study here.

There was only one way for the speedy rescue that was needed. Michael and I paid the bills. Hassan got his degree; and he and Mohammed came to our house for a celebration dinner. Hassan was radiant. Back in Jordan he found a job and sent me a watch in token of gratitude. But it was he who had given us happiness through his own.

Mohammed has been a good friend ever since, though he almost never writes. In the summer of 1989, he laid on a feast for our team of summer volunteers teaching English in the refugee camps in and around Amman. Once he told me of an experience he had had in Cambridge, when he was a heavy smoker. One evening he found that he had run out of cigarettes. It was late. He scoured the town for somewhere to get a packet. Suddenly he pulled himself up. "What am I doing, spending time and energy on this?" he asked himself. "I have become a slave to tobacco. It must stop." Since that moment, as far as I know, he has not smoked.

In 1974 we had no Palestinian visitors. I realised I needed to learn a great deal more myself about the situation in Palestine, and I had an urge to try my hand at TEFL (the Teaching of English as a Foreign Language). I offered my services as a volunteer teacher to UNRWA, was accepted, and after calling in on the UNRWA HQ in Beirut to be briefed by the head of English teaching for the Agency, went on to teach for a month on a summer course for teachers of English, held at Ramallah, in the West Bank.

While there, I lived in the Women's Vocational Training Centre (now a Community College), built with funds raised in World Refugee Year, on a hill outside the town. Ancient olive orchards cover the slopes below it; and beyond it you can walk up the hill into the rolling countryside. That is the place from which to watch the sun set, a pink glow spreading over the sky behind the interlocking hills. They grow dim in a translucent grey before the rapidly descending night.

I think that the conversations I had with the women teachers on the terrace after the evening meal were more valuable to them than anything they could learn from me in their classes. When they had got to know me a little, three of them asked, one after the other, "Can you help me to visit England?" And so it came about they did – like Tahrir.

During my stay in Ramallah there occurred two events which had far-reaching consequences. The first led to a new development for

Unipal – a development which gradually became as important a part of its work as the visits to England of teachers of English.

The Vice-Principal of the Women's VTC was Siham Atalla, and she was extremely kind to me. One Friday (the Muslim weekly holiday) she drove me through the hills to Deir Ammar, where there is a refugee camp dating from 1948. Just outside the camp, on a spur of the hills looking towards the Mediterranean over the plain below, is an UNRWA school; and beside the school an area planted with young trees, where a basketball court has been made, and a tiny swimming pool. About fifty boys, gathered from all over the West Bank and Gaza Strip, were enjoying a summer camp there. It was Open Day for friends and any of the boys' relatives who could manage the journey. We watched a fast game of hockey on roller skates and various other sports and gymnastics, and admired an exhibition of models for teaching geography made with the assistance of UNRWA schoolteachers and others acting as helpers on the camp. Among the helpers I noticed a young American and one or two Europeans. This gave birth to an idea. Why not get British students from Cambridge to go as volunteer helpers – next year, if possible? Living with Palestinians would give them an insight into the problems of the people; and if suitably chosen they would undoubtedly have skills to contribute. That too came about, through the goodwill of Mr Antranig Bakerjian ("Tony") a Palestinian Armenian and the UNRWA Area Officer in Ramallah, (quoted from in chapter nine), whose brainchild the children's summer camps were.

After the English course, I prolonged my stay, having found somewhere else in Ramallah to live for a few weeks. I was still involved tenuously with Amnesty International and had heard from other sources that there were Palestinian political prisoners in Israeli jails; but none, as far as I was aware, had been adopted by Amnesty. I decided I would try to get some first-hand information about these prisoners.

The Israeli lawyer, Felicia Langer, well-known for her defence of Palestinians in the courts (and later for her books *With My Own Eyes* and *These Are My Brothers*) seemed to me a good person to call on to begin with. Accordingly, I made an appointment. Her office was just within the old boundary of West Jerusalem, in a big office block. I was guided to her door by the sight of women in Palestinian dress entering and leaving. Inside, it was packed. I sat and waited. After a time Felicia was able to give me a few minutes. As we were speaking, a man came in and began saying something to her urgently in Hebrew. Felicia turned to me and said, "Go with that man!" I had no idea who "that man" was, but obeyed. He hailed a taxi and we jumped in.

Our destination turned out to be the headquarters of the International Red Cross in East Jerusalem. There the delegate, an interpreter beside him, was besieged by a crowd of women, obviously in a state of great agitation, each anxious to tell him something. We stood to one side, watching and listening for a while. When the hubbub subsided, a tall, dignified woman came up to us. "I think you are Dr Shahak," she said to my companion. "I would like to thank you for all you are doing on behalf of my people." That was my introduction to two outstanding persons of great courage: the Israeli academic, survivor of Belsen concentration camp, already well-known for his defence of Palestinians, Israel Shahak; and Mrs Nasir, the mother of Dr Hanna Nasir, President of Birzeit University[1].

Immediately, we were surrounded by some of the women who had been besieging the IRC delegate. They were the mothers, wives and fiancées of men who had not long before been picked up and imprisoned in a wave of mass arrests. Some of the men were lecturers at Birzeit. Eventually the women had learnt where the prisoners were held, and had been able to visit them – and been shocked at what they discovered. Those arrested had been tortured under interrogation. And their appearance showed it. Dr Shahak and I scribbled notes of what was said.

This, for me, was the start of one of the most disturbing experiences of my life. I was directed to a woman whom I could trust and who could help me find out more about Palestinian prisoners. I was driven with her to various places, the car always left at a distance from the house to be visited. Sometimes the visit had to be made after dark. I had wanted to find out about prisoners: I found out more than I had bargained for. It was horrible, like finding, under a large stone that has lain unmoved for a long time, something repulsive. Such cruelty – such pain inflicted by a people who had themselves only recently experienced the same at the hands of Nazi torturers! And I was scared – scared not only for Palestinians, but also for Israelis: one day, there might be terrible, and, this time, justifiable retribution. That atrocities had been committed was indubitable. There were the marks that I saw on bodies. And never shall I forget the meeting with an elderly man in Nablus who told me with curses, and with tears streaming down his face, how his son had been tortured to death in prison.

I produced a twenty-page report. Here I can only describe a few of the cases mentioned in it. They are of victims I met personally. There were many others. Once word got round about what I was doing, relatives and friends came to me, desperately anxious that I should hear what had happened to persons close to them, and, above all, that I should let the world know, when I returned to England. They thought this would help. Poor, poor people. One can only try and try – and go on trying, and hope that in the end the trying of many other, more influential people will eventually bring about a result.

I was taken to a village just outside Jerusalem, to a tiny stone-built house on a hillside. It had one room, though there were eight children. "The family are very poor," I wrote in my report. "The father is a tailor who mends, but does not make clothes. He is a communist; aged about fifty-six, he looks seventy. He came out of prison two months ago. He had been tortured so much that he had to spend ten days in hospital. Still bleeding from scrotum – with pus, so there must be an infection. The doctor's certificate (xeroxed copy in my possession) states: 'Severe headache and pain in scrotum…after beating…' He had been obliged to hold a chair above his head, standing on one leg for half an hour. Made to face wall; back of head struck so his forehead knocked against it; struck on sex organ; told, 'You'll have fifteen years.' 'Why?' 'You'll know later.' Family threatened by soldiers who held guns at the chests of his three- and five-year-old sons. They are still disturbed. Lawyer: Felicia Langer."

Western women, particularly if grey-haired and unglamorous, are often treated by Arabs as honorary men. After describing his torture, this man started to unzip his trousers to show me the effect of it. Suddenly, overcome with confusion, he did himself up again before I could see anything. There was an embarrassed giggle among those present. Then his wife mentioned she had constantly to wash his pants, and on my request produced a pair as yet unwashed.

An appointment was made to take me one evening after dark to a house in a Jerusalem suburb. There a man was brought to meet me who, also through an interpreter, told me the story of what happened after he was arrested – for an offence of which he maintained he was innocent.

> My eyes were covered, and my hands handcuffed behind my back. About ten Kg. of iron was fixed to my legs. I felt I was being taken to Gaza (I am familiar with the country). On arrival I was made to walk on a wall about 1.5 metres high, 45 cm wide, still blindfolded and my hands and legs as before. A soldier helped me up. Then dogs were let loose at me. I fell and skinned the side of my face. After that, I was put into a cell so small I had to stand all the time for two days. The walls were sticky (with paint, as it turned out). There was a chain from the ceiling to my handcuffed hands. Then I was taken out early one morning and kept standing blindfold, with hands and legs as before, in the sun all day without water or food, till midnight. It was August. I was made to hear water. Then I was taken to the torture room.

"You'd better give information," I was warned. "But I have nothing to tell." I was accused of association with Fatah[2], which I denied. I was hung up by the handcuffs, with my arms wide, as in crucifixion. The bench was pulled from under my feet. I was tortured for four successive days and nights in this way; my wrists were bleeding.

After four days I was taken to a room where there was a wooden bar-chair with electric wires from the ceiling. I was questioned again but I had nothing to say. An electric wire was clipped to my ear; when the current was released I was thrown across the room onto sand. This was repeated till I lost consciousness. Three nights of electric shocks. No water to drink; in the daytime I stood under the sun, a sack over my head, a rope round my neck. There was a hole for my nose. I was sweating and itching, and tried to throw myself against something to ease the itching. I struck my head, and bled; the hole moved, so my nose was covered. A soldier said, "As it's the first time, I'll put it back." Altogether the torture went on for twelve days. The last thing was torture on the sex organ and that finished me. I signed a confession in Hebrew which I do not understand.

He was beaten and kicked, but it was nothing compared with the rest, he said, though he was beaten so much on the soles of his feet that he could not wear his shoes.

He was sentenced in August 1969 to seven years; and spent three and a half in prison, but then was released, he thinks, because his house had been demolished.

The family's furniture, even clothes, were destroyed as well; his car confiscated. All his life's savings had now gone. He was back in the refugee camp from which he had extricated himself by hard work – in Germany and Kuwait. Before 1948 his family had owned land about thirteen kilometres west of Bethlehem. It was taken in 1948. In court he said to the judge: "Wouldn't you do something, if you'd been robbed? But I haven't done anything." His family were not allowed to visit him before the trial and were not allowed into the court. He could see his lawyer (Felicia Langer) only after his health improved.

He had three children, a wife and his elderly mother to support. But he told me he was unfit for work now. He could only do odd jobs, for he had diabetes and arthritis, especially in his wrists. The doctor had said it was due to lack of circulation in them while he was strung up.

Another day I was taken to El Bireh near Ramallah. The car was left at some distance from the rendezvous and we walked to a large house with two or three flats in it. Once again a man was brought to meet me. He looked very frail. He had been in prison for four years from June 1968, accused of giving food to *fedayeen* (guerrillas). He could not afford a lawyer to defend him, as he had seven children, a wife, and elderly parents to feed.

After he was arrested, there was a beating; but that was nothing, he said, compared with three or four days in a cell without food or water. His nails were pulled out. Electric wires were attached to his joints, and he was given shocks. So he said, "I let them spend a night with me without knowing they were *fedayeen*."

Two confessions were brought: one in Hebrew, one in Arabic. He signed the Arabic one. He thought, from the way he was treated in prison, there must be worse things in the Hebrew one. He was very ill in prison, and not allowed to see a doctor. On release he had to undergo two operations as a result of the torture. He was now unable to work. His wife did some embroidery to earn a little.

In Kalandia camp, in a small refugee shelter, a young woman said to me, "I may not be able to have children now, because of what was done to my husband in prison."

Then I was taken to see a torture victim in a hospital near Bethlehem – a boy of about eighteen to twenty, one of eight children of a poor refugee family. He was brought from bed to see me in a small office and was clearly in a very fragile state, both physically and psychologically – his right leg was shaking uncontrollably from the beginning of the interview and at the end of it was shaking much worse. He had been released from detention a month earlier lest he die in prison.

He had been arrested at night about three months previously and cruelly tortured: kept naked and beaten on his sex organs; blindfolded, handcuffed (behind his back) and hung upside down – there were rings on his ankles for the purpose. While in this position, they beat him. He cried out and spat so they gagged him. Then they caught him by the hair, dragged him round, kicking him. He was pricked with needles on the sex organs. A biro was thrust up his penis, which was beaten at the same time, so he urinated blood. At the same time they said, "Confess!" He was given electric shocks. At last they threatened to rape him; and a small bottle was thrust into his rectum. He lost control at this and flailed round with his arms, striking his hand against a window pane and breaking it, so his hand was cut. I saw an ugly scar there, and he had an ulcerated nail. There were bumps on his legs and scars on his abdomen from beating with wires and sticks, and red marks all over his torso where cigarettes had been stubbed out.

He was beaten many times till he lost consciousness; then came to, feeling water on his face. When he asked for water to drink, it was refused. It was shown him. Of the seventy days of torture, forty-six were spent in an isolation cell, which was dark – no windows. He was not allowed out to urinate or defecate; nor allowed a change of clothes, so he got lice. Bread was kicked into the cell. He had asked for books as he was supposed to be taking his *tawjihi* (school leaving exam), but they had been refused.

He had been in four prisons – in Bethlehem, Jerusalem, Hebron, and Sarafand. The specialists in torture – especially electric – are, he said, at Sarafand. During torture they would repeat names, most of which he didn't know.

He had refused to sign a confession in Hebrew. "I do not understand Hebrew," he told me.

The doctor who was present with us at the interview was taking a great risk. "I may be punished for this," he said. Not quite two years later he was deported – the worst punishment for a Palestinian. I met him again in Amman.

I took my report to Amnesty International, handing it to Katrina Mortimer of the ME Research Section – sure that there would be concern. I also took to Amnesty two "exhibits". One was a CS gas cylinder with printed on it "FOR OUTDOOR USE ONLY". Also printed on it was "Made in Pennsylvania". It had been shot, together with many more like it, among girls under fifteen *inside* their classroom in an UNRWA school, temporarily asphyxiating them. It had been given me by their headmistress. The other was the bloodstained pair of pants. Amnesty had accepted my report on Greek prisoners, so I waited hopefully. Once or twice I asked Katrina Mortimer what was happening. The answer was, "It's a conflict area. The prisoners may have been engaged in violence, or advocated it."

I had written this report on my own initiative; I had not been asked to do it, as I had for the Greeks; and nine years had passed since the Scheveningen AGM. Amnesty had grown in size and become more professional and so inevitably more bureaucratic. I did not give all the names of the released prisoners who had been tortured and whom I had interviewed – afraid of reprisals for them, (though I did give the names of others whose stories I had heard from lawyers and relatives). More important, of course, was that no one seemed able to entertain the thought that such atrocities could be committed by Israelis, by Jews. My report was quietly shelved. Unsurprisingly perhaps, the gas cylinder and the pants had no more effect on Amnesty International than my report.[3]

137

I also went to *The Times* and had an interview with the Editor, Rees Mogg, and Louis Heren, Foreign News Editor. I did not know then that Heren was a Zionist. Unfortunately, I was still new to the problem and could not penetrate their incredulity. In my report I had mentioned also that 17,000 Palestinian homes had been destroyed in the first five years of the occupation. "You expect us to believe that?" exclaimed Heren. "That would be as many as in a town!" I should have answered, "Go and see for yourself – where the villages Imwas (the biblical Emmaus), Yalu, Beit Nuba, Nebi Samweel and Jiftlik used to be. See the vast empty spaces in Jabaliya Camp, Gaza Strip; and the countless heaps of rubble in villages and towns all over the West Bank and the Strip." How sensible one can always be after the event!

Just before I went to Palestine in 1976, someone advised me to go and see *The Times* correspondent there, Eric Marsden. So on arrival I rang him, and we met in East Jerusalem at the American Colony Hotel, a meeting place for every nationality and particularly for journalists. Formerly an Ottoman pasha's palace, it is characteristic of traditional Arab architecture and very beautiful, built round a courtyard with a fountain, flowers, an orange and a lemon tree. On the walls of the spacious reception rooms are Palestinian pottery tiles – in their designs, a lovely blue predominating; on the floors, rich oriental rugs. Eric Marsden seemed pleased to see me. "I found your report *open* on my desk when I came back from holiday. I have been feeling very frustrated. I know this is going on, but I have been unable to get anything published. We must try the *Sunday Times*. I'll phone their London office from Cyprus. You go and see the Editor as soon as you get back." In the course of conversation he made a prophecy which has, sadly, already to a large extent come true: "It is Palestinian collaborators with the Israelis who will suffer vengeance first," he said.

On that trip I went also to Jordan and Kuwait (to Kuwait to try to raise money for the work), and was ill in hospital with suspected typhoid and a chest infection after I got back. A friend went to the *Sunday Times* office instead of me, with a copy of my report. A month or so later the paper sent Peter Gillman down to Cambridge to interview me. He was interested to discover that I was the same person whose name had appeared on *Inside Story*, together with that of his father-in-law, who had also "done time" for anti-nuclear activities. I think it was a kind of recommendation! Once accepted as *bona fide* I was asked to advise on procedure, and on who could help in Palestine and Jordan, where some of the tortured now were. Then a *Sunday Times* "Insight Team" made its own investigation; and in June, 1977, published a four-page report on Israeli torture of Palestinians, complete with photographs. Amnesty International was alerted. In recent years it has acted with considerable courage on behalf of Palestinians, producing reports on Israeli torture annually since 1989.

The American human rights organisation Middle East Watch produced a report on Israel's prison system in April 1991. More significantly, B'Tselem, the Israeli Information Centre for Human Rights in the Occupied Territories has issued its own reports. Its report of March 1991 contains unbearably shocking descriptions of tortures used on Palestinians, with illustrations. Other American reports on these practices have also appeared – that of the National Lawyers' Guild in New York (1978), and the US State Department has also become increasingly critical of Israel's treatment of Palestinian civilians in the West Bank and Gaza. All this does not seem to have had any effect on the US Administration, which boasts championship of human rights, or on the Israeli practice of torture.

Amnesty has not adopted as a prisoner of conscience the Israeli, Mordechai Vanunu, sentenced in September 1986 to *eighteen years' solitary confinement*[4], but has asked for his immediate release in view of the illegalities of his manner of arrest and detention and of all that he has suffered. Prolonged solitary confinement is a particularly cruel form of mental torture. (Mordechai is now allowed a few hours each day to be with other prisoners.)

Soon after the "Insight Team" report, David Holden, *Sunday Times* correspondent for the Middle East, was found murdered in Egypt. It was explained to me that Menachem Begin, the Israeli Prime Minister, was furious at the facts of Israeli torture being revealed, and assumed, because of Holden's position on the paper, that he was responsible, and so ordered him to be killed. The names of the members of the Insight Team were then published, in order to protect them.

Twenty years after that report, on 16th July 1997, *The Guardian* published an interview with Hermann Arndt, (Hebrew name Zvi Ahroni). He had been for about ten years head of Mossad's interrogation department; and the chief operator in the clandestine abduction from Argentina for trial in Israel of the Nazi criminal Adolf Eichmann. Arndt said in the interview:

> *"I took part in building the national security service. I was proud of it...Today I am disgusted by it. Let me tell you one thing: when I was head of the investigation department, nobody could touch a prisoner. Sure, you could use all kinds of tricks, you could bug them, listen in on their conversations. But beating them? Torturing them?"* He pauses to make an appalled face. *"Today not only is it done, it's legal. It's legal in my country...It's not my country any more."*

139

Sadly, there are many other countries where torture exists, including Arab countries; but Israel is the only country in the world where it has been legalised, a fact deplored by Amnesty International, which points out that Israel ratified the UN Convention against torture in 1991. Article 2 requires states to prevent "acts of torture in any territory under its jurisdiction". According to AI, "torture continues to be used in Israel because the majority of Israeli society seems to accept that the methods used are a legitimate means of combating 'terrorism'…the methods are acceptable because they are not used against Israeli Jews".[5]

In the summer of 1974 I had also gone down to Gaza. My intention was to find out if there was a possibility of residential children's summer camps being held there, on the lines of the one at Deir Ammar which had impressed me so much. It had struck me before when in the Strip that although it contained some of the most squalid of the refugee camps, it had one great asset: the sea. How wonderful it would be for the children to bathe under supervision and perhaps even learn to swim! I asked Mr Bakerjian if he could take some British volunteers at Deir Ammar the following year, and if he could possibly help UNRWA in Gaza with advice on how to set up similar camps in the Strip. "Yes," was the answer – he would do both! So I put the idea to the UNRWA American Director in Gaza. "No," was the firm reply. I decided to take the matter further when I returned home.

That summer too, a large shack was pointed out to me on the left side of the road leading north out of Jerusalem to Ramallah and Nablus. Behind the shack was rubble – all that was left of a two-storey stone house that had been the home of thirty-two people, members of the extended Mala'abi family. Seven boys had been arrested, accused of possessing explosives – four brothers had been released after torture. Three others were still in prison; one was reported to have become mentally deranged as a result of the treatment he had received. The Mala'abi boys were to be witnesses in the case of Archbishop Capucci – much in the news that summer. The Archbishop had been arrested for allegedly transporting weapons in the boot of his car, and the Mala'abi boys were suspected of being implicated.

When the chance offered, I was taken to visit the family in the shack which was made of hardboard with a corrugated iron roof. Friends had collected bits of furniture, bedding, and utensils for the homeless people, as everything they owned had been destroyed. Just an aunt, a

140

granny and two small boys were at home when we called. One of the boys was ill in bed with whooping cough.

For the practice of punitive demolition, frequently carried out by the Israeli military authorities, they invoke a British Emergency Regulation of the Mandate period (cancelled by the British when that came to an end). It authorises the destruction of the home of anyone suspected of possessing or using a weapon of any kind. The house is demolished before the suspect is brought to trial, when he may even be found not guilty. An Arab home is usually the home of the extended family: grandparents, parents, uncles, aunts and cousins may live under the same roof. Collective punishment was outlawed by the Fourth Geneva Convention (on the treatment of civilians under military occupation) – to which Israel is a signatory. Ironically, the convention was drawn up as a result of what Jews had suffered in World War II. This practice greatly intensified during the *intifada*, and continues to this day in the West Bank. It continued in the Gaza Strip until September 1993.

I saw other waste places where homes had once stood but been destroyed – sometimes for no better reason than the "security" or the convenience of the occupying power. In three refugee camps in the Gaza Strip, notably Jabaliya, 2,500 families had suddenly been made homeless in 1971: just spaces were left, with no more building allowed on them.

From the Nablus road, near the now overgrown rubble of the Mala'abi home, if you look to your left into the distance you will see still – most clearly if against the background of a glowing sunset – the black silhouette of the minaret of a mosque perched on the top of a hill. It is all that is left of the village of Nebi Samweel (the village of Samuel, the prophet). The destruction of this village was not a punishment for any alleged offence; but new Israeli settlements were to be built on the slopes of the hill leading up to it. Evidently, an Arab village could not be allowed to remain where it could *look down* on them!

---

1   Dr Hanna Nasir was soon to face his own grim experience. In November 1974, with four other arrested Palestinian intellectuals, he was driven handcuffed and blindfolded in a truck to the Lebanese border; there released and told, with a gun at his back, to walk. He spent nineteen years in exile.

2   The principal group in the PLO.

3   I was informed recently that Amnesty International had in 1970 brought out a report on the *Treatment of Prisoners under Interrogation in Israel*, as

had even the International Committee of the Red Cross, which rarely publishes its findings. These reports had drawn little attention: the press had ignored them.

4   See Chapter Seventeen, p197

5   *Israel/Occupied Territories and the Palestinian Authority. Five years after the Oslo Agreement: human rights sacrificed for "security".* Amnesty International Report, September 1998.

CHAPTER THIRTEEN

Two-way traffic between England and Palestine

Amneh and Najwa had both been in my English classes at the Ramallah VTC in 1974, and we had become more closely acquainted through the evening chats on the terrace above the olive groves. Amneh's home was in Nablus, the largest Arab town in the West Bank, and Najwa's in Beit Sahour, adjacent to Bethlehem. In January 1975 they both came to Cambridge. On arrival they both stayed for a time in our house, and then separated to live with different host families in the town. Amneh's English classes were only in the mornings; so in the afternoons she had a secretarial course, which she found very useful later. A particularly open, responsive and affectionate girl, she became a great favourite with everyone.

These two came in the middle of their school year, because it was easier for the Schools of English here to fit them in free of charge out of their "season" (the summer months when most foreign students used to pour into the country to attend language classes). Unfortunately for the two Palestinian teachers this meant foregoing their salaries for the whole period of their absence from school, as UNRWA could not afford to pay both them and their temporary replacements. The two girls had made this enormous sacrifice, realising what a valuable opportunity it was for them to come to England; but thereafter we saw to it that teachers came in their summer holidays, and language schools here have been very generous in giving scholarships at their busiest time to Palestinian teachers. That very summer, another UNRWA teacher came – Amal, from a refugee camp near Nablus. Tahrir and those three teachers have been followed by more than fifty others. They have come from the West Bank, Gaza Strip, Jordan, Lebanon, and Syria. We tried to have a "mix" each year, for the teachers welcome the chance, almost impossible in the normal way, to meet their compatriots from other areas of the Palestinian Diaspora, where each community has suffered in its own way the effects of the 1948 Catastrophe, and has developed – or been prevented from developing – according to the particular circumstances of its place of refuge. For once, too, they have been able

143

to meet people of various nationalities among fellow students; the teachers have seen something of Britain, visiting many places they have only read about in their school text-books, or of which they knew nothing; been to the cinema and theatre for the first time in their lives, and really enjoyed themselves. Siham, who came from Lebanon, wrote to us afterwards:

> During my stay in England I have lived the language and learned how to use it; but the most important thing I have learned is not to be fanatic...I have had the chance to meet many people of different nationalities and religions. I have learned to accept people who are supposed to be my enemies, and could talk to them without hatred, which I could not do before.

Siham came to us in the summer of 1983. She had lived and suffered through the Israeli siege of Beirut the previous year.

It was about this time that I had an urgent request for help from Anna Baidoun, English teacher at Birzeit University. She wrote on behalf of Hisham, a student who just before his final year was in urgent need of a major spinal operation which could not be performed in Palestine. A victim of polio before he was two, Hisham was severely crippled, and at ten years old had still only been able to crawl. No school would accept him, and his family were poor. But his mother never lost heart. "She wanted so much for me to be an educated person and to overcome this obstacle," Hisham said. "If not well in my body, I could be well in my mind." He eventually finished school at twenty-two; then his legs were operated on at the orthopaedic hospital in Bethlehem; and two years later he was admitted to Birzeit University. But the early years of crawling had caused his chest to be curved inwards. Now his spine was pressing on his lungs, and his life was at risk. Could Unipal help?

The cost of such an operation and long hospitalisation would be enormous. We just hadn't anything like the sum required. A friend suggested that I should write to the then Saudi Ambassador in the USA, who, she said, was kind and generous.

Late one morning, having done the family washing, I went up to the back bedroom-office. Before starting work I glanced into the garden and saw with satisfaction the long line of shirts waving their arms in the breeze. The telephone rang. "This is *Washing*ton..." For a split second I was nonplussed. But the voice continued, "How would you like the cheque made out?" In due course a big cheque arrived – enough to cover Hisham's hospital expenses, that of his mother who had to come with him to look after him when he came out, and that of his brother, who spoke English and had to look after *her*. Accompanying the cheque was a heart-warming letter from the Ambassador with the words, "I pray to Allah that the operation may be successful." Performed by Mr Gregory Houghton, one of the top two orthopaedic surgeons in the UK specialising in spinal injuries, who generously gave his services free, the operation was successful. Hisham went home with a straight back.

He told me later: "The surgery was very painful. It took me about two years to get over it. I spent two months in hospital in Oxford and met such good people – Arab and English. They encouraged me a lot, and helped me to recover."

Hisham completed his degree. He now has a good job in the Nablus Municipality Offices, speaks English well, and though still on crutches, moves with incredible dexterity up and down the steep flight of steps which leads to his home on a Nablus hillside.

When I was in the West Bank in 1974, Mr. Bakerjian had said he would welcome some British volunteers at his Deir Ammar summer camps and that he would help set up similar ones in the Gaza Strip; but the American Director of UNRWA in Gaza had said "No" to them. Sir John Rennie, the Commissioner General, who had written to Michael and me so kindly in 1969, came to the rescue. I had written to him about our difficulty and he opened the way.

In the summer of 1975 the first residential camps (one for boys, one for girls) were held in the Strip. We in England worked hard to raise the money, and Mr. Majdalawi, the UNRWA Palestinian Welfare Officer in Gaza, worked hard to organise the camp itself, to find Palestinian volunteers and donations in kind. The Gaza merchants contributed with equipment and provisions, as they did in the West Bank. The first British volunteers, after learning the ropes at Deir Ammar, also helped with the organisation in Gaza. Unipal owes a great debt to our pioneering volunteers. That first year they were Peter Crouch, Nicholas Turner, and Sheila Ward, graduates from Cambridge University, and Jane Lewis from Oxford.

In Britain, summer camps for the young fall roughly into two kinds: there are those for the privileged, who find it fun to rough it for a while close to nature, in tents; and for the under-privileged from slum areas for whom a spell of living outdoors and under canvas is also an enjoyable adventure. For Palestinian refugees, who have a totally different, very harsh experience of tent life, similar summer camps to ours are not very appropriate. The children need something else to make up for the deprivation they experience most of their lives, both at home and at school. The Deir Ammar and Gaza camps were quite sophisticated, and highly organised: particularly Deir Ammar. In Gaza there was the advantage of the sea; and swimming in it was always part of the programme. Our volunteers also taught crafts, drama, music (on pipe recorders), sports, and simple English through songs and games.

After the idea of the boys' camp had been accepted in Gaza, there had been opposition from UNRWA in having a girls' camp. I had had a distressing interview with Peter Holdaway, the chief Welfare Officer. "We have quite enough to cope with, without you giving us more," he told me severely. "A girls' residential camp in Gaza would be most unsuitable." He came round in the end! The following year (1976), when I was in the UNRWA Field Office in Amman, I got a message from him asking me to come and see him (he had moved there from Gaza). I went in some trepidation. "I owe you an apology, Mrs. Aitken," he said. "The girls' camp in Gaza was so successful, we have decided to have one here. The YMCA has been running one for some years for orphan boys; now we will have one for orphan girls!" Later, some of our volunteers with experience of the Gaza camps went to help in Amman. Deirdre Evans-Pritchard, who had graduated in Arabic from Durham University, was one. Deirdre, like other returned volunteers, also gave us invaluable help in interviewing candidates for voluntary work; she did so again in USA where she settled after marriage.

The work developed rapidly. By 1990 a total of over fifty teachers of English had been to England; and seven nurses from Lebanon had been here for extra training. The volunteer programme mushroomed as word went round among university students about this worthwhile and rewarding way to spend the summer vacation. Older people also applied; and we were particularly happy when teachers did so. In 1975 there had been four volunteers to go to Palestine. Ten years later there were seventy; and by 1990 a total of nearly 600 volunteers had been to the Middle East.

After five years, when the Gaza residential summer camps for children came to an end, volunteers helped on day camps for them in the refugee camps of the Strip. And sadly, when Tony Bakerjian retired, there were no more Deir Ammar summer camps either.

However, a variety of possibilities for volunteer work appeared. Early every year I would go to the Occupied Territories to "prospect" and on return, when candidates for the summer were interviewed, we would try to fit them into suitable projects. When volunteers had a special skill in demand it was satisfying for all concerned if they could be fitted into the appropriate "slots". Artists did wall paintings to enliven kindergartens and children's homes. Once the headmaster of a school for mentally handicapped children in England ran a training course in

146

the West Bank for teachers of the mentally handicapped there. A physiotherapist asked us for work with Arab children: she went to a centre for physically handicapped children in Jerusalem and stayed there for four years. Another time we were asked for an occupational therapist in Bethlehem in what was formerly a Cheshire home, but now run by the Bethlehem Arab Society for Rehabilitation. One was found who spent eighteen months there, and is still remembered with great affection. Other volunteers taught on summer courses in West Bank universities: English, biology, chemistry, geography. Volunteers have also worked in a university library, and helped to build a school. Twice, medical students have been able to do their "elective" in East Jerusalem hospitals. One girl's summer English teaching led her to work for a year with a Palestinian human rights association in Israel, and this help continued for some years to be given by lawyers in training.

One year, after the Israeli authorities had allowed municipal elections, the Ramallah town council opened a Children's Centre, where, during the long summer holidays, school children could enjoy creative activities, particularly in art. Unipal sent a volunteer to help. The Palestinian artist who lives in Ramallah, Vera Tamari, was a key figure in the running of the Centre. (Sadly, soon afterwards the councils were prevented from functioning by the occupation authorities and the Children's Centre was closed.)

Vera Tamari was a refugee from Jaffa, one of the two main ports of former Palestine, and its second city after Jerusalem. In her Ramallah flat is a ceramic piece which shows her father's home: the doorways, the windows, the trees in front. She told me:

> Recently some of my ceramic work has been inspired by Jaffa, but not by the present sadness of Jaffa…I was too small to remember Jaffa as it used to be. But after 1967 we were able to visit it. My impressions then were very confused. On the one hand there was this very run-down city; on the other hand I saw the terrible emotion of my parents as they sought out the familiar places of twenty years before. They were crying. They relived their youth, with their parents, their friends. I know Jaffa had a great history and that my parents were crying for that, too; but I could not see any of this in its present haggard appearance. But, strangely, when I went again, I absorbed Jaffa's past quite naturally, and the remains of its beautiful architecture. I longed for it as the home of my family and my ancestors, and I cried too. It has been terribly destroyed.

Lydda, (now Lod) was another ancient Palestinian town with the characteristic Arab architecture, appropriate for the country. In 1974 I saw it as it was being demolished, its beautiful, solid old stone houses, with arched doorways and windows, and high vaulted ceilings – the best for coolness – becoming ruins.

A few old homes in Jaffa have been kept and modernised for Israeli artists. That artists' colony is now proudly shown to tourists. A similar story, with even more heart-rending undertones, is that of the village of Ein Hud in Galilee. Ein Hud, a picturesque village on a hill, with a view to the Mediterranean, was not among those destroyed, but was appropriated by the Israelis, turned into a centre for the arts, and called Ein Hod. Some of the original inhabitants, employed to modernise their own former homes, cannot themselves enjoy them; they live nearby, in an "unrecognised" village with no services whatever. Ein Hud's story is movingly told by an Israeli author, Benjamin Beit-Hallahmi.[1]

The majority of the summer volunteers, university students, have taught English to Palestinians in their summer vacation. The first courses started in Gaza, and Unipal was greatly helped by the Chairman of the Red Crescent Society in Gaza, Dr Haidar Abd el Shafi (later leader of the Palestinian delegation to the first peace talks). It was not long before a whole team of students would go to Gaza for this purpose, and a few years later another team to Nablus. They would live in a school lent by UNRWA, sleeping in the classrooms and catering for themselves. Every day they would disperse to take classes in the refugee camps.

And then Palestinians asked us for systematic teaching of English throughout the academic year. So from 1980 onwards it became one of Unipal's main activities – starting in Gaza, just as our work with children and the summer English teaching had. These "long term" volunteers had to be qualified in TEFL; and once again language schools here which run training courses in TEFL for native speakers of English generously came to our aid: providing the month intensive course free of charge for our prospective volunteers.

The Gaza Strip has for good reason been a main concern of Unipal's. For eighteen years (1948–67) it was under Egyptian control, but separated from Egypt proper by the Sinai desert and on its other sides by the new state of Israel and the sea. It had been completely cut off from Jerusalem and the West Bank, which was under Jordan, and which had all the advantages of famous Muslim and Christian holy sites, and therefore not only drew the tourist and pilgrim traffic but most of the educational and medical work of various religious bodies. Gaza was relatively neglected. It had, too, the highest proportion of refugees to residents: about two thirds of the total population.

Moreover, in the early years of the Israeli occupation it was the most active centre of resistance and suffered brutal repression. Consequently, the Israeli authorities fear Palestinian resentment there more than anywhere else and have actively discouraged foreign groups of visitors. For all these reasons the Strip is an exceptionally needy area. When it is understood by Gazans that volunteers have come to give help, the welcome given is particularly warm.

In the early 80s we also sent long-term volunteers with a TEFL qualification to teach English in Palestinian universities and educational institutions: Birzeit University (BZU), where Dr Hanan Ashrawi was then Chairman of the English Faculty, and particularly co-operative. Other volunteers taught in Hebron and Nablus universities, Dar el Tifl School for Girls and the YWCA Secretarial School in Jerusalem.

In 1987 there was a rather different candidate from the others for summer volunteer work with Unipal. Scott Faigen, an American Jewish concert pianist, living and working in Germany, had heard of Unipal when on a visit to Sweden. What he wanted above all was to learn, and to see if he could contribute anything to mutual understanding between Jews and Palestinians. He was so keen that he came for interview, from Germany, on crutches: he had broken his foot. He did not easily fit into any of our usual projects but he seemed to me too valuable to lose. I told him I could not promise anything, but would try to arrange a special programme for him. So when I went out a few weeks later to Israel/Palestine I sounded out Palestinian friends in different walks of life. There was a willing response.

Thanks to their hospitality, Scott was able to meet Palestinian actors, musicians, doctors, teachers, and lawyers. He stayed in refugee camps, villages and towns; and even had the distressing experience, with the help of an Israeli Palestinian lawyer, of seeing the inside of an Israeli prison and tortured Palestinian detainees. But he also took a "master class" in piano for the Palestinian music teacher, Nadia Abboushi – in this way rendering his own bit of practical service. He stayed with Hanan Ashrawi, Nadia's sister; and when Hanan became well-known as spokeswoman for the Palestinian delegation at the peace talks, he was proud to be able to say that he had had the honour of playing scrabble with her!

Nadia Abboushi's pupils play Chopin, Mozart, Beethoven. She says:

> I want to build up a core of students who will become qualified to teach music in schools. When we have a free Palestine, we will have a music institute, maybe a conservatory where we can train students properly. Personally, I'm not involved in Arabic music, but I encourage my students to take an interest

in it, and I am on the board of a centre for folk music and dance. It is doing a serious work collecting folk songs and dances in order to develop our tradition further.

Nadia and musician colleagues have already started a music institute; but, under occupation still, they are having a very difficult time.

A key person in arranging Scott's programme was Fateh Azzam, then Director of the Hakawati Palestinian National Theatre in Jerusalem. He himself had Scott to stay for a time; and, having spent years in America, he was the right person to introduce an American to the Palestinian situation, and explain to him some of the difficulties of life under military occupation. The Hakawati Theatre had, in particular, to struggle for survival under strict censorship. One of over 1000 Military Orders, Order 101, says that a gathering of ten or more people for political purposes or what *may be interpreted* as political purposes in any public place, social club, café, is illegal and punishable by high fines and up to ten years imprisonment. "When you have a community wanting to express itself in a difficult situation," Fateh said, "much of what it has to say is bound to be political." Forbidden to perform at all in the West Bank or Gaza Strip (Jerusalem, annexed by Israel, comes under Israeli civil law), the Hakawati may take plays, if it can afford it, to Galilee and even abroad.

In September 1991 an English version of the play *Ansar III* toured the United States, Canada and UK, and was well received throughout its three month tour. To be allowed to travel, however, the Israeli authorities forced the main actor to sign an undertaking not to return home for at least one whole year. *Ansar III* depicts some of the horrors of the tented prison camp in the Negev desert, where Palestinians are kept in 'preventive detention', i.e. without charge or trial, for six months or more.

Fateh, well versed in international law and familiar with the human rights violations under Israeli military rule, became Director of Al Haq in Ramallah, the human rights organisation affiliated to the International Commission of Jurists. A Palestinian whose family originated in Nazareth, he has American citizenship, and is only allowed to stay in Ramallah on a visitor's visa, which has to be renewed every three months. "I cannot under any circumstances," said Fateh, "get permanent residence in my own homeland."

Nearly six years later, Scott Faigen had not forgotten his experiences in Israel/Palestine. In February 1993 he came over from Germany at his own expense to give, with the violinist Peter Fisher, a Benefit Concert in Cambridge for Unipal. Both are fine musicians and delighted the audience. The proceeds were earmarked for the Library on Wheels operated by the Palestinian Centre for the Study of Non-violence in Jerusalem. The books, for children, are taken to refugee camps and villages in the Occupied Territories. That same year, another Jewish volunteer, violinist Anne Solomon, gave her time as did pianist Murray McLachlan and cellist Veronica Henderson, for a concert in Cambridge to benefit the Union of Palestinian Medical Relief Committees.

Preventive medicine, health education and community participation are emphasised in the work of the UPMRC. "Even if you do marvellous things in a hospital," says Dr. Mustafa Barghuti, the chairman, "these marvellous things may be an achievement for you, but not an achievement for the patient." Without basic facilities in village or refugee camp the patient may have continually to return to hospital for treatment. UPMRC mobile clinics and health centres have increased in number with doctors, nurses, health workers and pharmacists working voluntarily one day a week, now numbering hundreds. They are often harassed; even imprisoned in Ansar III. But the infrastructure for a national health service is being established with a blood donor system, family planning and a community based rehabilitation service for the injured and disabled. Sadly, since the Oslo Accords, funding from abroad has dropped disastrously: the Palestinians' troubles are thought to have been solved! Some clinics have had to be closed. A few Unipal volunteers, mostly "medics", have had the privilege of an assignment with the UPMRC.

Volunteers have had an experience not available to tourists and pilgrims to the "Holy Land", for they have worked alongside the local people and for a time have shared their lives. On more than one occasion they have been deeply shocked and distressed, as when a student has suddenly been missing from a class and they have learnt the reason. In 1980, a young man teaching at Bethlehem University learnt, only two days after he had started work, that one of his girl students had been killed – shot in the back of the head by an Israeli soldier as she got into a bus to come to her class. When the *Intifada* began, seven years later, such tragic happenings became more frequent.

In the villages of the West Bank and within the Green Line (i.e. Israel) there are Palestinian charitable societies trying to help the village youngsters educationally. We were soon asked to send volunteers to teach English in villages in both the West Bank and Israel as well as in refugee camps and universities. Julia Slater, our first long-term woman volunteer in Gaza, at Michael's suggestion planned our first English courses for Palestinian communities in Israel.

It is worth recording some of the impressions which volunteers have brought back. Peter Smith, who taught English one summer in Gaza, wrote:

> It was a hugely fulfilling experience, but harrowing as well: living with and making close acquaintances among the Palestinians draws you into painful empathy with their frequently humiliated and violated state. Despite this…overwhelming hospitality, as well as great charm, articulateness, and humour.

Tim Barnes:

> In many ways I felt I gained a lot more from Gaza than I was able to put in. My overwhelming feeling is one of gratitude.

and Sarah White, who was also in Gaza:

> The encounter with a different culture I found extremely enriching. For me it was the first time I had got outside the European/American eye view, to see a different kind of society, a different way of thought and action. This was made possible by the incredible welcome I was given by the Palestinians themselves. Throughout my stay I felt greatly my privilege at being welcomed among them as a sister.

Esther Howard, who helped on the Deir Ammar girls' summer camp in 1977, put her finger on the most valuable contribution a volunteer can make:

> I have grown so clearly to realise the importance of sharing a concern or care just by being present in such an area. To be repeatedly thanked for being there and *listening* I found distressing. But I feel the real importance of people like ourselves is to be witnesses to the situation, to spend time opening ears and minds to people who, not surprisingly, feel the world has forgotten them…and, through our own experiences, *to arouse concern in people here.*

Esther returned to teach English for an academic year at An Najah University, Nablus.

The situation of Palestinian refugees in the Gaza Strip struck David Styan with particular force:

For the visitor, the shock of a summer in Khan Younis is not the appalling conditions within the camps nor the fact that camps such as Khan Younis can be ignored by everybody outside. The shock and tragic irony is that whilst the inhabitants have remained huddled together without adequate facilities and services for thirty-five years, I can now stand with friends from the camp staring through the barbed wire surrounding the new modern buildings of the [Israeli] settlements.

This was in 1983, since when the situation has greatly worsened.
   Back in England, another volunteer wrote:

Returning to England I was surprised to find how uncomfortable I felt for a while in what suddenly seemed like a greedy and self-indulgent society. It was a privilege to be allowed to share the lives of people of the Gaza Strip. The only way to repay their kindness seems to be to communicate what I saw – so few people have any idea of what is happening out there.

That same year we had this message from a Gazan student:

Happy Christmas, Unipal! I am writing to thank you. But it is not only the English classes I am grateful for. Above all, it was a wonderful opportunity to make friends with people from outside. If ever you are in Gaza, my house is your house.

Hundreds of thousands of young Westerners have worked on *kibbutzim* in Israel. Unipal's volunteer contribution to the area was minuscule by comparison; but at least it gave an opportunity to a few to learn something of "the other side". Quite a high proportion of those who applied to us had previously been on a *kibbutz*. It is to their credit that they had sensed "this is not the whole story".

Audeh Rantisi

Audeh Rantisi, a Palestinian Anglican clergyman, is married to an Englishwoman, Patricia (Pat). They used to run a boarding house in Ramallah for poor Christian Palestinian boys attending the mixed school across the road. The building of the "Evangelical Home for Boys" is very splendid. It was erected on a rocky, steep hillside, so the land was going cheap. (The money came from Oxfam.) Volunteer labour, including a little through Unipal, helped the Home in various ways. The building was destined to serve the community as well as the boys who lived there, with a department for vocational training, a library, a gymnasium, and a clinic. When I asked Audeh if I could record his story, he said, "Take what you want from my book." At that time he was very busy…The building is no longer used now as a home for Christian Palestinian boys, and Audeh is retired.

✳

Audeh's family had lived in Lydda, Palestine, now Lod, Israel, for at least 1,600 years. In 1948, when he was eleven years old, they were forced to leave. Audeh describes how.

> The horror began when Zionist soldiers deceived us into leaving our homes, then would not let us go back, driving us through a small gate just outside Lydda. I remember the scene well: thousands of frightened people being herded like cattle through the narrow opening by armed soldiers firing overhead.
>
> In front of me a cart wobbled toward the gate. Alongside, a woman struggled, carrying her baby, pressed by the crowd. Suddenly, in the jostling of the throngs, the child fell. The mother shrieked as the cart's metal-rimmed wheel ran over her baby's neck. That infant's death was the most awful sight I had ever seen.
>
> Outside the gate the soldiers stopped us and ordered everyone to throw all valuables onto a blanket. One young man and his wife of six weeks, friends of our family, stood near me. He refused to give up his money. Almost casually the soldier pulled up his rifle and shot the man. He fell, bleeding and dying while his bride screamed and cried. That night I cried, too, as I tried to sleep alongside thousands on the ground.[2]

The thousands of inhabitants of Lydda, and of Ramle, a neighbouring town, were not given time to prepare for their expulsion. The Zionist soldiers drove them eastwards without food or water in the searing July heat.

> Still branded on my memory is a small child beside the road, sucking the breast of its dead mother. Along the way I saw many stagger and fall. Others lay dead or dying in the

154

scorching midsummer heat. Scores of pregnant women miscarried, and their babies died along the wayside.

The exhausted people eventually reached the hills and Ramallah, about ten miles north of Jerusalem, and at that time little more than a village. The multitude of refugees sheltered under trees and the people of Ramallah did what they could for them.

On my return from the Middle East in 1972 I would talk everywhere I could about the Palestinian refugees. I was invited to Yorkshire, to address the Friends' Monthly Meeting, held in Scarborough. Someone in the audience protested that I was not speaking the truth: no Palestinians had been evicted from their homes. The next day, Sunday, I attended the Quaker meeting in the village of Kirkbymoorside, and was introduced to an elderly lady who knew Ramallah. "I was temporarily headmistress of the Friends Girls' School there," she said. "It was just at the time when thousands of refugees poured in from Lydda and Ramle. They were in a pitiable state. I used to tell the Jordanian soldiers to bring to us any babies they found lying by the roadside."

"And when you came back to England, did you tell people what had happened?" I asked.

"No, I didn't think it would be appropriate to do so."

I could have wept. The silence on the part of many who *saw*, who *knew*, has contributed to the convenient myth that the refugees "fled voluntarily" or "obeyed orders from their leaders".

But another Friend, Christina Jones, wife of the headmaster of the Friends' Boys School, also in Ramallah at that time, has left a vivid record in her book, *The Untempered Wind, Forty Years in Palestine, 1922–1962*, published by Longmans in 1975.

Audeh and his family were fortunate in being offered a place to stay temporarily, at the Friends' Girls' School. Each classroom held five families, one in each corner, one in the middle. Audeh's extended family of thirteen members occupied a corner. Others lived on the landing of the stairs.

The UN Mediator, Count Bernadotte, came to Ramallah, and recorded in his diary:

> "Never have I seen a more ghastly sight than that which met my eyes here at Ramallah. The car was literally stormed by

excited masses shouting with Oriental fervour that they wanted food and wanted to return to their homes. There were plenty of frightening faces in that sea of suffering humanity. I remember not least a group of scabby and helpless old men with tangled beards who thrust their emaciated faces into the car and held out scraps of bread that would certainly have been considered uneatable by ordinary people, but was their only food."

In his report to the UN Bernadotte urged that the refugees be allowed home; he expressed, too, his concern about the behaviour of the Zionist soldiers, their "large-scale looting, pillaging, and plundering".

Shortly afterwards Bernadotte was assassinated by members of the Stern Gang (Lehi), the Zionist terrorist group led by Yitzhak Shamir.

When classes started again in the autumn, the refugees had to move out of the Friends' School and into tents provided by the Red Cross. There followed a bitter winter, with rain and snow. Five thousand refugees died from exposure and insufficient food.

Audeh did what he could to help his family, selling kerosene and little cakes which his mother managed to bake. For eighteen months he worked in a carpenter's shop. When he was fifteen, opportunity came to him.

A Lutheran philanthropist from Michigan, USA, had sold his business to open a boarding school for Palestinian boys. Audeh applied, and was accepted. Free at last from the refugee camp, he was thrilled to go to school.

In spite of his painful memories, Audeh hopes and prays for reconciliation between the people who caused so much suffering, and his own, the Palestinians.

After more than four decades I still bear the emotional scars of the Zionist invasion. Yet, as an adult, I see what I did not fully understand then: that the Jews are also human beings, themselves driven by fear, victims of one of history's worst outrages, rabidly, sometimes almost mindlessly searching for security. Lamentably, they have victimised my people.

---

1   Benjamin Beit-Hallahmi, *Original Sins: Reflections on the History of Zionism and Israel*, Pluto Press, London, and Concord USA, 1992, pp 95-96.

2   The quotations unless otherwise stated are from *Blessed are the Peacemakers*, by Audeh Rantisi, Eagle, 1990.

CHAPTER FOURTEEN

India again

In 1975, the year the Unipal volunteer programme started, Martin and Janet were volunteers in India. Like their father, they were neither of them careerists, and for a long time voluntary work had a particular attraction for them. While at school and university they had gone in the summer to international work-camps abroad organised by UNA (United Nations Association) or IVS (International Voluntary Service).

On leaving Durham University, Martin worked as a volunteer with the newly formed Cyrene community in Cambridge, living in a refuge for homeless men and women who in some way had fallen through the net of the social services, and reached the bottom.

Every five days, pale and exhausted, he would come home for a short break. It was a twenty-four-hour-a-day job, with many problems. The work included such things as clearing up the vomit of a resident who had come in drunk, or remaining calm while one of them held a knife at his throat. We could not help being relieved when after five or six months he called it a day.

After that, he took a postgraduate Diploma in Development Studies, then worked for a time as a hospital porter, earning enough money to go to India in search of his own Voluntary Service Overseas. In 1974 he joined a group led by an enterprising young man, Ashley Butterfield, who had made the organisation of overland journeys to India – (now, just in India) – his life's work. They travelled the hard way, by local public transport, staying in cheap hotels overnight, through Turkey, Iran, Afghanistan, and Pakistan.

Arrived in India, Martin sought out a useful job. To begin with he worked at Agrindus, a Gandhian Ashram in Uttar Pradesh. There he was asked to help with a survey of the needs of surrounding villages. While on the survey, he had an adventure – more alarming in retrospect to a mother than it was at the time to him. One evening, on his way back to the Ashram through the jungle, he went astray without realising it. The sun was sinking fast and had reached the tops of the trees. Night falls suddenly in the tropics and it would soon be quite dark. On the

157

path he met miraculously, as it seemed afterwards, a villager to whom he explained that he was making for Agrindus. The man pointed out that he was walking in entirely the wrong direction.

His work at Agrindus ended, Martin went to Delhi to await his sister's arrival there and took the opportunity to find out about suitable work projects for her.

Janet, after graduating from Sussex University, had trained as a nurse and midwife. India, and voluntary work there, had drawn her as it had Martin. She too came overland in the same way; but it was winter, and as they crossed the Afghan mountains the party nearly froze – taking it in turns to sit on each other's feet in an unheated bus with broken windows. She and Martin travelled the length and breadth of India for her to find a project to which she could give her energies. It was found eventually in a remote district of Bihar, in a famine and earthquake prone area, among neglected and impoverished tribal people, mainly Santals. Years before, Pierre Cérésole, the Swiss founder of Service Civil International (International Voluntary Service), had himself set up a branch in India (still known as SCI there) in the days following an earthquake in Bihar. It was with SCI India that Janet decided to work. After two years her contract ended. The two other volunteers also left. Janet came home for a rest and then returned after a visit to China with a medical group. She lived in the village, treating patients, delivering babies, educating villagers to become in their turn health workers and educators, and initiating family planning. She worked there as a volunteer for eleven years.

Meanwhile Martin had found more work for himself in the South – in Tamil Nadu. In the plains, not far from the city of Madurai, is a farm settlement for destitute boys, a "Boys' Town", founded by Joe Homan, a Peterborough man. Martin found a place there. When Joe returned to England for six months to raise funds, Martin was left in charge.

Towards the end of 1975, Martin and Janet invited Michael and me to come and visit them in India. When we received the invitation, I was excited. To see India, and our children again after months of separation, would be wonderful. For Michael it would mean taking his annual holiday in the winter, as it would be better to go in the cooler weather; for me it would be difficult, as I had, after much pressure, gone back to teaching Russian for a time: the modern language master at the comprehensive school in Royston was to have a year's sabbatical leave, and he had been unable to find a replacement for his Russian classes, so I had finally agreed. And Unipal was growing fast. However, in January and early February 1976 there would be a lull in its activities; and I managed to find someone to take my classes for four weeks at the school. I wanted Michael to go to India with me, but he tried to persuade me to go alone. Eventually he thought of what Albert Schweitzer used to do when in a dilemma.

He opened at random a New Testament in the Moffat translation, and put his finger, also at random, on the open page, where he read, "Have we no right to travel with a Christian wife?" So it was decided we would go together! Everything fell into place.

We all, Martin included, stayed with Janet in her mud hut in a tiny hamlet, ten miles from the nearest small town, and saw her at work; and then we all travelled south by train to Tamil Nadu to visit "Boys' Town". From there, we made a pilgrimage to my birthplace in the Palni Hills. I considered myself very fortunate to have been born and to have lived the first two years of my life in such a beautiful place; and, as in my earliest memory and in dreams, the forest-covered mountains rose like pyramids from a wide, flat plain.

From Calcutta to Madras had taken three days and two nights. A long railway journey in a slowly moving train is a very good way to see India: the amazing variety of its scenery, the villages near the railway, the social life in them and in the railway stations, where people literally live on the platforms. Sometimes beggar children would come to the window when the train stopped. We would give them any food we had with us, and they would picnic there and then. Once a leper came to join them, and they helped him down onto the lines. A train whistled past. I was dreading what we would see when it had gone. But the children were still there, laughing at our anxious faces. As we moved off, they waved cheerfully. How they had avoided being killed, I really do not know.

We were making our way out through the crowd in the station at Madras when I noticed a little girl lying on the platform, and huddled by her side a tiny baby. Both were grey with dirt and dust, and fast asleep. They must have dropped down where they were, exhausted. Travellers were milling round, and it seemed the little bodies must get trampled on. Some well-dressed young men were standing by, doing nothing. I asked if they could not move the children to a safer place, but they just laughed. I did not know what to do: the family had disappeared ahead. I left a few bananas close to the girl's hand, and was about to hurry away when a ragged urchin came up. "He is sure to take the bananas," I thought as I looked back. But he bent down, roused the little girl for a moment, placed her hand round the bananas, and went on. Thank God for the generosity of the very poor, and of children!

There were also destitute children who frequented the railway junction at Madhupur, the nearest town to Janet's place of work in Bihar. Once, when we gave some food to a few of them, they collected up others to share it; and only then began to eat.

159

On his return from India Martin had a job as a hospital social worker. For some years he combined social work with anti-nuclear activities and then with work on a thesis – on the rôle of peace-keeping forces in international relations; but finally decided social work and a thesis do not mix well and decided to concentrate on the latter.

In Bihar Janet was supported for her last eight years by Quaker Peace and Service. One day I hope she will write a book about her experiences there, and about the people: so primitive in western eyes – hunting with bows and arrows, trying to placate evil spirits with offerings and rituals; and so much superior to us in many ways: content with almost nothing; self-reliant, long-suffering, caring for their old people and each other in spite of deprivation; and enjoying traditional festivals, dancing and gaiety whenever possible. Their ill-nourished children start work very early, looking after the animals or making leaf plates for sale in the town; but they also make their own games in the sand with sticks and stones and dried berries for marbles.

Eleven years Jan lived in that isolated spot, usually, but not invariably, coming home for a while in the hottest weather. There was no telephone (about once a year she would phone us from Calcutta, a day's railway journey away); no made-up road; her only means of transport a bicycle; and until Manan joined her the nearest doctor ten miles away. Always there was the risk of infection – from patients, insects, impure well water (which had to be boiled thoroughly before consumption) or even rabies. Jan was once in very close contact with a rabid dog. Unknowingly, she had even nursed it – for it was a favourite dog which had once guided her home through the jungle when she had lost her way after attending a patient. It had the "dumb" form of the disease of which Jan was unaware. She had to go to Calcutta, where she gave herself the fourteen injections into the abdomen which were then necessary. Just at this time the government here was conducting an energetic campaign against the possible spread of rabies into England from abroad, through animals smuggled in. There were posters everywhere depicting a skull and crossbones with, in lurid red letters, the words RABIES IS A KILLER. The injections too, one learnt, could have horrible side effects. It made one sick with anxiety. And once, Janet was very ill with typhus, and had to treat herself. She told us this only long afterwards.

In the monsoon snakes came into the compound or even indoors. Janet was oblivious of comfort, and slept on a plank bed. For Michael and me she had seen to it that there were village-made string beds. One night there was a crunching of bones under mine: the cat was eating one of the rats which frequented the premises.

Manan Ganguli was a Bengali doctor from Calcutta, who came to work with Janet in Bihar. They married, carrying on the health work

160

together and adding to it tree-planting, for the countryside there is being rapidly turned from forest into desert. They also gave support to a much-needed anti-nuclear movement in India, Janet writing the intermittent information pamphlets. At last she returned to stay in England with her first child, Sushila, and Manan has joined her here. So my daughter has an Indian husband: one of many mixed marriages today. Times have changed in that respect since the days of my youth!

In the late 70s a Palestinian acquaintance, Leila Shawwa, an artist from Gaza, was visiting us in Cambridge. As she was leaving she asked Michael, "Why don't you take more interest in your wife's work? You should visit the Occupied Territories!" He was silent. He had other concerns. I also tried to persuade him. Once again he opened the Moffat New Testament. This time he read, "Take the road that leads south to Gaza"! Still he held out; and instead of going south he drove north – to Scotland, to visit his cousin in Glasgow. On the way he had a nasty accident with the car, his life saved only by his safety belt. Taking it as a judgement, he decided he must go to Palestine. "But only as a pilgrim," he assured me. "Not for any other purpose." However, observant and sensitive as he was, he could not but be shocked and distressed by what he saw and learnt – in Gaza, in Nablus, and even in Jerusalem and Bethlehem. "It's a police state," he said on his return. He came onto our committee. From the beginning he had helped generously with financial support that had covered administrative costs and more (for there were no salaried employees for twelve years). Now we had the advantage of his wise advice. He was, too, an excellent interviewer for volunteers, with long experience of summing people up. When warden of the training centre for overseas relief workers where I first met him, he had had to write for Friends' House thumb-nail sketches of the character and qualities of the trainees (including mine, which I did not altogether like!). They were extraordinarily perceptive. Since then, he had had still more experience of people through probation work. He interviewed for Unipal till within a few weeks of his death. Martin and Janet also interviewed when they were available: they have something of their father's shrewd perception of character and years of volunteering behind them.

But whenever I inveighed against the Israelis for the cruelties they have inflicted on Palestinians, Michael would always check me and remind me of what other governments and peoples have done, including our own. "Judge not," he would say. It is difficult: this particular injustice has gone on so long, with the suffering and hardship increasing year by year. And the Western world, still oppressed by guilt in relation to Jews, prefers to close its cowardly eyes, or look the other way. One day the guilt of aiding and abetting the persecution of

Palestinians, or of doing nothing to prevent it, will also surely weigh heavily upon us.

Michael and I made further trips to India separately. Each time I found myself thinking, "Aren't the needs of the poor in India even greater than those of the Palestinians?" In India there is hunger, disease, and grinding poverty in both town and country; utter squalor for thousands of pavement dwellers in the big cities. In Calcutta it was shocking to see a tiny child picking over a heap of garbage in search of something to eat, or something to sell.

The same kind of question has sometimes lurked in the minds of the concerned and altruistic young people who have applied to Unipal for voluntary work. Educated to think about Third World needs, it could come as a surprise, sometimes even a shock, to learn that poverty has not been the Palestinians' worst affliction – though it has been growing disastrously since the Gulf War, an additional burden. It is especially so now, since the government of Israel has cut them off from employment possibilities in Jerusalem and within Israel itself.

The main problem facing the Palestinians has been the obstinate refusal or inability of Western governments (and Westerners in general) to recognise that the people of Palestine have been, and still are, the victims of a cruel injustice – one that affects every aspect of their lives: in the West Bank and Gaza Strip, which together with Arab Jerusalem have been illegally under harsh military occupation ever since their conquest by Israel in 1967; discriminated against in Israel; pounded by Israeli bombs and shells in Lebanon. Palestinian suffering stems from brutal violation of the human rights supposedly guaranteed them by international law. Israel has signed the Universal Declaration of Human Rights and the Fourth Geneva Convention – the latter designed specifically to protect people in the position in which Palestinians now find themselves in the Occupied Territories. Britain signed too. One of the obligations of signatories to the Convention is to ensure that no signatory violates its provisions. Tragically, Western governments, including Britain, have ignored their obligation, so the violations continue unchecked.

CHAPTER FIFTEEN

Lebanon

Dr Said Dajany was in charge of the PRCS (Palestine Red Crescent Society) Nursing School in Beirut. It was suggested to us by Peter Crouch, one of our first volunteers, who after he left Cambridge was Oxfam representative in Lebanon, that Unipal should contact Dr Dajany with a view to our helping with nursing training. I did not meet Said till he came to Cambridge a few years later. He was a delightful person to work with. Small, rotund, with a smiling friendly face, he was always co-operative and helpful. He felt sure we could, somehow, help to raise the general standard of nursing for Palestinians. Good nurses were desperately needed in Lebanon – in particular to treat the many injured both in Israeli air-raids and in the appalling civil war (1975 to 1990).

Seven nurses came to England in the next few years. After a month's intensive English, they spent six months in a hospital where they were given a course tailor-made to their needs, to qualify them as clinical tutors. Two of them, Ahmed Shehadeh and Olfat Mahmoud, became like members of the Aitken family.

The Unipal Newsletter for the winter of 1981-2 began: "Our last annual Newsletter reported an exceptionally hard year for Palestinians in the Occupied Territories and Lebanon. 1981 has seen even more tragic developments. The bombing of Beirut by the Israeli air force in July 1981 hit the headlines here. After it, Ahmed wrote to us:

> We were doing our final exams, but left everything and went to the hospitals. In half an hour we had about fifty cases of children, elderly, and a few young men and girls. Our work was to stop the bleeding and give A-T (anti-tetanus) injections. We put a stamp on the patient's hand to show he had the A-T..."

Much, much worse was to come.

In June 1982, the Israelis launched a full-scale invasion of Lebanon.

They had been bombing South Lebanon intermittently for ten years. I was in Beirut when, in the early summer of 1974, they had carried out particularly heavy air raids on the refugee camps in the south. Nabatiyeh and Rashidiyeh camps suffered massive destruction. The terror caused by these raids drove thousands of Palestinians and Lebanese to the north towards Beirut; and the flood of destitute Muslims into this area helped to destabilise Lebanon, never really stable, relying as it did on a very precarious confessional balance of power; and with an apparently endemic reliance on armed strength in the rival groups.[1]

The destabilisation was further assisted by the Israelis arming and training the Falangist "Christian" Maronite militia. (The Falangists were an extreme right-wing party, led by Pierre Gemayel. They leant towards Europe, particularly France; their leaders preferred to speak French, and despised Arabs – Palestinians most of all. In 1936 Pierre Gemayel visited Germany and was favourably impressed by German discipline. He may not have deliberately copied Hitler's methods, but the cruelty of the Falangists against those they considered their opponents is strongly reminiscent of that of the Nazis.) So both directly and indirectly, by her actions, Israel helped to precipitate the hideous civil war which began the following year and lasted for fifteen years. When the IDF (Israeli Defence Force) had invaded in 1978, the renewed displacement of population ensured that the destabilisation continued. After it partially withdrew, it left a strip of Lebanese territory along the Israeli border in control of a renegade "Christian" officer, Sa'ad Haddad (succeeded on his death by Antoine Lahad), thus making it impossible for a reconstructed Lebanese Army to take control of the south and effectively preventing UNIFIL (United Nations Interim Force in Lebanon) from fulfilling its mission. (This strip of Lebanese territory, in addition to one occupied by Israel, provides a launching pad for sporadic attacks on Israel by justifiably angry groups such as Hizbullah, and suffers revenge attacks or "pre-emptive strikes" of a bigger kind from the Israelis.)

Back in 1920, Chaim Weizman, the driving force in Britain of the Zionist movement and the first President of Israel, had argued with the British Government that the northern frontier of the new Jewish "Home" should be the River Litani in Lebanon – for the sake of the water, the most vital commodity in the Middle East. The invasions of 1978 and 1982 gave the Israelis an opportunity to achieve their aim.

The horrors of the 1982 invasion were vividly reported by Robert Fisk in *The Times*; and the British public were shocked by what they saw of it in lurid colour on TV. Particularly horrifying was the ferocity of the siege of Beirut, where widespread destruction and carnage were caused by bombing and shelling. The Israelis tried out horrendous new American weapons: cluster bombs, phosphorous bombs, and vacuum bombs. Worst of all they cut off water and food supplies. Eventually, even the US administration was revolted. It obliged the Israelis to stop, and persuaded the PLO leadership (under Arafat) that protection would be given to the Palestinian civilian population if its guerrillas withdrew from Lebanon. Accordingly they did so.

During the night of 17th September 1982, I was listening to the BBC World Service, as I often did when sleepless. There was an announcement so shocking and horrible it was almost unbelievable.

The inhabitants of Shatila refugee camp in Beirut and the adjacent area, Sabra, had been *massacred*: men, women, and children slaughtered wholesale by Falangists. For three days and nights the killing had gone on. The people had been left defenceless.

Acre and Gaza hospitals, where some of "our" nurses worked, including Ahmed, stand at each end of Shatila camp.

Our Winter Newsletter of 1982 recorded that the invasion "has left 20,000 dead (Lebanese police figures), mainly civilian; at least 40,000 injured; and countless thousands homeless. Over thirty years of UNRWA work has been destroyed: schools, clinics, and entire refugee camps are in ruins. At the time of writing, schools that are habitable are still full of homeless families, so classes cannot be held. Many doctors, nurses, and teachers have been killed or imprisoned...The Palestine Red Crescent Society has suffered an even worse fate than UNRWA, for in the south it is unable to function at all. In Beirut its hospitals have been severely damaged, and stores of drugs and medical equipment seized. The fate of the PRCS nursing school at Acre hospital is still uncertain. We have heard that Ahmed is alive, well, and working harder than ever. We do not yet know the fate of the other nurses."

I felt I must find out; find out, too, how our teacher friends had fared in the south of the country, from where up till that time they had all come.

There was a lull in the fighting when I arrived in Beirut in January 1983. But eight years of civil war, and then invasion, had left devastation in the city.

I had Dr Dajany's telephone number and he kindly called to see me at the hotel into which I had booked. It was too expensive for me, so he helped me to find another. In the morning he took me to the nursing school at Acre hospital. There I saw the damage and learnt how whole truck-loads of drugs and equipment had been removed by the Lebanese Army, including the electricity generator, an essential item in view of the constant cuts in the electricity supply. Twenty ambulances had been driven off.

Ahmed was there to meet me. He had become a vital worker, teaching in the nursing school during the day; on duty in the wards at night, snatching a few hours' sleep when possible. He introduced me to Olfat Mahmoud, who had been nominated to come to England in her turn to train as a clinical tutor, and came a few months later. They told me how they had both narrowly missed being killed during the massacre. When the Falangists had stormed in at the main door of Acre hospital, they had jumped from a ground floor window at the back and run through bullets to a place of safety.

Together we picked our way along the muddy central road that ran through the ruins of Shatila camp, passing a mass grave on our right with here and there little wreaths of flowers on it, to Gaza hospital at the far end. It had been raining heavily. Children were wandering among the puddles, garbage, and rubble; a few were trying to play.

The desolation of a destroyed refugee camp has a special poignancy. All through that time in Lebanon I was choked by grief and outrage. Were these unfortunate people *never* to be allowed to rebuild their lives?

Ahmed pointed down an alley to our left, and I saw a bank of earth running along the edge of the camp, parallel to the central road we were on. "Israeli soldiers were standing there during the massacre," he said. It could have been no more than about fifty yards away. The soldiers must not only have heard the screams but seen very clearly what the Falangists were doing. In fact, after dark, as we had soon learnt, they had sent up flares to assist the murderers in their grisly task.[2]

We went through the wards in Gaza hospital. The first patient I saw was an old man bolt upright in bed staring at the wall opposite. He did not turn his head at our entrance. His throat had been cut in September and he'd been left for dead, but his life had been saved in this hospital. His wife, an extraordinarily cheerful little body, was there to attend on him. She had a bowl of soup in her hand, which she was cooling carefully before feeding him with it. His throat still could not take any hot or any solid food. In another ward lay a man, very ill, whose two legs had been smashed. The wall of his little house had collapsed on him as he was trying to repair it, and he had suffered great loss of blood. Ahmed thought there was some hope that he would recover. A Lebanese woman in another ward had lost a leg. She had been holding her baby daughter in her arms when an older child, a little girl of four, had come in holding something in her hand and had said, "Mummy, catch this lovely ball!" It had pretty colours on it, attractive to children, but it was a cluster bomb. The baby had been killed, the mother lost a leg, and the little girl who threw it lost a hand. There were two little paraplegic girls, one paralysed as a result of injuries in the massacre. She had been left losing blood for two days and was still in trauma, crying every night; her father had been killed in front of her; she was Lebanese too. The other paraplegic was a fourteen-year-old Lebanese girl, with a sweet, extraordinarily pretty face, but very pale, who looked like a seven-year-old. She had come from a village in the south, and had been taken from hospital to hospital, but none would take her without payment except this PRCS hospital. She had had terrible bed-sores from lack of care. She whispered to Ahmed (he translated for me), "I feel much better now." PRCS hospitals are the only ones which give free treatment. Lebanese patients make up over seventy per cent of the total; but the Lebanese Army, dominated by "Christian" Falangists, had made it almost impossible for the PRCS to function. After all, the patients were only poor Muslims.

In the UNRWA office I met Zeinab, a teacher of English who had come to England through Unipal. She had arranged to meet her husband, who worked at the Palestine Research Centre in Beirut, and took me with her. She had not had any particular intention of showing me the place; but as we were leaving, I peeped into a room with the door ajar, and saw rows and rows of empty metal book-cases. When I asked her about them, she explained what had happened. The Israelis had looted the building, taking away not only all the books (thousands of them) but even the chairs! In the fridge where drinking water was kept, she said they had left the bottles filled with urine. Upstairs, families' flats had also been looted and made filthy with excreta.

The Palestine Research Centre was devoted to the history and culture of Palestine. It was therefore a focus for Palestinian national identity and, as such, it must not remain. The painstaking and devoted work of years was stolen, and the place treated with contempt. (The archives were returned fourteen months later in exchange for six Israeli POWs. Exactly two weeks after my visit a bomb destroyed the building itself: this time the work of an extremist Lebanese group. Twenty people were killed, a hundred injured.)

The following day, as Zeinab took me south by "service" (i.e. communal taxi) down the pot-holed coast road to Saida (Sidon), I noticed at one point some large pipes lying near the roadside. They had been intended to carry the water of the Litani into Israel. The work had started during the invasion of 1978: the Israelis had very nearly achieved the aim cherished by Zionist leaders since before the establishment of their State – unimpeded access to this good water supply. Although most of the West Bank water was already being taken by them in 1978, it was still not enough for people accustomed to plenty, as in Europe.

Ein el Hilweh, the largest refugee camp in Lebanon, on the outskirts of Saida, was three-quarters destroyed. The wide empty spaces where the ruins had been cleared away reminded me of Le Havre in 1945. Some refugee shelters remaining on the edges were patched with a dark green UNRWA tent serving as a roof here, a wall there. One or two men were clearing ground and starting to rebuild, but it was mainly women and children at work, for most of the menfolk had been carried off to Ansar, a prison camp set up by the Israelis.[3] 5,000 Palestinians and 1,000 Lebanese were being held in Ansar.

Seven of the eight UNRWA schools in the camp had been completely destroyed. The eighth was damaged, but full of homeless families. We went into one classroom – cold and dark because the broken windows were covered with any remnant of cloth to hand. A woman was living in a corner of it with her eight children; the youngest, twins of a year old. Her husband was in Ansar. She said a Christian friend of her husband's was helping her to support the family. Washing was hanging desolately on a string outside in the rain.

The three other women teachers of English who had up to that time been to England – Fat'meh, Nabila, and Imtiaz – were all safe, and their families too; but Fat'meh's husband and two brothers were in Ansar, and all had had their homes badly damaged. The walls in one room where Fat'meh lived were black from phosphorous burning.

Once again, as thirty-five years earlier, the children went to tented schools: big marquees which take up to ninety pupils each. In them you chose between darkness and cold. If the flaps were open some daylight came in, but so did the wind. Three shifts operated in each tent. The children could have lessons for only two hours a day.

I visited one UNRWA school in downtown Saida. Most of it was occupied by homeless people. Women were cooking in the far corner of the wet courtyard. The lavatories stank. Dirt and litter were everywhere. In the four rooms available where classes were going on the litter was ankle-deep. That, at least, seemed avoidable, and I couldn't help saying so. My criticism was accepted with amazingly good grace. "It will be better when you come next time." I felt ashamed. There were three schools operating in shifts in these cramped quarters, each for two hours a day, and the teachers had to try and get through their syllabuses somehow.

Zeinab took me to visit her brother Mahmoud in Mieh Mieh refugee camp. He had recently come out of Ansar. He told me his story:

I was at home on the 24th June last year when loud-speakers announced that all men between fifteen and sixty were to go to a public square in Saida. Then about seventy men at a time were chosen haphazardly and made to go up one by one to a table at which sat three Israeli officers. Behind the table, parallel to it, was a large vehicle with six hooded men sitting inside. The hoods covered their heads and faces entirely; there were holes for the eyes. As each prisoner came up, the hooded men would knock if they meant "Yes, detain this man". Sometimes, if not one of the six knocked, the man would still be taken prisoner because there was a group of Falangists standing by who would indicate to the Israelis that he should be. I was unlucky; five of the men didn't tap but the sixth tapped. To begin with we were taken into Israel where the conditions were even worse than later in Ansar. Interrogations were accompanied by beating. I was interrogated by two committees in turn. They kept asking me, "Were you in Fatah?[4] Were you in the PFLP?[5] or the DFLP?[6]" I had been in Fatah because, as a student, I had been a member of the Palestinian Students' Union, but had never been trained for arms. However, as I had a BA in English Language and Literature, they questioned me about authors – Walt Whitman, Wordsworth, Edgar Allen Poe, etc. I was able to answer correctly and to quote from their books, so they insisted that I must be an officer. I had more beating to make me admit it. "You must tell the truth" – then a beating with sticks, very hard. Then, "All Arabs are liars, you must be an officer," etc. etc. I was sprayed with insecticide.

I became the leader of a section. A prisoner had thrown something white from his section into a neighbouring one. An Israeli officer who had seen this from his watch-tower insisted that it was a stone. He asked me to tell him the name of the prisoner who had thrown the stone. I said it was a cigarette. I was beaten, this time with an electric whip with wires in it so that every time I was beaten, I got a shock. I had twenty-five strokes. I stood my ground that it was a cigarette, not a stone, and I would not give the name of the prisoner.

169

Electric whips such as Mahmoud describes are manufactured by Britain for export: part of our shameful arms trade.

One day as Zeinab and I were squelching through the mud of Ein el Hilweh camp, we met a girl whom she said I should speak to, as I had expressed concern about the prisoners in Ansar. The girl's fiancé was held there. I had mentioned to Zeinab that I was going to be in Palestine the following month and would try to enlist the help of sympathetic and hopefully influential Israelis on behalf of the prisoners. As I was taking down some details about the prisoner, an elderly man came up, in his hand a card issued by the International Red Cross Society with the name and number of his son, also in Ansar. Then a woman with her son's card, then another. In no time at all we were surrounded by women all holding worn little IRCS cards with the names and numbers of husbands, sons, brothers…Zeinab became alarmed and said, "Let's go." Without her translating, I was helpless. A crowd of women followed us back, pleading, weeping, tugging at my arms. I felt my own tears coming. When we arrived at the house, Zeinab went out to speak to them. She explained to them calmly and at length that there was not much I could do. They slowly dispersed. Zeinab then indicated a young man who had been watching. "See him?" she said. "He is an informer. We have to be careful."

Another time a car stopped by us. The occupants had recognised Zeinab and asked us to join them to visit a young couple to whom a baby had recently been born. It is the Arab custom for friends and relatives to go and congratulate on such an occasion. We entered a room full of people, who were all of course talking Arabic. Zeinab whispered to me, "There's someone here you can talk to." She introduced me to the new father, a doctor working with UNRWA. It turned out he had had his medical training in Moscow, and so spoke fluent Russian. We had an interesting conversation. "No," he said, in answer to my question, "I did not find that political pressure was put on me. I was just grateful for the training I had. I spent seven years in the Soviet Union. Before I could start my medical course, I was obliged to spend a year learning the language."

While in the south I was taken by an UNRWA supervisor of English to a number of schools to meet teachers with a view to selecting one or two for courses in England the following summer. Renewed troubles, though, made it impossible for them to come until two years later.

In the few remaining days I had in Beirut before returning home, I was able to choose two more teachers for a study-visit to Britain. One was Siham, from whom I have already quoted (Chapter Thirteen, p 144). The other, Nuha. They endeared themselves to everyone they met in England. On the way back to Lebanon they were stuck in Cyprus for a time, as there had been more fighting and Beirut airport was closed. Nuha took the opportunity to write to us from Larnaca:

> In England we felt there is still goodness in the world and people who really help and care for us. Being teachers, we'll try to convey these facts to our pupils, to lessen their feeling of being left alone in the midst of a jungle. We ourselves had a period of relaxation which we were deeply in need of after the long, long, terrible and miserable situation. Our greetings and love to all the nice people who welcomed us.

Alas, the torment of the Palestinians in Lebanon not only did not ease but very soon increased. After the Israelis and Falangists came the turn of the Amal (Lebanese Shiite) militia to wage a cruel war against the refugee camps in Beirut, subjecting them to shelling and in one case (Bourj el Barajneh) a long and terrible siege.[7] Our Newsletter of Spring 1987 reported:

> Shatila Camp: every home reduced to rubble. 35, 000 have fled south in search of shelter, food, and water. Bourj el Barajneh camp: 35,000 trapped; 35% of homes destroyed. (Figures are approximate.) Infectious diseases rampant. People reduced to eating cats, dogs, and grass. "Our" Olfat is working there.

> In South Lebanon Rashidiyeh camp still under heavy fire in fifth month of siege. El Bass camp: the kindergarten supported by Unipal has been burned down.

> Ein-el-Hilweh camp: suffered heavy attack. Many people have fled. Mariam, a teacher who came to us last summer has written:

> *"My first night home was spent in a shelter. We were obliged to leave our house. We are living the worst days in our life. In spite of the bad situation I feel I am living in England in my imagination, in my memory, with my photos. Thank you very much, you gave me the chance to live the happiest days of my life...to live with some of the kind families in England who helped me to change my opinion about the English people."*

171

During that short Lebanon visit of January 1983 I kept wondering about the attitudes of the different parties to the conflict. Israelis patrolled Tyre, Sidon, and the refugee camps in groups, on foot, guns ready to fire, eyes suspiciously roving. Israeli military vehicles drove as fast as possible along the roads, guns all pointing outwards. Any of these armed men could storm into homes at night to search and arrest. It was all as it has been in the occupied West Bank and Gaza Strip. The Lebanese had never fought against them. The Palestinians had kept their word and for nearly a year had not fired a shot against Israel. Did some of the men inside Israeli uniforms feel the cruelty of pursuing and slaughtering them, and destroying even the poor little homes they had managed to establish in a foreign land? Some did; and some protested against the war on their return to Israel. One even paid for his protest with his life, when an Israeli terrorist threw a grenade into a crowd demonstrating outside the Knesset.

Jacobo Timerman, an Israeli journalist, has written of the Shatila massacre "...all of us realised it had been organised by our army."[8] His son, Daniel, who had served as a soldier in Lebanon, refused to go back for a further spell of duty and was confined to a military prison for twenty-eight days. Before making his decision, Daniel had questioned his father gently about life in prison, for Timerman had been in prison in Argentina. He writes:

> Listen to the reply of an Israeli father, and reflect on the degree of abnormality, alienation, and depravity that has overtaken daily life in Israel:
>
> "Son, you can't compare an Argentine gaol to an Israeli gaol. In our gaols, only Arabs are maltreated, and you are a member of a superior race. It's true that once we were the people chosen by God to be witnesses of his truth; but now that we have girded ourselves for the murder of another people, we are a superior race since, as our government says, nobody can defeat us. They won't torture you in gaol. Once you can arrange your daily routine, thirty or sixty days pass quickly."[9]

Timerman ends his book with a cry for help:

> Only the Jewish people, I believe, can now do something for us. The Diaspora Jews who have maintained the values of our moral and cultural traditions, which have been trampled on by intolerance and Israeli nationalism, should establish a

Jewish tribunal to pass judgement on Begin, Sharon, Eitan, and the entire general staff of the Israeli armed forces. This alone could be the means of working free of the sickness that is destroying Israel, and, perhaps, of preserving Israel's future.

What is it that has turned us into such efficient criminals?

I fear that in our collective subconscious, we are not perhaps repelled by the possibility of Palestinian genocide. I don't believe we Israelis can be cured without the help of others.[10]

Israel Shahak has answered, at least in part, the question Timerman has asked. In a book recently published, Shahak shows how Jewish fundamentalism affects Israeli politics and the behaviour of its powerful army: Gentiles, particularly Arabs, are inferior to Jews, and it is wholly permissible – even to be encouraged, if that is in the Jewish interest, to discriminate, persecute and kill them.[11]

And the attitude of the Lebanese? Everywhere we drove there were checkpoints manned by armed men of one of the Lebanese militias; or in the south by Haddad's followers. I was not good at distinguishing one lot of soldiers from another. Among civilian Lebanese I was able to speak with, there were widely different attitudes. One woman staying in the same house in Saida as I was owned to being Lebanese with something like regret. "I am not proud of it these days," she said. She was working with a charity which included Palestinians. But to my dismay it was in beautiful Brummana, in the home of a Lebanese family closely connected for many years with the Quaker School there, that I heard expressions of intense hatred. Brummana had certainly been in a difficult situation, as had surely every place in Lebanon; but it had escaped unscathed. There was not a bullet hole that I could see in any of the fine school buildings. A very prosperous young man, the eldest son of the family, said to me, "I *hate* Palestinians; I don't want to see one walk down the street; they must go."

I asked, "Where can they go?"

"I *don't care* where they go!" Not one member of the family expressed any horror about the Shatila massacre: on the contrary, they approved the fact that those responsible were still in positions of power and that there had been no Lebanese enquiry.

It is not for British people to judge. Our government was mean and cruel when Jews desperately needed refuge from Hitler: with an eye no doubt to votes, the British taxpayer was given priority, and every Jew had to be sponsored financially. Lebanon (like Jordan), has had to cope with a flood of uninvited impoverished refugees. Palestinians with skills or money have been an asset, but most have been discriminated against from the first. In Lebanon they were not allowed to have jobs in any government service or in banks. When the guns arrived, after Black September 1970 in Jordan, the PLO was able to insist on Palestinians getting jobs. In any case, it provided them itself with its network of welfare services, schools, hospitals, workshops. To my mind, weapons degrade all human beings who resort to them; and the more they are used the greater the degradation. Palestinians have their violent young men, as do other nationalities. And violence is often the fruit of desperation. What hope had young Palestinians for their future? What hope have they in actual fact now, in the late 1990s? In Lebanon the situation for them has become desperate indeed.

---

1 A detailed and well-informed description of the Lebanese situation is given in David Gilmour's *Lebanon, the Fractured Country*, Sphere, 1983.

2 The Israelis had actually arranged the massacre with the Falangists, and encircled the camps to assist them, according to reliable sources:

(i) *Israel in Lebanon, Report of the International Commission to Enquire into Reported Violations of International Law during its Invasion of Lebanon*, Ithaca Press, 1983;

(ii) Michael Jansen, *The Battle of Beirut: Why Israel Invaded Lebanon*, Zed, 1982;

(iii) Jacobo Timerman, *The Longest War*, Alfred Knopf, 1982, Chatto and Windus, 1983.

"On Friday afternoon, a group of at least 400 people seeking refuge in downtown West Beirut and carrying a white flag approached Israeli soldiers. The civilians said a massacre was taking place; they were turned back into the camps at gunpoint." (*Time*, 4th October 1982, quoted by Jansen, p 105. Similar accounts are found in the report of the International Commission.)

3 David Shipler gives a description of Ansar in his book *Arab and Jew, Wounded Spirits in the Holy Land*, Marshall Pickering, 1990, pp 327-333. This prison camp has given its name to two others: Ansar II on the beach in the Gaza Strip; Ansar III in the Negev desert.

4 Fatah – the main group in the PLO.

5 Popular Front for the Liberation of Palestine.

6 Democratic Front for the Liberation of Palestine.

7 Described by Pauline Cutting in *Children of the Siege*, Pan, 1988

8   Jacobo Timerman, *The Longest War*, Chatto and Windus, London, 1982, p 157.

9   *Op cit* p 158

10 *Op cit* p 159-160.

11 Israel Shahak, *Jewish Religion, Jewish History: the Weight of Three Thousand Years*, Pluto Press, 1994, especially pp 26-27.

CHAPTER SIXTEEN

The Occupied Territories; Israel

From Lebanon I flew to Cyprus; and from there to Tel-Aviv, as I had done in 1974, nine years earlier, for there was no normal direct travel between Arab countries and Israel, just as there was no postal or telephone communication. I took with me a list of fifty-nine UNRWA men teachers from the Tyre and Sidon area still held in Ansar, including Fatmeh's husband. (Three weeks later, on the flight back to London, I met Uri Avnery, the Israeli journalist and former Knesset member well-known for his contacts with Palestinians and for his efforts on their behalf, and gave the list to him.)

I had been told that an Israeli lawyer, Leah Tsemel, had undertaken the defence of the headmistress of an UNRWA girls' school in Ein el Hilweh, who was detained in Ramle prison, Israel: her third period of detention there without charge. I had met Leah years before and knew of her dedicated work on behalf of Palestinian prisoners. She kindly agreed to see me at her home on her day off, the Sabbath.

Leah told me that she had a good hope that Abla, the teacher in question, would soon be released. In the course of our conversation over mugs of coffee I mentioned to Leah the poem by Erich Fried[1] which years before had struck me so much. "It was that poem," she said, "which first opened my eyes to the way our rulers behave to Arabs who are in their power."

As usual, my visit to Jerusalem and the Occupied Territories involved visiting teacher friends who had been to England, looking for new ones to come, and seeking out "projects" where British volunteers were wanted for the summer.

I went to Jalazone camp on a hillside outside Ramallah; and made my way through its narrow alleys to Iftikhar's home. She had been one of my keenest students on the UNRWA summer course for teachers in 1974, and had come to Cambridge two years later. That hot summer of 1976 we had both agonised over the terrible situation of Tal al Za'atar, the cluster of refugee camps in Beirut being besieged, then overrun and the inhabitants slaughtered by Falangists. (Only a few managed to

176

escape. Among them were two teachers of English who came to us for courses ten or twelve years later.)

On my previous visit to Iftikhar in 1978 she had told me her seventeen-year-old brother was in Ramallah prison and the family were worried about him. I had asked her if they would like me to try and see him, and she had been pleased with the idea. Could I find out how he was being treated? He had been rounded up one night with a number of other young men in Jalazone, accused of setting fire to a truck used to transport men each day to work in Israel. "But when the truck was burnt," said Iftikhar, "he was with me here doing his homework. He is preparing for his *tawjihi*." I went to the military HQ and was admitted to see the Governor. He wanted to know how I knew Khaled's family, and I explained. He told me if I came the following Tuesday at ten a.m. I could see Khaled. I kept the appointment, and was asked to wait while Khaled was brought from his cell in the prison. Sitting by the open door of the Governor's office I saw a young Arab pass along the corridor, his shaven head hanging low. There were two Israeli soldiers behind him, guns pointed at his back. I went out and asked if the prisoner was Khaled. Yes, he was, and I was told I could speak with him in the corridor. But it was November, and on my way to the prison a bitter cold, furious wind had suddenly blown up, starting a dust storm. At the end of the corridor the window was wide open and a gale was sweeping through. I had no jacket and was shivering, so I asked if we could go into a room. This was allowed, and a soldier accompanied us in and sat in a corner. Conversation was difficult. I knew almost no Arabic, and Khaled's English proved to be minimal. How could I find out how he had been treated – and in front of the Israeli soldier? After a few polite exchanges I asked, as simply as I could, "Were the soldiers *good,* or were they *bad?*"

Khaled looked at the Israeli: "Good," he answered, then turned very red and hung his head. Clearly he was not used to lying.

Then I too looked towards the soldier.

"*Not me!*" he said. He had a kind face; and both Khaled and I found ourselves asking him for help with vocabulary. He spoke English and some Arabic.

Now, four years later, I was in Jalazone again. I found Khaled at home, unrecognisable as the young man I had seen at the military HQ. His black hair was thick and curly, and he had an upright, dignified bearing. He had become a teacher. But the camp, as usual, had had more misfortunes. An Israeli settlement across the road, opposite the entrance to the camp, was a constant source of friction. Palestinian children would throw stones at passing settlers' cars or military vehicles; and both settlers and soldiers retaliated with shooting, for settlers too

177

are armed. Sometimes, at night, boys scrawled slogans on walls inside the camp or even on the outside wall. This was forbidden.

Iftikhar told me that there had recently been a spate of slogan writing, and consequently military reprisals. About a dozen boys aged fourteen and fifteen had been rounded up one night and hauled off to prison, where they were still, a month later. Parents had just been allowed a first visit. They found their sons had been put into solitary confinement, hooded, stripped, and made to stand outside, or in a corridor with the window open one end and a door at the other, and then douched with cold water. It was winter; and in the hills of the West Bank winter is very cold indeed. The treatment was designed to make the boys confess, or to name other boys.

I was shocked to hear that schoolchildren had been forced to suffer in this way, and felt publicity at home might help. I phoned *The Times* correspondent, Christopher Walker. He said he had not time to look into the matter, and recommended David Shipler of the *New York Times*. After several tries I managed to contact Mr Shipler. When we met in his office he offered to take me in his car to Jalazone. I was a little worried – he lived and had his office in West Jerusalem, had an Israeli secretary, and with his long beard he looked Jewish! His name sounded rather Jewish too. How would he be received? How would he report these events? I discovered he did not speak Arabic. Iftikhar would have to act as interpreter as well as guide. However, his conversation on the way to the camp was reassuring. When we arrived in the right street, I suggested it would be best if he did not park just outside the house, and I went in first to warn and reassure Iftikhar. She hastily threw a scarf over her head before meeting a strange man, and then welcomed us both in. David Shipler was conscientious about his task. We went from one family to another, up and down, round and about the little crooked streets, and in every home he took careful notes.[2] The result of his investigation was an article in the *New York Times*, in which he named one or two of the boys. I was anxious lest their families might suffer in consequence. On my next visit to the West Bank I went to Jalazone again to find out. Nothing untoward had happened. Indeed, one of the families had received a sympathetic letter from a New York Jew enclosing the equivalent of £10.

The early 80s saw two important new developments for Unipal: we began to send volunteers to Palestinian communities within the "Green Line"[3] (Israel) and, in answer to the urgent request of friends in Gaza, the teaching of English on a long-term basis had at last been started in the Strip.

Clive Robson had applied some time earlier to work in Palestine with Unipal, but had gone instead to teach for two years at St George's School, which is attached to the Anglican Cathedral in Jerusalem.[4] In his free time he had taught in a West Bank village. Now he was back in England. I asked him if he would like to go to Gaza and pioneer a long-term project there. He agreed; and after a month's intensive training in TEFL he set out. A few months later he was joined by Richard Locke and Julia Slater. For years after that Unipal had volunteers teaching all the year round in the refugee camps of the Strip. Clive, Richard, and Julia have been followed by others.

The Unipal Newsletter Winter 1984 records, "The long-term English teaching project in the Gaza Strip has made a good beginning. We hope to maintain the high standard of teaching skill and commitment which has characterised the first year of the project. English is fast becoming the principal language of communication in the world. For this reason, as well as for higher education and for jobs, it is of prime importance to Palestinians."

✳

Our first volunteers to Israel worked in a village in the north of Galilee, not far from the Lebanese border, Deir el Asad, and in Ibillin, a large village some miles inland from Haifa.

I had been directed to Deir el Asad by a young Quaker, Jed Williams, who had been a volunteer in Israel with another "sending agency" (now folded) – "Volunteers for Palestine". There was a Community Centre in Deir el Asad run by public-spirited residents who were trying to improve conditions in the village, and organise suitable activities for young people. I was invited to stay in the home of one of them, Yahya Dabbagh. To my relief he spoke excellent English; and I was happier still to find that he was by profession a probation officer. We at once had an interest in common. He told me he had spent a year in England, sponsored by the British Council, for further experience in his field. There had been probation officers from various countries on the course. I pricked up my ears and asked, "Were there any from Japan?"

"Yes, there was one."

"Was he called Sachio Yamaguchi?"

"Yes," replied Yahya. "He went to Cambridge for part of the course, to be attached to a probation officer there for practical work, and I went to Canterbury. I am sorry to have lost touch with Sachio."

"I can put you in touch," I said. "Sachio has written to us every Christmas since he stayed with us." Soon after, Yahya was happy to receive a letter from Sachio. Strange to think how narrowly Michael and I had missed getting to know Yahya years earlier.

For several years volunteers went to Deir el Asad. They did manual work – helping to build a playground one year; another year a containing wall for one of the steep winding roads. They taught English; and one summer helped with art and crafts on a day camp for young children. After a lapse of some years, volunteers went to Deir el Asad again (Summer 1990); and I am glad that this happened before Yahya Dabbagh died from heart failure some months later – for it was he who had once again asked for them. I had gone then to see him primarily to get his story – that of a Palestinian who had managed to stay in his village at the time of the Catastrophe in 1948.

Yahya Dabbagh

Yahya had retired from the probation service when I met him in Acre in May 1990 and recorded what follows in a room beside the courtyard of the great Acre mosque.

On 29th October 1948 the Arab army left. The Israelis were very close. I tried to persuade people not to leave the village out of fear. Some people didn't listen to me and left the village at night. We are between thirty and forty kilometres from the Lebanese border, so they could cross into Lebanon. The next day we formed a committee and contacted the Israeli army. Its representatives promised us they would enter the village peacefully. They came the next day, and were very harsh. They collected all the males and divided them into two groups, old and young. I was in the group of younger men. Then they chose four young men, whom they took aside and shot dead: cold-blooded murder. The older people they told to collect their things and go, and they fired shots behind them to force them to leave. Us younger men they took prisoner. We were taken on foot for about twelve kilometres and then put in buses to go to a detention centre. I stayed in prison for five months, until the end of March 1949.

It wasn't only at Deir el Asad that they killed people to terrify the rest of the villagers. It happened in other villages too. They would kill people in front of all the others. But the inhabitants of Deir el Asad did not all leave the country. They only went into hiding in the hills, living under the trees.

After a while a delegation from among them went to a neighbouring Druse village with which they had good relations; and it was through the good offices of the Druse,

180

who in their turn had good relations with the Israelis, that they were allowed to return to the village.

So the village was not deserted for long and was not destroyed as other villages were. The military government was very harsh, not only in the way it restricted our movement but because they took away our land. They interfered in every aspect of our lives; and that went on for eighteen years from 1948 to 1966. We were not allowed to market our agricultural products, except with a permit. Life was very hard. I worked for a time as a teacher; but then I was kicked out, as I was not approved of by the military authorities. Fortunately, I was accepted for training as a social worker and was sponsored by American Friends (Quakers). This was for three years; and then I joined the Probation Service. The British Council gave me a scholarship for a year, to join an academic course, and I went to England. I met on that course people from all over the world, from Africa, Asia, Japan. It was a good group.

For the next twenty years, I worked from Acre and lived in Deir el Asad. It's a village of about 2,000 people; but we have no library, no social club, no sports facilities. Together with friends, we established a Community Centre. With voluntary donations, some of them from abroad, we bought two dunums[5] of land and we built the Centre. It was through the Centre that I came to know Unipal. We do not have the same services in our villages as the Jewish villages do, and besides, our community is the youngest in the world. More than sixty-five per cent of the population is under eighteen.

The Israeli authorities don't care about us at all. Till recently there was nowhere for the children to play. We have a school in Deir el Asad, but the standard is very low. The building is inadequate. Fourteen rooms are rented in different places in the village, and these are not good rooms; they lack ventilation and light, and they are very crowded. Last year, there were some bad epidemics amongst the children.

In the Community Centre we try to cater for some of the minimum needs of the villagers. There is a kindergarten; a sports club, with karate and volley-ball; and an embroidery group which the girls take part in. One boy did attend for a

181

while, but then felt it was not very masculine. We have started a library.

One of the activities was to organise work camps in the summer, to undertake work that was needed in the village and which the local authority could not provide, because it did not have the money. We needed proper roads, and because Deir el Asad, as you know, is on a steep hillside we had to build containing walls for the roads. So, at these work camps in the summer, we invited volunteers. We had international volunteers from abroad; young Israelis wanted to help us; and Unipal sent us volunteers too.

In 1962, 4,500 dunums of land were expropriated from three villages including Deir el Asad. Deir el Asad owned the lion's share, 2,500 dunums. Two years later, the Israelis started to build the town of Carmiel. Carmiel is a modern town, very nice, very clean, it has everything, though it is only twenty-five years old. It is much more presentable than Deir el Asad, which is 500 years old. Only Jews live in Carmiel. A few Arab families did buy apartments there, and a great fuss was made: they weren't wanted. I personally own forty dunums of land in Carmiel. It was mine before the town was built. I was offered compensation for the land, but it was very little, a fraction of its value. I didn't accept it, so they just took it.

From the heights of Deir el Asad you can see Carmiel in the distance on the plain below. It appears white against a background of fields; and *looks* beautiful in the rays of the evening sun. Yahya took me there to catch a bus for my journey south. I was seated in the bus, talking to Yahya standing in the gangway. There was only one seat vacant, by me, and I moved towards the window to make more room as an Israeli woman prepared to take it. She looked at Yahya, then me. With an expression of extreme distaste she drew her skirts around her and sat down on the edge of the seat as far from me as possible. Bishop Winter, who was expelled from South Africa for his opposition to apartheid, once went to visit Yahya Dabbagh. He told Yahya that he wanted to write a book about Arab/Jewish relations in Israel, because he saw a great similarity in what was going on in the two countries. Unfortunately he died before he was able to complete the book.

Father Elias Chacour (Abuna)

Abuna (Arabic for our Father) is a Melkite priest, and an exceptionally busy person, for apart from his religious duties, he has worked unceasingly to provide better educational facilities for the children and young people, both Muslim and Christian, of Ibillin and surrounding villages. Unipal volunteers have helped him in his work.

In the spring of 1990, in a room behind his church in Ibillin, he told me, "We need volunteers desperately to help us build an extension to our school. We are expecting 350 new pupils and must have room for them. Once again I have no permit to build. When I asked for one, it was refused. 'If these children cannot go on with their schooling,' I said, 'they will be on the street with nothing to do; they may take to drugs or become delinquent.' 'Then you will have to build a prison for them, won't you?' was the official's reply! Can you send me four strong and willing young men this summer?" I said I would try; but I was no longer running Unipal. When I asked if I could record his story, he said, "I'm sorry; I have no time. Take what you like from my books." So that is what I have done.

Elias Chacour was seven when the events took place which so tragically affected his family and his village, Biram, in northern Galilee, in the late 40s. Till then the inhabitants had lived a simple, peaceful life, cultivating their fields and orchards and worshipping in their ancient stone-built church. One evening Elias's father brought home a lamb; and over supper, with his six children gathered round him, he explained why.

Jews who had escaped terrible persecution were coming to their village and must be welcomed hospitably. They might carry guns, because they were fearful; but no one need be afraid of them. The soldiers came, and stayed in the Chacour home and other homes in the village. A week later the villagers were told to move out for a few days for their own safety, as there might be fighting. They were promised that nothing would be touched if the keys of the houses were left with the soldiers.

Obediently, the villagers moved out and camped in the olive groves under the trees. The weather became cold and wet. After a couple of weeks a delegation from among them went back to the village to ask if the people might return to their homes.

> Before long, the men came running back, their faces a confusion of anguish and fear. The horror of their report spread through the grove.

Upon entering Biram and passing the first house, they had seen that the door was broken in. Most of the furniture and belongings were gone. What was left lay smashed and scattered on the floor. At the next house, it was the same, and at the house across the street. Chairs were smashed, curtains shredded, dishes shattered against the walls.[6]

Soldiers stopped the village emissaries, and levelling their guns at them, ordered, "Get out! The land is ours."

The unarmed Biram people could do nothing against armed soldiers. They needed shelter, and decided to climb the next hill to the village of Jish. They found in it an eerie silence. Jish was empty, apart from ten elderly inhabitants, who told them what had happened. Soldiers had arrived in trucks, and with machine guns levelled, had simply told the people to clear out. One old man said he had heard gunfire just outside the village. Jish had been pillaged, but the Biram villagers were welcome to such shelter as there was.

As they settled in uncomfortably, they heard of other villages in Galilee being emptied systematically by the Zionist soldiers. A fearful question remained unspoken. What had happened to the people of Jish?

One day, two of the boys found a soccer ball; others joined them and they had a game with it in a sandy space of ground on the edge of the village. A boy kicked it out of bounds. Elias raced after it. It had settled in a stretch of loose sand.

> Oddly, the ground seemed to have been churned up. I stooped and picked up the ball, noticing a peculiar odor. An odd shape caught my eye – something like a thick twig poking up through the sand. And the strange color…
>
> I bent down and pulled on the thing. It came up stiffly, the sand falling back from a swollen finger, a blue-black hand and arm. The odor gripped my throat…
>
> "Elias, what's wrong?" Someone was hollering in the reeling distance…
>
> Later, the shallow graves were uncovered. Buried beneath a thin layer of sand were two dozen bodies. The gunfire that the old man had heard had done its bitter work.[7]

Soldiers came again to Jish. Elias and some other boys were playing just outside the village when they heard the rumbling of trucks, and scattered in terror. The trucks reached the village and a voice blared on a loudspeaker, "All men must show themselves at once. Come outside with your hands on your heads." The men were then ordered into a large circle.

Immediately the soldiers began to accuse. "You are rebels. Tell us where your guns are hidden. We know you are fighters – Palestinian terrorists."

These words scorched me. Father, my uncles, cousins and the *mukhtars* – "terrorists"?

On and on went the interrogation as the heat of the day built to a searing brightness. The men began to squirm, drenched in their own sweat as the sun poured down. There was no water. Neither could they relieve themselves. Without ceasing, the soldiers demanded that they surrender their weapons. There was nothing to give up; there were no guns anywhere in our village. Still the soldiers harassed them through the long afternoon. Men weakened and some dropped as the heat and accusations pounded at them.

And suddenly, as the afternoon sun waned, it was over. The commanding officer barked abruptly: "Go back to your homes. But don't try to escape."[8]

That night the loudspeaker blared again, summoning all men to come out and give themselves up. They were herded into trucks as the women wept, and babies and small children wailed.

As the last tailgate slammed shut, the loudspeaker called out to the women. "We are taking your terrorists away. This is what happens to all terrorists. You will not see them again."[9]

Father Chacour has told elsewhere how Bishop Desmond Tutu of South Africa once said to him: "The plight of the Palestinians is worse than that of black South Africans. In my country, they want us to remain as the white man's slaves. In your country they do not even want you to remain."

But the story of the Chacour family did not end that terrible night.

Three months later, when dark had once more settled on Jish, and the children were almost asleep, someone was heard trying to open the door of the tiny one-room house, and a muffled voice hissed from outside: "Let us in. Quickly. Open up!"

"Go away!" called Elias's mother.

"It's Michael. Let us in. We're home."

The door was quickly opened.

> Four men pushed inside. I was startled for a moment, as if we had been tricked and these were strangers crowding in before us in the flickering candlelight. They were very thin – almost emaciated – their cheeks sunken behind unkempt beards. Their clothes were dirty and ragged, and the worn shoes were nearly falling off their feet. In the eyes of my three brothers was a wary, hunted look. Only Father seemed as calm as if he had just spent a pleasant day in his fig orchard, though he was obviously exhausted.[10]

He told their story. The four had been driven with the other men to a spot just north of Nablus, near the border of the "West Bank" which had come under Jordanian rule. There shots fired just over their heads forced them to run.

They had headed at first towards Amman, then Damascus, and then south-west into northern Galilee. They had lost sight of brothers and uncles, and the few men they met from Jish were too frightened to return. Strangely, in Jordan and Syria, they had not met the customary Arab hospitality, but were treated as vagabonds and had had to walk for days with little or nothing to eat. Near Jish, they had waited till dark in case there were soldiers still in the village, then had crept through it until they had found the right door.

Towards the end of 1949 the village elders heard that the new Israeli agricultural settlements were hiring Palestinians to work for them. Elias's father's fig orchard was bought from the new government by a settler who needed men to care for the trees till harvest time. Elias's father applied for the job for himself and his three eldest sons.

> And so, three years after our expulsion from Biram, Father and my brothers were hiring themselves out as labourers – just for the chance to touch and care for Father's beloved trees. I did not know the word *irony* then, but I could understand pain. [11]

186

Chacour has written elsewhere

> Mobile Western people have difficulty comprehending the
> significance of the land for Palestinians. We belong to the
> land. We identify with the land, which has been treasured,
> cultivated, and nurtured by countless generations of ancestors.
> As a child I joined my family in moving large rocks from the
> fields. We lay with our backs on the ground and our feet on
> the rock and pushed, *pushed*, all together. Little by little, "slow
> by slow," the rock was moved to the side of the field.
> Perspiration rolled off our bodies, and blood often streamed
> from our feet, soaking into the ground. It took months to
> clear the stones from just a small field. The land is so holy, so
> sacred to us because we have given it our sweat and blood. It
> rewards us with wonderful immense crops. Father could
> collect up to three tons of dry figs from his fields. Palestinians
> are at one with their land, and part of them dies when they
> must be separated from it.
>
> One of the Zionist myths is that Palestine was a wasteland
> when the State of Israel was established. The Palestinian
> farming techniques were not modern ones, of course, but
> they were tailored to the land. Beautiful terracing with hand-
> built stone walls surrounded the hills, utilising and protecting
> the land. The olive, fig, and almond trees were carefully
> tended, the fields lovingly cultivated.[12]

Late in 1950, the Biram villagers received the wonderful news that the
Israeli Supreme Court had given them permission to return home.
The elders of the village took the official letter to the commanding
officer at Biram, who shook his head, saying, "This letter means nothing
at all to us. You have no right here." The elders argued in vain.

For them it came as a great shock to learn that in the new state of
Israel the Supreme Court could be overruled by the military.

When he was ten, Elias was given the opportunity by the Melkite Bishop
to go to a boarding school in Haifa. One day his elder brother Rudah
came to see him and give him news.

For a second time, the Israeli Supreme Court had given permission
for the Biram villagers to return. When the commanding officer at

Biram had seen the new order, he had simply said that the soldiers needed a little delay to pull out. "You can return on the twenty-fifth," he had added. That would be Christmas Day!

The villagers had joyfully made their way to Biram on Christmas morning. To their surprise, the soldiers were still there, and had seen them.

A cannon blast sheared the silence. Then another – a third. The soldiers had opened fire – not on the villagers, but on Biram! Tank shells shrieked into the village, exploding in fiery destruction. Houses blew apart like paper. Stones and dust flew amid the red flames and billowing black smoke. One shell slammed into the side of the church, caving in a thick stone wall and blowing off half the roof. The bell tower teetered, the bronze bell knelling, and somehow held amid the dust clouds and cannon-fire. For nearly five minutes, the explosions rocked Biram, home collapsing against home, fire spreading through the fallen timbers.

Then all was silent – except for the weeping of women and the terrified screams of babies and children.

I could not absorb Rudah's words. He told me that another village, Ikrit, had also been bombed at about the same time. I was simply cold.

Alone that night, I was frightened by my own thoughts. I did not know how to handle the anger. More than anger. Rage. I lectured myself, wishing that I could be just like Father, who was my indelible example of spirituality. But I was me – a young man with a growing awareness that the world seemed bent on my destruction.[13]

Elias studied further – in Nazareth, in Paris, and finally at the Hebrew University in Jerusalem. He has struggled unceasingly to achieve twin aims: through education, to restore dignity to his humiliated fellow Palestinians; and in so doing help them (and, I believe, himself) to be more willing and able to overcome bitterness and resentment against the newcomers in the land. At his school in Ibillin, now "The Prophet Elias Community College" with vocational training also, there are both Jewish and Arab teachers. He has received at last the permit for the building. But he had had, *unofficially to buy* it.

1   *Hear O Israel,* p 116

2   He alludes to this episode in *Arab and Jew: Wounded Spirits in the Holy Land,* pp 411–412.

3   Israel has no internationally recognised frontier. The Green Line is the boundary agreed by the armistice of 1949.

4   St George's has a high reputation for the education it has provided for Muslim and Christian Palestinians alike. Among its well-known alumni are Professor Edward Saïd and other distinguished Palestinians. "Our" Dr. Dajany, a Muslim, was a pupil there. When I took him to Evensong at King's in Cambridge, it moved him to tears: "It has reminded me of my schooldays," he said. Like most Palestinian refugees outside the country, he has not, of course, been allowed back to Jerusalem.

5   4 dunums = 1 acre.

6   Elias Chacour, *Blood Brothers,* Chosen Books, 1984.

7   *Op cit.*

8   *Op cit.*

9   *Op cit.*

10 *Op cit.*

11 *Op cit.*

12 Elias Chacour, *We Belong to the Land,* Marshall Pickering, 1990.

13 Elias Chacour, *Blood Brothers,* Chosen Books, 1984.

CHAPTER SEVENTEEN

The Intifada

In the small hours of the morning, on 12th June, 1985, Michael died suddenly of a heart attack. In a few terrible moments my best friend and my loving companion for over forty years was gone.

Inevitably, Unipal suffered. Our home had been its home too for nearly thirteen years and continued to be, for two more. The small back bedroom which served as office astonished the first Palestinian teachers who came. They had imagined that the UN in our title – often written UNIPAL – was connected with the United Nations, and they had expected spacious offices like those of UNRWA! Yet from that little room a great deal of work went out; and every spring practically the whole house was pressed into service for the weekly Saturday interviewing sessions which were held for potential volunteers: enthusiastic, intelligent young people – some perhaps slightly apprehensive about what they might be letting themselves in for. A few would eventually be disappointed at not being chosen; but we always tried to make the day interesting and enlightening, so that everyone could go away feeling it had been worthwhile. In the sitting-room where candidates waited, there were books, journals, maps, pictures, photographs, and the reports of former volunteers for them to look at. If the weather was fine the garden too was used in coffee intervals and for picnic lunch. Occasionally, when the number of candidates and interviewers (mainly ex-volunteers) exceeded a total of twenty-five, there was overflow accommodation for interviews in the garden shed. When these were over there was a "briefing" session, and candidates had a chance to ask questions. Some said on leaving that, even if not selected, they would still think it had been worth coming for the day.

Debbie Dorman, who started with Unipal in January 1985, became a popular and dedicated volunteer programme organiser; but the increasing workload obliged us in 1986 to appoint another to help her. Trouble then began. My morale at that time was at its nadir. Carmen, the Chilean refugee who had been the invaluable part-time office helper and successor to Margaret Deakin as accountant, had had to leave; I had become totally debilitated through grief and illness (an operation for breast cancer, followed by radiotherapy which reduced me to a jelly); and I was, of course, by 1987, getting old: I was seventy. It was a difficult, very unhappy period; there were misunderstandings and bad temper on both sides. It was time to hand over responsibility to younger, more vigorous people.

Unipal left our house, and Cambridge, towards the end of 1987. It has had since then several addresses, faced various vicissitudes, and had various people running it.

Sometime in 1992, as I was musing painfully over the unexpected repercussions, like the Chinese whispering game, which followed the decisions we, the trustees of Unipal, took in 1987, a letter arrived from an early volunteer who had loyally remained in touch. In it she referred to "the many, many good volunteers who have gone out over the years, quite a few of whom are still working for Palestinians in one way or another," and "many more of whom are probably doing their bit to spread the word". It is true. And that is what Unipal was created for.

Individual volunteers, after their return, wrote books and articles based on what they learnt through first-hand experience; were responsible for television documentaries on life under occupation; active in the academic world; and in many other ways tried to enlighten a public largely ignorant and prejudiced against Palestinians as a result of highly efficient adverse propaganda.

To go back – not altogether irrelevantly: a few days before Michael's funeral Martin and I were at the undertakers', sitting beside the open coffin. I had been full of remorse for having given, as I thought, too much attention to Unipal and not enough to Michael. Why, for instance, had I not insisted he should see a specialist after the mild heart attack he had had six months previously? I thought also of how a friend had, unintentionally, upset both of us a week earlier. Suddenly I heard, very distinctly, Michael's voice say – *There is no blame!* Astonished, I turned to Martin and told him what his father had just said.

Some time afterwards Martin and I went to talk with a Quaker friend about a "Testimony" (obituary) for Michael which she had been asked to write for the next Yearly Meeting of the Society. She herself was slowly dying of cancer; but was looking forward to her new life. I told her what I had heard Michael say at the undertakers'. "Why, that is just as in the *I Ching*," she exclaimed. We did not know the *I Ching*: the 5,000 year old book of Chinese wisdom and divination. Martin immediately went and bought a translation of it. Sure enough, every few pages, introduced in one way or another, there are the words: "There

191

is no blame". On p 71 this sentence stands out alone. The meaning seems clear to me: from the perspective of the eternal and of complete understanding, there *is* no blame: only love and forgiveness.

I am not psychic, I am sure; but I do not need a medium, even if I could bring myself to use one, to know that Michael is alive – as Michael; and that in perplexity he is there as ever to help, *if I inwardly ask and listen.*

With son and daughter away from home I found comfort in carrying on some of Michael's work, and returned to my old ploy of editing, giving the office staff more responsibility for the running of Unipal. He had written a great deal of verse. "It's not *poetry*," he used to say, "it's only playing with words." I began to make a selection of the "poems". They were very varied – a "mishmash" he had called them.

The first publisher I sent *Mishmash* to accepted it, albeit reduced a good deal. We agreed between us that a proportion of the profits would go to charities that Michael and I had been involved in. One evening, at the end of 1990, during the Gulf crisis, friends rang me up. "Did you watch the news on BBC 1?" (I hadn't.) "One of the hostages in Iraq read a poem from *Mishmash*!" The BBC eventually sent me the video. An elderly couple in that frightening situation were being interviewed at the British Embassy in Baghdad. "I have found comfort in this poem," said Mrs Wright; and taking up a little green volume which I recognised, she read *Help!*

Some of Michael's poems which had previously appeared in *The Friend*, had been set to music by a Quaker composer, Tony Noakes; and this brought music into my life again – something Michael had always hoped for. Music was important to him; he composed a little; and he had just started giving me piano lessons. The first person to play and record some of the verses, as songs, was the Scottish pianist Murray McLachlan. Another gifted pianist, Beate Toyka, the wife of a Unipal committee member, played the accompaniment for them when they were sung at a memorial concert for Michael.

For two years after Michael's death I did not make my annual visit to Palestine. But in May 1987 I decided to go back, to see friends. It was the first time that I had had to leave without some words of blessing on my trip that Michael always used to write, to cheer me on my way.

I visited people with whom we had worked – those who had received volunteers, teachers of English whom we had helped to come to England, and others. It was both a heart-warming and a harrowing experience. Heart-warming was the welcome given; harrowing was the sight of the obviously intensified oppression of a long-suffering and courageous people: the ever-growing solidly-built settlements on confiscated Palestinian land, and the arrogant, provocative presence everywhere of heavily armed soldiers.

It is always a matter for grateful wonder, experienced by many besides myself, that after a visit to the Occupied Territories one returns with morale boosted, even feeling better physically. The Palestinians, in spite of all they suffer, never fail to be kind and hospitable; and they can still *laugh*. The things we complain of in our smug and greedy society dwindle into insignificance.

It was on this visit that I found the Palestinians willing to receive and help Scott Faigen, the American Jewish concert pianist; and I became acquainted with an exciting new venture – the PCSN (Palestinian Centre for the Study of Non-violence), founded by Mubarak Awad, a native of Jerusalem, and his American Quaker wife, Nancy Nye, formerly headmistress of the Friends' Girls' School in Ramallah.

The Centre was discovering non-violent means to counter the injustices from which Palestinians suffer in the Occupied Territories; and was attracting the co-operation of liberal and dissident Israelis who took part alongside Palestinians in demonstrations of a very practical kind.

One day I accompanied a mixed party (Palestinians, Israelis and expatriates) to El Khalil (Hebron) on a special shopping expedition: to buy goods from Palestinian shops which the Israeli military were trying to deprive of custom in order to make the owners leave "voluntarily". (The premises were coveted by settlers who had already taken possession of the upper floors.) A fence along the front of the shops with soldiers at each end intimidated local would-be shoppers.

On 24th May I was with a similar international group who were supporting the defendants at a trial in Jerusalem. Nearly eighteen months previously the PCSN had mounted a massive olive tree planting exercise at the village of Qatana. Centre workers, villagers, sympathetic Israelis and others had planted olive saplings to replace two thousand olive trees that had been uprooted by Israeli soldiers preparatory to seizure of the land. The saplings too were uprooted, and a number of demonstrators arrested. Thirteen Israelis accused of "trespass" were in court that day in May. In the group gathered to give moral support were Qatana villagers and Israeli rabbis.

Thanks to the wife of an Israeli rabbi, I was able to talk with one of the villagers whose olive trees had been uprooted. She spoke English, and the Palestinian knew a little Hebrew. This woman had gone by night to pick some olive branches from the stolen trees which had been transplanted in Jerusalem – in the avenue named, irony of ironies, *Martin Luther King*. She distributed them among those present.

Mubarak Awad, Director of the Centre, was forcibly deported not long after these events. The Israeli authorities seem to fear both the non-violent pursuit of justice which they do not appear to understand, and Palestinian-Israeli co-operation. Mubarak's place was taken by Nafez Assaily, a former teacher of English who had been to England through Unipal for a language course. Nafez too is dedicated to non-violence; and he is a brave man, with, mercifully, a wonderful sense of humour.

In March, 1988, I was again in Palestine. The *Intifada*, the *shaking off* of the occupation, was just three months old. A spontaneous, unarmed uprising, it was sparked off in Gaza, when five Palestinians were crushed by an Israeli army vehicle. The movement quickly spread to the West Bank and gathered strength. Palestinians felt enough was enough, and were determined to make a bid for freedom. They suffered intensely in the following years.

In a Gaza hospital lay a young man with a bruised, swollen face: all his teeth knocked out. On his stomach were the marks of an army boot. Ever since Golda Meir's notorious statement that there was no such thing as Palestinians, Israeli politicians have felt free to show their contempt for them. "Grasshoppers" Menachem Begin called them, "drugged cockroaches" has said another. It is no wonder that nineteen-year-old soldiers of occupation stamp on Palestinians when they have the chance, or otherwise humiliate them.

"Many times," said the headmaster of an UNRWA school, "I have been stopped by Israelis and asked for my ID [identity] card. Sometimes the soldiers throw it on the ground and stamp on it. Then they say, 'Kneel, and pick it up.'"

One morning some friends and I were visiting Amal, a teacher in a refugee camp in the West Bank. While we were talking, we smelt gas. "Something is starting, you'd better go," said Amal. Before leaving, we looked cautiously out of the window – she warned us not to put our heads out. Down the main road along the side of the camp a small crowd was standing still, the women waving their white head-scarves. We heard the chant "Allahu akbar! Allahu akbar!" ("God is great.") "It's the funeral of the boy who was shot yesterday," said Amal. Then we heard shooting. We made our way down a side alley towards the main road where the friend who had brought us had parked her car. Already a large group of soldiers had descended from a truck about 100 yards from the mourners. In front of us in the road five or six boys were throwing stones at the soldiers – the stones all seeming to fall short. Our friend's car was between the stone-throwers and the soldiers. She made a dash for it, turned it round, and we got in. As we left, scores more soldiers, guns at the ready, came running towards the motionless funeral crowd. They passed on each side of our car. We did not see what happened to the boys; they must have scattered quickly.

In the afternoon we visited a hospital. No sooner had we arrived than ambulances started coming in. Young men who had been waiting at the entrance hurriedly carried in stretcher after stretcher bearing blood-covered and groaning men and women. We learned that five of them were from the camp where we had been in the morning. A young man from the camp, aged thirty-three, died some hours later, from gas fired into the room in which he had been sitting. That afternoon the hospital admitted seventeen casualties, twelve from other camps and from villages. And it was like that, day after day.

In November that year, it was raining in Nablus when another friend drove me round on my visits. In one street, through a gap in the houses, I noticed a cluster of wet tents clinging dismally to the steep hillside, and asked her about them. "A young man in each of the five families," she said, "was suspected of throwing a Molotov cocktail or of intending something of the sort, so the families' houses were destroyed. The Red Cross gave the tents."

But even more damaging to Palestinians as a whole than this harsh treatment – meted out all too often – was what was happening to thousands of children and young people. Not only were many becoming homeless, being killed or maimed; but *all* were being hurt by the closure of schools, colleges, universities, even of kindergartens. Birzeit University was closed for four years, other universities for almost as long. In Nablus I saw five schools being used as barracks for Israeli soldiers. Alternative education, given by parents and teachers in pupils' homes, was declared illegal. Even UNRWA was forbidden to distribute the teaching packs which had been prepared to limit the damage to children's education. It was as if the Israeli authorities positively wanted school children and students to be on the streets to throw stones at the soldiers and so be gassed and shot. From the terrace of my friend's house we could see, in the valley below, a refugee camp. There was trouble there. Helicopters were dropping poisonous blue clouds of gas; and then came the sound of shooting. Red Crescent ambulances appeared on the road to the camp – and were stopped from entering.

Three things, as I have learnt, are especially dear to Palestinians: their land – now mostly taken from them; education, their lifeline and hope for the future – which has been mercilessly attacked; and family ties. Under occupation many families have been forcibly separated. All this happened before the *Intifada*. But the Israelis, determined to crush the spirit shown in the uprising, intensified their oppression.

The headmaster of an UNRWA school told me

> One day there was a demonstration in the school compound. About twenty-four soldiers came. The boys threw stones at them. As I stood at the gate I saw a soldier shooting indiscriminately into their midst. Rawi, aged fourteen, was wounded in the leg. I went to rescue him and took him to my car. To my surprise, there were already three other boys in it, and teachers were looking for me to take them to the UNRWA clinic at the camp. So I put the fourth into the car, and made to drive out – but someone at the gate told me that soldiers were waiting and had blocked the road to the clinic. So I had to drive to another camp. The doctor there gave them first aid and then transferred them to the Ahli hospital in Gaza. When I reached home, my mother had a shock. My clothes were covered in blood.

> If the soldiers did not come to the schools there would not be any trouble. The boys would never go to look for them! If the military authorities really wanted quiet, they would make sure soldiers kept away from schools. As it is, of course the boys are provoked by the soldiers coming.

An old friend, a teacher who lives in one of the refugee camps in the Gaza Strip, told me how he had asked his nine-year-old son to go and buy some yoghurt from a nearby shop. The boy was picked up by patrolling soldiers and taken to their military base. There, he was handcuffed with his hands behind his back and kept sitting in this position all night. Once he asked for a drink of water; he was offered urine. At last, in the early morning, while it was still dark, he was released and told to find his way home. An acquaintance of the family found him crying in the street and took him back. But that is not the whole story. The boy's father deliberately left home for the night, for he knew what would happen. Soldiers would come and demand a big ransom for his son: a sum he could not afford, for he has a large family. He hoped they would release quite quickly a nine-year-old child – for what use could he be to them?

There is a stunningly beautiful rehabilitation hospital for the disabled in Beit Jala (near Bethlehem), built recently through the vision and energy of Edmund Shehadeh and his friends of the Bethlehem Arab Society for Rehabilitation, founded years ago by Leonard Cheshire, but since then run by local people.

The original old building is still in use. Lying in a room there, I saw a pitiful victim of the crushing of the *Intifada*: the shrunken motionless body of a young woman who was completely paralysed. She could not speak, only whimper. Zouhriya, just married, had been sitting one evening on the balcony of her new home when a passing Israeli soldier had casually lifted his gun and shot her in the head: in an instant turning her into a near vegetable, her life and that of her husband shattered – for nothing.

I looked down at the little whimpering body, and was moved to useless tears. An impulse made me stoop and kiss her cheek. When I looked down again, a radiant smile had spread over Zouhriya's face. "She needs love," said Edmund.

The Israelis who struggle against the injustices and cruelties committed by their government have the respect and appreciation of Palestinians who know about them.

In September, 1986, a young Israeli technician, Mordechai Vanunu, had been lured by a *Mossad*[1] agent from London to Rome. In Rome he was kidnapped, drugged, and taken in chains secretly to Israel, where he was tried *in camera*, and condemned to eighteen years solitary confinement. His crime? He had revealed to the *Sunday Times* the extent of Israel's nuclear arsenal, because censorship in Israel prevented him from warning his compatriots and the world in any other way of the danger this threatened. He had felt people must know, and that in a democratic society they had a right to do so. He had previously worked on the nuclear plant at Dimona in the Negev desert and had signed an undertaking not to reveal what he learnt there. Some time after leaving the plant, however, he had felt that his allegiance was to a higher law. Perhaps his becoming a Christian influenced him. That could not help him with the Israeli authorities, any more, it must be supposed, than his advocacy of the rights of Palestinians. When he was in Dimona he had taken photographs of the weapons and of the equipment that was used for the production of the nuclear bombs.

It has long been, of course, an open secret that Israel does manufacture nuclear weapons, though to what extent was not suspected till Vanunu's revelations. If officially acknowledged, the US might be obliged by its own law[2] to suspend aid to Israel. This would spell political disaster both for the US Administration and the Israeli government. Therefore they turn a blind eye to what is being done at Dimona. Illogically enough, the Israelis have branded Vanunu as a traitor, while denying to the world their nuclear arms capability. In 1963 Shimon Peres told President Kennedy, "I tell you forthrightly that we will not introduce atomic weapons into the region...Our interest is in de-escalating the armament tension, even in total disarmament." (!) That lie would become the official Israeli response for many years to questions about Israel's nuclear capability.[3]

While in Jerusalem in 1988, I sought out Asher, one of Mordechai's brothers, to find out more about his conditions of imprisonment and ways in which we could help him. I met the brother by appointment at a street corner one evening. A good place to talk, I thought, would be the hostel nearby, where I was staying. It so happened, too, that I had made the acquaintance there of a Dutch theologian and his wife. It occurred to me they were just the sort of people who would take up Mordechai's cause, but they would certainly be going to bed early, as they were leaving for Holland in the small hours the next day. We hurried to the hostel. The iron gate was closed as it was already dark – but not locked. As we went in, the sound brought out the gatekeeper, who immediately recognised an Israeli. Never have I seen such fear and horror on a man's face. He raised his hand, the palm towards us, his fingers spread out. "No, no, no!" he exclaimed. "It's all right, Ali," I said. "We're in a hurry to see someone. You needn't be afraid of this man. I'll explain afterwards!"

Ali let us pass. We were in time to have a talk with the Dutch professor. When I had seen my visitor off the premises, I turned to Ali who was standing by and said, "I expect you know about Mordechai Vanunu, Ali. That was his brother."

"Oh, Mrs Aitken," he said with a broad smile of relief, as he shook me warmly by the hand, "I am so sorry. Please forgive me!"

In at least two Western countries, critics of government policy to develop nuclear power – inextricably linked, through its production of the deadly substance plutonium, with nuclear weapons manufacture – have paid for their questioning with their lives. In USA Karen Silkwood was killed under very suspicious circumstances. In England, Helen Morell, who was researching the incidence of cancer and leukaemia in children living near a nuclear power station, was found murdered at her home, her papers stolen. Appeals for a full independent enquiry have been ignored. Willie McCrae, an outspoken critic of nuclear power, met a similar fate in Scotland. Nuclear power has shown itself to be a threat to democracy.

"I'll pick you up at ten o'clock tomorrow morning," Nafez said immediately when I rang him at the PCSN office on my arrival in Jerusalem at the end of March, 1990. "I want to introduce you to a nice Jewish family."

Anna and Amnon lived in an attractive little house which they had built themselves on a hillside just outside West Jerusalem. The couple were among other Israeli citizens deeply disturbed by what their government was doing in the Occupied Territories. They were campaigning for the reunification of Palestinian families forcibly divided by the military authorities. Wives had been taken from home at night by soldiers acting under orders to deport them, because they had not obtained the requisite permit for living with their husbands resident in the West Bank or Gaza. (Such permits were extremely difficult to obtain.) Given a few minutes to pack a bag, a wife would be made to take any child not entered on her husband's ID card, then put into a "service" taxi for which she had to pay, and driven, together with other wives in her village or camp in similar circumstances, to the Allenby Bridge – never to see her husband again on the western side of the river, where he belonged and had his work.

We had a friendly talk with Nafez's Israeli friends, who gave us coffee and cakes and described how they wrote letters to Israelis in positions of authority – much on the old pattern of Amnesty supporters who campaigned for prisoners of conscience. One such letter was read to us. It expressed their dismay at the lack of humanity shown in the forcible separation of their "adopted" family and urged that the wife be allowed her natural right to live with her husband. "The practice of separating families is bad for Israel's image," they had added.

Anna told me about the difficulties at school encountered by her teenage daughter who shared her liberal views. "They are not approved of by her teachers and class mates; but Gerda stands her ground well." I met Gerda and Anna again the following Friday in Jerusalem, when I joined the silent vigil in a West Jerusalem square of the "Women in Black" who were protesting week after week against the occupation and its brutalities. And the following day Anna and Amnon were present at a meeting in a *kibbutz* to which Nafez took me as an observer.

Every fortnight Israelis and Palestinians from the occupied West Bank had been meeting for friendly dialogue: alternately at the *kibbutz* and in Ramallah, from which most of the Palestinians came. That Saturday only five Palestinians were present, for Ramallah was under curfew. The five had braved it, and somehow made their way out, to come and meet their Israeli friends. We sat in a wide circle in a spacious comfortable common room and drank mugs of coffee, while matters of mutual interest were discussed; and afterwards walked round the *kibbutz.* It was well planted with trees; and the spreading lawns were green, as in England. There was a swimming pool, too. Thinking of the dry West Bank, and how until recently there was no swimming pool in the whole town of Ramallah for want of water, and how vital Palestinian crops have perished for lack of it, I felt a pang. (Israel taps for its own benefit the underground West Bank aquifer, so West Bankers suffer.) But the five Palestinians showed no envy or resentment whatever. As one of the welcoming kibbutzniks (a young man who had served as a soldier in the army of occupation) showed us the *kibbutz* sheep farm and picked up a lamb, one of the young men from Ramallah discussed with him the possibility of some mutual trade in meat. "If you prefer the fore-quarters we could buy the hind," said the Palestinian. Four out of the five Palestinians had been educated at the Friends' School for Boys and learnt about peacemaking. The young kibbutznik invited us to his house for tea and chocolate cake baked by his wife. A British Jewish couple, former kibbutzniks, were also there, having come from Jerusalem for the dialogue. It was all so friendly, so civilised, it seemed obvious that these two Semitic peoples, given a chance, could live together happily, or at least in mutual tolerance, as they had done for centuries before the Zionist take-over. I left Israel/Palestine that time more hopeful than I had ever been.

As Nafez drove his fellow worker and me back to Jerusalem, the sun was setting behind us – spreading a warm red-gold light over the whole of the western sky. The trees of the *kibbutz* were silhouetted black against it.

A few months later Saddam Hussein invaded Kuwait; and there followed "Operation Desert Storm". The clock was set back many years as darkness spread over the Middle East. The Palestinians entered the most cruel period of their tragic history, with thousands more refugees from Kuwait pouring into Jordan, and those who could, returning to Palestine. The economy in the West Bank and Gaza Strip, already undermined by occupation and confiscation of land, fell into total ruins. Remittances from the Gulf dried up; unemployment became widespread.

Nafez I did not see again for three years. I found him then less full of jokes and fun. In October 1991, Israeli soldiers had massacred twenty Palestinians in Jerusalem at the Haram al Sharif – the Noble Sanctuary, where stand the two great mosques, the Dome of the Rock and Al Aqsa. The PCSN organised a peaceful, sit-down protest. The Israelis launched gas. A grenade of it fell between Nafez's knees, exploding in his face. Two years later, after much treatment, his lungs were almost normal again; but he had lost sixty per cent of the sight of one eye. Now he is concentrating his work in the "Library on Wheels" which takes books to children in refugee camps and villages, where there are no libraries; through these books and in other ways, such as puppet shows, still propagating the principles of non-violence.

---

1   The Israeli secret police which operates abroad.

2   Seymour Hirsh, *The Samson Option: Israel, America and the Bomb.* Faber, 1991 and 1993, p 119.

3   The Symington Amendment to the Arms Export Control Act initiated by Senator Stuart Symington in the late 70s, states that no country manufacturing nuclear arms is entitled to US economic aid. Israel receives over US$4 billion annually – apart from the $10 billion loan guarantee which Rabin secured on becoming Prime Minister. A clever escape clause for the US in the Amendment provides that countries involved in the transfer or sale of nuclear materials prior to the Bill are exempted. Symington apparently was a Zionist. Israel had collaborated with South Africa over nuclear technology and nuclear materials since the early 60s. The Amendment also provides that the President can override the law if he decides the termination of such aid would be damaging to American national security. Israel's nuclear capacity was then considered necessary in view of the Soviet threat. The law was applied twice to Pakistan. *Op cit*, pp 262-3.

CHAPTER EIGHTEEN

From guerrilla fighter to peacemaker

Anwar Abu Eisheh's home was in Hebron, where his father was a bus-driver. A schoolboy at the time of the "six-day war" in 1967, he remembers the heated discussions between those Palestinians who wanted to leave and those who wanted to stay.

Some said, "I'll die in my own home and will never be a refugee," others said they wanted to remain alive even if outside Palestine; and some decided to flee lest their daughters should be dishonoured – for in 1948 Palestinian women had been raped by Israeli soldiers. Anwar's father decided to stay. On 8th June the family had their first visit from Israeli soldiers.

> They rummaged everywhere and requisitioned all vehicles. My father's bus could not be taken as the battery was flat. That day he was wearing a khaki jacket of military style. The soldiers took it and all his money: 45 dinars, which was in a pocket – a month and a half's salary.

> On 27th August at one a.m. there was a knocking on our door. About eight Israeli soldiers stormed in, pushed my father about, then some took him outside, while others roughly searched the whole house. We heard a cry from my father. My sisters were terrified; on her knees my mother begged the soldiers not to hurt him…After they had gone, and my father came back to us, blood was gushing from his mouth. I burst into tears and vowed that I would avenge him.

Anwar decided to join the *fedayeen* – the freedom fighters – in Jordan. He made one abortive attempt to do so; but was persuaded to come home to take his "tawjihi" (school leaving certificate). Finally he succeeded in joining Fatah, the main group in the PLO, in Amman.

We had military training; and also political lectures which seemed to us very strange. The difference between Jews and Zionists was explained to us. I confess that till then I had made no distinction between them. We new recruits were immensely struck by the fact that anti-Zionist Jews visited us.

We made several incursions into the occupied territories, patrolling these for several days at a time.

By July 1970 clashes between the Jordanian authorities and the Palestinians had begun to multiply. Often these clashes were provoked by the Jordanian secret police. Here's an example: one day in August a Jordanian officer who sympathised with Fatah came to our base in a raging fury, saying, "I've just been attacked by your *fedayeen*." We went to the spot where our comrades were said to have set up a barrage from which to shoot. The men we found there were not *fedayeen*, but members of the Jordanian secret services. If the officer had not been a Fatah sympathiser, his soldiers would have attacked us without our knowing why. Jordanian agents in the guise of *fedayeen* were constantly humiliating Jordanian soldiers.

On 17th September the Jordanian army attacked the Palestinians and tried to encircle Amman. I was at a base right out in the country when we received the order to return to Amman to defend our positions there…Six of our men refused to budge, saying "We are not cowards."

Anwar and his companions found them dead when they returned from the battle in Amman.

From 17th to 20th September no one could sleep in Amman. After a week there rose a stench from the corpses. There was no water, no food, and hundreds of civilians dead. The Jordanian army had shelled residential quarters with heavy artillery while we had only light artillery. During that month of September, 1970, it is estimated that 20,000 Palestinians were killed.

That year Fatah was granted many scholarships for study abroad and Anwar was one of 100 young men who went to Algeria. There he found he had to become used to spoken Algerian Arabic which differs slightly from the Levantine, and learn a new language, French. Realising how much a couple of months in France would help his French he decided to spend his summer vacation there, and wrote to a Frenchwoman who had visited the Fatah base in Amman. Danièle and her husband Marc invited him to stay with them in Paris. After a few days Anwar realised that Marc was Jewish. This period was a happy and fruitful one for him. During the whole of his stay in France he avoided all contact with Arabs as he wanted to speak only French.

The following academic year Anwar studied law; and at the beginning of July, after his exams, rejoined Fatah in Syria.

He was entrusted immediately with a mission to the occupied West Bank. When he had crossed the Allenby Bridge the Israeli soldier on duty found his name on a black list.

Anwar was arrested and underwent a thorough search. Nothing was found on him. For two days he was in solitary confinement in Jerusalem and then transferred, blindfold, to Hebron. There the tortures began.

> 16.7:   I make the acquaintance of my interrogators. One of them, Abu El Abed, bestows on me a mocking smile and makes me undress...For two hours he talks; then for six or seven hours he hits me...This first session is tolerable; and back in my cell I think I will easily be able to bear the pain.

> 17.7:   Abu El Abed again interrogates me. I am naked – as is usual during a torture session. Another person is present who seems to be an instructor in torture. Repeated blows with the fist, long stretches of time in tiring positions – holding a chair with arm extended, standing on one leg.

> 18.7:   Second stage of torture with commandant Jony. There are two witnesses there who have been tortured and make accusations against me.

> Jony threatens to arrest my father (who never engaged in politics) if I will not talk. As I still refuse, he brings my father and we are tortured, naked, in front of each other.

> Towards ten p.m. I am taken to a cell where I find another prisoner who is very kind to me. My father has been put, on purpose, in the cell opposite me, where I can see him.
> The cell which I share is tiny: 2m x 1m. My companion, Walid, tells me that every prisoner ends up by cracking; so he will

not confide anything to me lest I tell the Israelis, for I too may crack. This encourages me to trust him: the more so, that when I complain of terrible colic pains after being forced to drink salt water, he sympathises, lets me smoke two or three of his cigarettes, and tells me of the torture he has endured. I believe him when I see the marks on him of burns from lighted cigarettes. They look genuine.

19.7: I am woken at 4.30, taken into the yard and douched with icy water. I am made to drink salt – slightly dissolved in water, which makes me vomit. Then I am made to lick up the vomit. That makes me more sick than ever. Finally I have to wipe it all up with my clothes which I then have to put on.

20.7: A terrible day. Before being taken to the torture room, I am introduced to the "abattoir" – the "slaughterhouse": the room set apart for sophisticated torture, where there are ropes, clubs, iron bars. The "keeper", who has blood on his overall, warns me that if I do not talk during the next session, I will be brought to him.

This day I am hit with a club, kicked, and again made to drink salt water. Then the torturers stick a match up my penis and I cannot control the urge to vomit. I am made to lick it all up.

Back in my cell, Walid tries to convince me I will not be able to stand it much longer. For the first time, I think about talking. I am losing courage; I can no longer bear the look of the torturer.

21.7: After three hours of torture, I reach the end, and give the name of a comrade. It is the worst mistake I made in my life: because of me, this friend was to spend four months in prison and would be tortured maybe worse than I was. In addition, his mother, who had cancer, and whom he had come to visit in Palestine, died a fortnight before his release; and he was not even allowed to attend her funeral.

I am returned to my cell – and there, a surprise announcement. Walid is to be deported to Amman, and has been given one hour to collect his things.

It is at this moment that I ask him to take the detonators which are still in my shoes. After a little hesitation, he agrees. Half an hour later I am transferred back to Jerusalem.

There follows a very long interrogation, till four in the morning. There are a number of torturers and many of them are drunk. Their leader is called Youness, and he has one thumb cut off which is noticeable when he hits me. He asks what, exactly, I intended to do in occupied Palestine.

22.7: Saturday – the Sabbath: so no interrogation, no torture; I can rest.

23.7: After being forced again to drink salt water, I have electric torture. I am hit on the genitals with a club and with fists.

In the evening I am taken to another cell, where to my surprise I see someone I know well: Bassem, who was with me in Algeria, and who was also arrested at the Allenby Bridge. Before we have any discussion we search the cell thoroughly to discover if it has been bugged. Although we find nothing, we talk only of trivialities. Bassem has been told he will be released the next day, as he has been imprisoned by mistake. I ask if he will get my uncle to find me a lawyer.

24.7: What Bassem had been told, we discover the next day, was just a trick to make me give him information which he would pass on to the Israelis: for the next day he is tortured even more than I am.

[Fifteen years later, Anwar told me, Bassem was killed in Cyprus by Israeli agents.]

Through the questions they ask us, I realise that Walid was a traitor and that he gave my detonators to the Israelis. (I learnt later that soon after my transfer to Jerusalem, he went barefoot into another cell to spy on a new prisoner.)

25.7: I am burned with cigarettes. I still have the marks.

26.7: My body is pricked with red-hot pins…In the evening I am taken to yet another cell which is divided in two by a grille. On the other side of the grille is an Israeli who is completely insane: he talks loudly and unceasingly, and urinates into my side of the cell. He, unlike me, can come and go as he likes. I am allowed out once in twenty-four hours, to have a drink of water and go to the toilet.

27.7:   Torture during the day; the madman all night.

28.7:   A little after midday I am tortured by a man who spits into my mouth and makes me swallow his saliva. My nerves are finished, and I tell him I will talk. After a few minutes' rest I confess to him that I was carrying detonators and that I gave them to Walid in the Hebron prison to take to Amman. I succeed, I think, in convincing the Israelis that the detonators were just for my own use. I imagine they will stop torturing me.

29.7:   I am left alone but I cannot sleep because of the madman and because I keep thinking of what I have done. For the first time since I was imprisoned, I weep.

30.7:   I am tortured even more than before as they doubt my confession and want to know more. They get nothing from me; and think I am finished.

1.8:   I have a medical examination. I have lost nine kilos since my arrest, seventeen days earlier. And it was not from going on hunger strike.

Anwar was transferred back to Hebron and kept in solitary confinement till 23rd September. There was no more torture nor interrogation; but he was not allowed to wash and could go to the toilet only twice a day. The cell, being under the roof, was insufferably hot and airless. During that period he began to understand how the system of traitors worked. They were used as decoys. He realised why Walid had not looked too unhealthy – he was allowed out of his cell during the day.

On 23rd September Anwar was allowed down into the main prison and was happy to be with other prisoners. At last he had a shower and a change of clothes. He discovered from his companions that he had experienced by no means all the forms of torture there were.

For his trial in October his family had found a very good Israeli lawyer (who cost the equivalent of a year's salary for his father); he was condemned to only twenty-four months including fourteen months remission under surveillance; and the four months already spent in jail were deducted from the remaining ten. (Anwar thinks that if it had all happened in, say, 1981, the sentence would probably have been ten years. But in 1972 the Israelis thought that the Palestinian resistance was crushed after "Black September", 1970, in Jordan.)

A representative of the International Red Cross, a Swiss, who visited the prison, refused to believe what Anwar told him about the tortures. Unfortunately only one man, Daoud Al Jaba'ari, whose left arm was paralysed as a result of them, was sufficiently unafraid of reprisals to confirm Anwar's account.

Anwar was released on 13th May, 1973. He worked at various jobs, but began to be harassed by the Shin Bet (secret police). He wanted very much to continue his studies abroad, provided he could have a permit to leave *and* come back. This was refused him, as he had not consented to act as an Israeli agent. He hoped the Mayor of Hebron, Sheikh Mohammed Jaba'ari, would help him; but the Mayor preferred to listen to the Shin Bet and the military Governor, and refused. Anwar sought the help of lawyers.

Finally he was called to the office of the military governor, where he was told: "Either you stay and stop bothering us with lawyers, or you leave permanently." Anwar replied that he wanted to leave. Thereupon he was given three blank sheets of paper to sign. Seeing his hesitation, the officer repeated, "Sign – or you cannot leave." Anwar signed; but still does not know what the blank sheets were for. He was told to leave Hebron quickly.

In early July 1974 Anwar left Palestine. He completed a Master's degree in law in Oran, Algeria; and then, in 1977, thanks to the advice and help of a French friend there, he went to Paris – to study further.

In 1984 Anwar was in Cambridge through Unipal for a course in English which he needed for his work. He had been appointed the PLO representative for cultural exchange between Palestinian and European youth. The year before, he had been shot in the leg when with Issam Sartawi who was assassinated; but to our relief had recovered enough to ride a bicycle – something of a necessity in Cambridge. He was immediately popular: friendly, humorous, and helpful.

He gave me a copy of his book *Mémoires Palestiniennes,* published in 1982 in Paris by Clancier-Guénaud (a firm now folded) from which the extracts quoted above have been taken.

Issam Sartawi had, on behalf of the PLO, been seeking dialogue with the Israelis, and trying, with the help of European politicians and diplomats, to find a way to a settlement other than by force.

Exactly how and why had Anwar, a freedom fighter, become an adherent of non-violence, and a seeker for justice and peace through mutual understanding? Surely, I thought, this man who had suffered so cruelly from the Israelis was someone of unusual magnanimity and realism; of insight and courage.

So in March 1991 I went to Paris to see Anwar again, and to learn more from him.

His story continues as he told me it then.

It had been the fault of Europeans and Americans that Israel was implanted in our country and most of us were expelled. In third world countries, in my case anyhow, we associate people with their governments, with the political system. For me, French people used to be those who were killing my brothers in Algeria and supporting Israel. As a boy I threw stones at tourist buses. But when I met French people I understood that the reality is another thing.

There have been many landmarks in my life.

The Israeli occupation in 1967 was the first. It was a big hammer-blow on my head and the head of others. When they beat my father, it was the spark which fired me to resistance, for they beat my father unjustly. It was part of a collective punishment for a cut telephone wire.

I went to Jordan and joined the freedom fighters; there, the years 1968–70 laid the foundation of my political education. From Fatah I learnt to distinguish between Zionists and Jews. Israel wants us to make no differentiation. Jews coming to support us opened my eyes.

In Algeria, where I was sent to study at the University of Oran, my political ideas developed further: there was a good professor of politics, an Iraqi, who had been a devout Muslim, who taught us Marxism–Leninism.

I was in Amman in 1970. The Palestinians, a people who had been humiliated and frustrated, now had arms in their hands. The battle of Karameh had shown for the first time that the Israelis could be defeated. After that the Palestinian organisations made mistakes. We were still raw and inexperienced. The King was afraid for his throne; and the

US on the one hand, the USSR on the other, could not allow another Vietnam in the Middle East – which might happen, if the Resistance became too powerful. I have already described how the King and his organisations acted to break down the Resistance.

Then prison: perhaps the most valuable time of my life. What was good? The many days in solitary were hard. After that, I was with the élite of society. It was perhaps one of the happiest periods of my youth. I was with *good* people; and I was put in charge of the library. I had the right to take books to different cells, and met members of different political groups: Fatah, DFLP, PFLP [Democratic Front for the Liberation of Palestine; Popular Front for the Liberation of Palestine]. We read, talked, debated – always like brothers. I think the guards did not bother about political discussions; but they took anything they found written. I increased the number of books to about 3,000. The Red Crescent Society, my family, and released prisoners helped: physics, maths, geography, literature – were no problem. In prison I discovered Jean-Paul Sartre, Victor Hugo, Shakespeare, and Tolstoy – translated into Arabic. It was a big experience for me.

The questions that I had begun to ask myself earlier – when the first friend I had in France, still like a brother to me, was a Jew; when I lived with French people in Oran among whom was Roland Machet (now a professor in Dijon University), a Christian, very non-violent – these questions, and more, now grew in my mind. If you ask yourself questions, it is a beginning.

But I was still for the military struggle. In 1976 came Tal al Za'atar. The PLO appealed for volunteers to go and fight the Syrians who were supporting the Falangists – the Falangists who had besieged Tal al Za'atar for months, destroyed it, and slaughtered the inhabitants. We set out by boat from Libya. It was dangerous, as one out of three or four boats was stopped by the Israelis. But we arrived at Saida, and met refugees from Tal al Za'atar. There was a woman there, out of her mind; she was unable to weep. She showed us the blood on her dress. "My children had their throats cut on my knee by the Falangists," she said. We soldiers, standing round her, wept. "I will avenge your children," I said.

We had our first battle. The Syrians attacked us like a steam-roller. There were about 3,000 of them; only a few dozen of us. They charged us *singing.* It was a great shock. I had thought they would be sad to be forced to fight their Arab brothers. That singing drove me mad. I had hesitated to shoot brother Arabs – now I began to shoot – shoot – shoot – I shot every bullet I had.

["Comme j'étais sanguinaire!" Anwar exclaimed at this point to his wife. "Je ne me reconnaissais pas." – "How bloodthirsty I was! I didn't recognise myself."]

After that, I began to ask myself questions about the big ideas – about Arab unity, the common struggle, and all that. What do they *mean*? I began to think of dialogue: of the possibility of speaking to people and trying to understand. I had thought the Syrian régime was a progressive one, unlike the Jordanian – under which we schoolboys had been shot when we held demonstrations on 15th May, the anniversary of the State of Israel.

But worse fighting followed. One day seven wounded Palestinians in an ambulance were passing through a certain village. The Falangists – a majority in the village – killed them all, and burned the ambulance. So we attacked. The battle lasted three days. We lost a lot of men. I was in the front of the attack. Then there was fighting in the narrow streets. It was horrible. Afterwards I had terrible stomach pains from the things I had seen. The battle itself had been proper: soldiers against soldiers. My group had sixteen men. The last moment of the attack, when you run the remaining twenty metres and climb the barricade, is the most dangerous. Four men were killed by shots in the face. When I saw my dead comrades *I began to hate war:* to hate it most when I saw Palestinians and Lebanese allies of ours, who had not been first line fighters, come up and shoot everything that moved, even cows, and to loot. We, first liners, stopped them: we even had to shoot in the leg. I have some perspective on this phenomenon now. Israeli friends have told me the same things happened when they were in the army. These second and third line soldiers are called "La résistance de la 25ième heure" – "25th hour resistance fighters". It's international. Our military orders are clear: not to touch civilians, not to steal;

but the men coming up behind feel they have to say, "We have no more bullets." The same thing is happening in Kuwait now. Kuwaitis who did nothing before are calling themselves the Kuwaiti Resistance and are killing and torturing Palestinian civilians. [Anwar is speaking in March 1991, just after the end of the Gulf War.]

When I came to live in France after my studies in Algeria were finished, I began to be active for Palestinians. Every Sunday I went to the market with some friends. There we had a stall with books. French people, Arabs, Zionists, non-Zionist Jews – would come and talk. I became President of GUPS (General Union of Palestinian Students) and took part in many meetings and debates. I read the European press a great deal. It is a very great privilege to be in a European country and to hear every kind of opinion. I can read a paper from Iraq, Syria, Algeria, or Israel. If you are in an Arab country, you have only what is allowed.

I began to develop – to believe in the non-violent struggle; to believe in an Israeli State and a Palestinian State.

And through the press I discovered Issam Sartawi. I think he was a man of vision. He understood what we can have and what we cannot have. I think he came to his beliefs in a way similar to mine. He had been a fighter – in fact the head of our military organisation after 1967. He suffered as a soldier. Bit by bit he saw we must be more realistic and change our strategy.

I asked if I could work with him, and he accepted. Then I began to see there was another world than mine in GUPS: that there was important diplomatic work going on in the wings, and that that is necessary for a struggle like ours. For me it was a new opportunity and a rich experience. I worked with Sartawi for a long time. We made contact with Israelis, with important European personalities, and especially the Socialist International.

But because of his contacts with Israelis, Sartawi had a lot of enemies: those Palestinians who were against dialogue with the Israelis. Sartawi was a pioneer in this endeavour, which was unacceptable to some Palestinians, in particular to those in the political line of the Syrians and Iraqis. I didn't worry about that then. Sartawi's political line was that of the PLO: the most important element in PLO policy. There is nothing unusual about that: one must have contacts, dialogue, with one's enemies.

Issam Sartawi hated to be protected. The only time he shouted at me was when I told him that in France he must have guards. He finally accepted, but every time he could get rid of his bodyguards he did so.

When we were in Albufera, the village in Portugal where the Congress of the Socialist International took place, a tiny village south of Lisbon – I don't know why – we neglected this question of protection. We were very, very busy and far from any town. I believe God decided what happened.

It was the last day of the Congress. I was in charge of a petition to allow Sartawi to speak from the platform, and was collecting signatures. He had not till then been allowed to speak, even from the floor. I had collected some hundreds of signatures, and was looking for people who had not yet signed. I had my back to Sartawi, for I was looking out of the door and he was looking in, joking with some people.

It happened so quickly you couldn't realise anything. I must have been shot from behind: the bullet went into my leg – here, and came out – here, the other side; and I fell down. When I looked up Sartawi was lying on the ground, shot in the head, also from behind. There must have been more than one person involved in the killing.

I don't know what the investigation discovered. No one has told me. One man was caught and imprisoned for just three years. For me, the actual killers are not important. They are just mad people. The important thing is "who gave the order?"

It is clear that it was Abu Nidal.[1] He killed Sartawi.

When I felt I was shot, I saw Sartawi and crawled up to him; but after a few seconds I was pulled away – I was holding onto his jacket.

213

Alone in the ambulance I looked up at the ceiling and felt guilty. "He died, and I am alive. What will he think of me? He must be angry with me." I was taken to Tunis for treatment for some months. I realised that everyone who hated Sartawi was trying to silence me too, to prevent me from doing anything. Sartawi had been very courageous. He had criticised certain people in the PLO openly. There are many tendencies and rivalries in the PLO.

The biggest shock for me was when I discovered that Ibrahim Souss, at that time PLO representative in France, circulated a rumour giving the impression that I perhaps was party to Sartawi's murder. It was the most painful thing I have ever experienced. I became fed up, and asked for my present post.

When I had been President of GUPS, I had seen attendance at meetings begin to dwindle and had tried another way to rouse interest. I had arranged for a Palestinian football team to come from Lebanon and Syria to France. It was a successful visit. Now my job is to foster contacts in sport. We also have a folklore group; we work with Scouts; and I help also in a sponsorship scheme for Palestinian children. There are still debates; and I see journalists.

I completed a doctoral thesis – on land in Palestine from the Islamic period to 1987. This period of work allowed me to study Zionism, everything on the land question relating to international law and civil law. The thesis matured me, I think, and I was happy to do it.

During this period also I learnt about PCSN – the Palestinian Centre for the Study of Non-violence in Jerusalem. I became its unofficial representative in Europe – unofficial, because I'm in the PLO. It is a voluntary work that I do.

I believe firmly now in the methods of non-violence. I am convinced that we Palestinians, especially, must struggle in a non-violent way. If you look at the *intifada*, you will see that ninety per cent of its methods are very non-violent. Stone-throwing is the most violent part of it. I would prefer it not to be used. 100% non-violence would be better. But you cannot force people to be non-violent, especially when you see the extent of the oppression they suffer. In my country there is a very long tradition of stone-throwing against oppressors.

The situation is much worse now, since the Gulf War. Many people are in despair because of the long, long humiliation; and in the international order there are two weights, two measures.

When you look at the Palestinians you see we are a people like any other – with our good, honest, dedicated people, and our rogues and those who are self-interested.

I hope that the peace movement in Israel will grow. My aim is to live with all the people in my country, with equality in rights and in duties, without regard to religion or race. What I want is to return and live in the LAND of my ancestors.

Anwar is now back in Hebron and teaches law at Al Quds University.

---

1   Abu Nidal has been the Palestinian archterrorist. Patrick Seale, in *Abu Nidal: a Gun for Hire* (Hutchinson, 1992), gives a convincing explanation for Abu Nidal's successive murders of Palestinian "doves". In this carefully and courageously researched book Seale points out that it is in the interests of some Arab régimes to keep the PLO weak, and in the interests of hardline Israeli governments to make use of a criminal in order to blacken the PLO as a terrorist organisation with which one cannot negotiate: for genuine negotiation would involve giving up territory. "The truth is," Seale writes, "that the PLO has for years been the main victim of terrorism rather than its perpetrator – the antithesis of the popular perception encouraged by Israeli propaganda." – p 320.

CHAPTER NINETEEN

Conclusion

Towards the end of 1991 I received a letter from Gaza:

My dear mother Eleanor,

It was a great moment in our history to see our delegation in
Madrid sitting with the other delegations to negotiate for
peace. I'm sure you remember Dr Abd el Shafi. He used to
talk to the volunteers in the orientation week. I'm a strong
supporter of the Madrid Conference and I do believe it will
lead in one way or another to lift the occupation off our heads
and shoulders. I was one of the thousands who went to
welcome the return of our delegation at the check-point at
the border of the Gaza Strip. We welcomed them with olive
branches and white flowers. It was a moving scene, and many
of the [Israeli] soldiers were affected. One of them said to us,
'I don't believe this!'

Dear mother, we all pray for peace. Then I can travel wherever
I want. Surely I'll visit you and other English friends as well.
My mother, my sister and my brothers send their love to you,
to your son, and your daughter and her family. Our hearty
congratulations to Janet and her husband on having the new
baby boy safely. He must be proud of being called Michael
after his grandfather. Please for my sake whisper in the ear of
the new Michael to be faithful to the name he's carrying. I'll
never forget the old Michael.

With very best wishes
Your affectionate son
Mohammed

However, in the peace talks with the Israelis, the Palestinians were handicapped from the start. There was no balance between the two parties. Israel, the dominating power, decided which Palestinians would be allowed and which not allowed to be in the Palestinian delegation: there should be representatives only from the West Bank and Gaza Strip – none from the refugees outside the borders of Palestine, nor, perhaps even more hurtfully for Palestinians, from their capital, East Jerusalem. The Israeli demands were backed up by America. (The Palestinians had no say at all in the composition of the Israeli team.) Nevertheless among the Palestinians at the talks were individuals of distinction, who worked hard for a just, comprehensive peace settlement.

The conciliatory and statesmanlike introductory speech made by the leader of the Palestinian delegation, Dr Haidar Abd el Shafi, met with stony unresponsiveness from the Israeli Prime Minister, Yitzhak Shamir, and that set the pattern for the course the talks were to take. They became more and more difficult through Israeli intransigence.

Events on the ground suggested Israel was not really interested in a just peace. Peace is not possible without justice. Persecution of Palestinians in the Occupied Territories increased, with more killings, beatings, imprisonments, and demolition of homes; 415 Palestinians were deported, without charge or trial (from their own country, by a foreign occupying force) to a barren mountainside in South Lebanon in the depth of winter; to cap it all, the entire populations of the West Bank and Gaza Strip became virtually imprisoned: cut off from East Jerusalem – their capital, their cultural, educational, religious, commercial and medical centre – and from each other; able to move only with permits – as with the "pass" laws of apartheid South Africa. Students from Gaza enrolled at Birzeit University (West Bank), had to hide in the hills to avoid arrest and being forcibly sent back; some made their dangerous way swimming up the coast (along that shore the sea is full of treacherous currents, and the Israeli military are always on the watch), continuing the journey clandestinely, in order to study at their university. Few workers were allowed into Israel, the main source of employment and earnings since the Palestinian economy was made subservient to Israel's in the wake of the 1967 war. Already Palestinians' jobs in Israel were being taken by Russian Jews, Eastern Europeans, and South-eastern Asians.

Yet on 13th September, 1993, Yitzhak Rabin, then Prime Minister of Israel, was seen on television, at the White House, Washington, shaking hands with Yasser Arafat, leader of the PLO – the "terrorist" organisation. Was it a mirage, or a breakthrough? Would the limited agreement reached at Oslo lead to the much, much more that is needed for genuine and lasting peace?

Since then the Oslo Accords (or Declaration of Principles) look like a betrayal of the Palestinians. At Taba, Egypt, in May 1994, Arafat, apparently under Israeli and Egyptian pressure, signed away the free democracy that Palestinians had longed and suffered for (Oslo II). One wonders why Arafat initiated at Oslo such a flawed secret deal behind the backs of the Palestinian negotiators. In the past five years the situation for Palestinians has steadily deteriorated.

Great hope was generated by the first Palestinian elections ever, in January 1996, but that hope is gradually being crushed.

Palestinians outside the occupied territories of Palestine in Lebanon, Syria, Jordan and Israel feel themselves forgotten. In Lebanon, their situation is desperately insecure. The Hariri Government, in its endeavour to rebuild a ravaged country, favours big business. In the tragic refugee camps of Beirut, Palestinians are reduced to squalor, penury, and hopelessness: nothing must be done which might encourage them to stay, so they have no citizen rights whatever. (But where else can they go?)

In South Lebanon, Lebanese villagers and townsfolk share with Palestinian refugees the shelling and bombardment that comes from Israeli forces in occupation there ever since 1978. The Lebanese Hisbullah retaliates on northern Israel with rockets; and this in turn brings Israeli retaliation. Mid-April 1996, when Peres launched his massive bombing onslaught "Grapes of Wrath", saw a terrible re-enactment of the panic flight northwards in 1974 of thousands of civilians. Power stations in Beirut were also bombed. At Qana in southern Lebanon, an Israeli helicopter gunship deliberately destroyed a UNIFIL post – i.e. a United Nations post – sheltering Lebanese refugees. A hundred people, mostly women and children, were killed.

In the Gaza Strip Israel still controls over forty per cent of the land in this tiny densely populated area; takes most of the water; the settlements are intact and protected by a re-deployed Israeli army.

True, Israeli soldiers more rarely enter parts of the Strip meant to be for Palestinians only. (But when they do it can be with lethal results. "Last Saturday, 4th March [1995], they opened fire on traffic going along the main road to the camps. They killed a popular headmaster in the Strip, and injured some others," I was told in a letter from Gaza.) There are no more curfews or strikes; Palestinians can even at last go freely to the beach – except where it is reserved for Israelis. They can have control over education and health. They have been allowed their own police; but the Palestinian police are armed to take over the policing rôle of the Israeli military, a rôle that was becoming increasingly irksome for the soldiers in occupation. Arafat has had strict instructions to crack down on Islamic Jihad and Hamas, cost what it may in

Palestinian lives. By February 1995, twenty Palestinians had been shot by their own police; more have been since. Appalling reports continue to emerge of the arbitrary brutality of Palestinians against Palestinians. (By August 1998 twenty Palestinians had died through torture while in Palestinian custody.) In Israeli jails there are still hundreds of political prisoners, the number replenished when some are released.

The Strip has been turned into an enclosed ghetto, which because of its overcrowding, squalor and unemployment (above fifty per cent) must be a breeding-ground for frustration and anger. Now hunger threatens the Palestinians of the Occupied Territories. "As this issue goes to print," wrote Adam Keller, the Editor of *The Other Israel*,[1] in March 1995," a new Rabin-Arafat summit has taken place at Erez Checkpoint [on the border between the Strip and Israel] – the latest in a series of 'last efforts' to shore up the collapsing peace process. Afterwards, it was announced that 15,000 hungry Palestinian workers would be graciously allowed to go back to being overworked and underpaid in Israel. (A bare three years ago, some 120,000 Palestinians worked in Israel on a regular basis.)" The situation is now infinitely worse. There is a total blockade.

Rabin's delays over implementing the Oslo Accords did not greatly help the "peace process". He was however, assassinated by a young Israeli of extreme orthodox views who resented the handing back to the Palestinians of any piece of the "Land of Israel". Many Israelis applauded the murder. Many others were deeply dismayed. The peace process began its terminal decline. Rabin's successor, Shimon Peres, was no peace lover either, as his bombing onslaught on Lebanon showed. The advent of Netanyahu as Prime Minister has been a total disaster.

"Israel's closure of the West Bank and Gaza Strip has prevented the free movement of people and goods in and out of the West Bank and Gaza Strip…The closure devastates the Palestinian economy and causes losses which are greater than the amount of international assistance being provided."[2]

In the West Bank the indigenous inhabitants of Palestine are confined to small enclaves; Israel has an enlarged land area together with its natural resources. Only splinters of their former homeland will be left for the Palestinians, splinters separated from each other by new roads for Israeli use. Rampaging and violent settlers, who terrorised Palestinians with increasing impunity after Oslo, are, in fact, being rewarded for their efforts. A fragmented West Bank, cut off from the Gaza Strip and both of them cut off from Jerusalem, will make, of course, a viable Palestinian State impossible.

Palestinian homes continue to be destroyed within the Jerusalem area as Zionist Israel strengthens its hold on East Jerusalem. Thus are pre-empted the promised talks on the final status of the city – left, in the Oslo Accords, to be discussed last, among other vital issues such as water and the refugees (refused repatriation since the wars of 1948 and 1967). The illegal, solidly-built settlements around Jerusalem are, contrary to the Accords, being strengthened and expanded in order physically to cut off the city from the inhabitants of the West Bank and Gaza.

There are reports of corruption in circles round Arafat. Hanan Ashrawi has resigned in disgust her position as minister for higher education. Dr Haidar Abd el Shafi resigned his post a year earlier. A *casino*, costing around $150m, "a vast, multi-facility complex with swimming pools, tennis courts, exquisite restaurants" apart from a huge gambling hall, has been built at Jericho. (Just down the road are two large Palestinian refugee camps with *nothing*.) Islam, like Judaism, forbids gambling; but the casino is for Israelis and wealthy Palestinians as well as foreign tourists; and it has been built on land belonging to the *Waqf* i.e. it is on Islamic religious property.

In early 1996, a truce was in force between the PNA (Arafat's Palestine National Authority) and Hamas, which was beginning to favour political rather than violent action. The Israeli government under Peres chose that moment to assassinate two popular Islamic leaders. There followed a series of suicide bombings causing dreadful carnage among Israeli civilians. The first was timed to coincide with the anniversary of the massacre in February 1994 of twenty-nine Palestinians at prayer in the Ibrahimi Mosque, the principal mosque in Hebron, by a fundamentalist Israeli settler from America, Baruch Goldstein. On that occasion, the occupation forces had punished, not any settlers, but the entire population of the city by slapping on a curfew and greatly adding to the number of civilians killed. This time the Israelis inevitably embarked on an even more iron-fisted policy of collective punishment, strongly backed by the Clinton government and by Arafat as well. An Israeli spokesman said they would hunt the Palestinian needle, even if it meant "burning the Palestinian haystack".

Since the suicide bombings, Palestinians from the West Bank and Gaza Strip have been banned altogether from working in Israel: 1,400 Thai workers have been imported to take over their jobs. Around 400 Gazan university students studying in the West Bank have been rounded up and forcibly returned to the Strip to join the ranks of young men doomed to enforced idleness and bitter resentment: possibly to produce yet more suicide bombers? Where is the *sense* of it? Is it not a cruel and a dangerous thing to rob the young of hope, and drive them to despair? Despair can be deadly.

Netanyahu, Prime Minister of Israel, who balks at implementing even the flawed Oslo agreements, seems to be dealing a final death blow to hopes of genuine peace. He has continued more brazenly the annexationist polices of his predecessors. On 14th January, 1997, under outside pressure, he initialled together with Arafat an agreement for partial Israeli withdrawal from Hebron: twenty per cent of the city – its heart – will remain for 400 Israeli settlers and army – and for 20,000 Palestinians the surrounding area. Hardly, one would think, an arrangement for enduring harmony.

Ariel Sharon, with a criminal war record as Defence Minister (He masterminded the 1982 invasion of Lebanon, orchestrated the massacre of Shatila and Sabra, and as Housing Minister has been responsible for the great increase in settlements.) has been appointed Foreign Minister to assist at peace talks. He was at the Wye Summit in USA, October 1998.

"Seven years ago – as sanctioned by the Madrid peace conference – the international consensus on resolving the Arab-Israeli conflict was 'land for peace'. Not any more. Peace is now to be traded for Israel's unconditional security, and whatever slithers of occupied territory it feels it can dispense with." (*Middle East International*, 30th October 1998.)

Also at the Wye Summit was the head of America's CIA. *The Guardian* reports that half the deaths under torture in Palestinian custody have occurred since CIA training of Palestinians began. The CIA specialises in espionage, information gathering and interrogation. Its help given to Pinochet in Chile and to the junta in Greece shows what that can mean. Israel and USA insist on this CIA "help".

While not mentioning the CIA specifically, Amnesty International's Report of September 1998 indicates how much American and Israeli pressure affects Palestinian detainees.[3]

Long, long ago, Israel was to be "a light to the nations". What is she now? Greedy and cruel, she has become like South Africa was: one of the very worst of colonialist nations, racist and oppressive. Most alarming of all, she has become a serious threat to peace not only for the Middle East, but for the rest of the world also, because of her nuclear and chemical arsenals, and the uncritical support of the world's only remaining super-power. To date, Israel has refused to allow international inspection of her Dimona plant, (there are now other nuclear installations also), and refused to sign the non-proliferation treaty. No Western pressure is brought to bear to oblige the Israeli government to do either. On the contrary, to pursue her ambitions, Israel receives all the funds she asks for from America, and, under President Clinton, even more than she asks for – between two and six billion dollars annually, in various forms, far more than a Third World country such as India with its 600 million people.

On each side of the unhappy divide are individuals struggling for change, for humanity and understanding. They shine like candles in the darkness. A few have been named in this book.

"If only the Israelis would say they are sorry for what they have done to us, we would forgive them," Tony Bakerjian, the veteran UNRWA official, told me; and Doris Salah, Director of the YWCA in Jerusalem, "Reconciliation is not a problem for Palestinians. For centuries, Christian, Muslim, and Jewish Palestinians have lived together in harmony. For over forty years it is the *Palestinians* who have been wronged and suffered injustice: and yet it is they who have already shown they have forgiven, and have come forward with a peace plan – the Declaration of Independence in November, 1988, when the PLO recognised the State of Israel, but demanded recognition for the Palestinian people also. They will not try to put the clock back: Israel is a reality; but we too are here!"

Palestinians are practised in the art of forgiveness: they have had to be, in order to survive many centuries of conquest and foreign rule. But never, as far as one can tell, has their situation been as dire as it is today. Can their patience hold out much longer, or will there soon be a worse explosion of angry desperation leading to total disaster both for them and the Israelis?

Dr Haidar Abd el Shafi of Gaza was asked in an interview with the Third World magazine, *South*, for a message to the international community. This is what he said: "Please make every effort to understand the truth about the Palestinian-Israeli conflict. I am convinced that when people know the truth, they will stand by it. Truth has its own force; and our suffering stems mainly from the fact that it has been distorted for so long, masked by Zionist propaganda. It is now no longer difficult or impossible for people to know the truth, if they want to. *Please try to know the truth.*"

Dr Abd el Shafi's message must surely include the Israelis as part of the international community.

One longs to cry out to Israel's political leaders, "For God's sake, from your position of strength – acknowledge the justice of the Palestinian cause. Treat Palestinians as the human beings they are: not angels, any more than Jews, but of equal value to Jews. Do you not see the resemblance between your assumption of belonging to a superior race with superior rights and the doctrine of the Nazis? Do not let this be your legacy to history! The Palestinians too have committed crimes; but the original, the great crime, from which all others have stemmed – yours and theirs – was committed by you Zionists, not by the Palestinians, who were and are its victims. You robbed them of their heritage; and then compounded the felony by the fabrication of myths

– of lies – to conceal it both from your own people and from your Western allies. Have the courage to acknowledge your guilt, and make amends. For the sake of your children, listen to your own prophets, among you now. Then indeed swords could be beaten into ploughshares, and the lion lie down with the lamb. Where is your best security if not in making friends with your Palestinian neighbours, whom you have wronged?

"A searching of your hearts leading to a confession of the truth could take you, like Ariadne's thread, away from the monster of fear and hatred towards the freedom of understanding and trust, and so towards genuine peace for all the people of Israel-Palestine."

It could lead, even, to equal rights for all citizens in a unified state, without artificial internal frontiers – inappropriate for a tiny country. Now, in November 1998, that seems an unrealisable dream. But it will surely take shape one day. There may be much pain for both sides in the interval, a very long interval perhaps; but truth, the strength of the human spirit, and mutual forgiveness must conquer in the end. The possible alternative is too frightful to contemplate.

---

1 *The Other Israel,* PO Box 2542, Holon, Israel 58125.

2 Christian Aid Report *Action for Partners, five years since the Declaration of Principles,* Sept 1998.

3 Amnesty International Report, Sept 1998, *Israel/Occupied Territories and t he Palestinian Authority. Five years after the Oslo Agreement: human rights sacrificed for "security".*

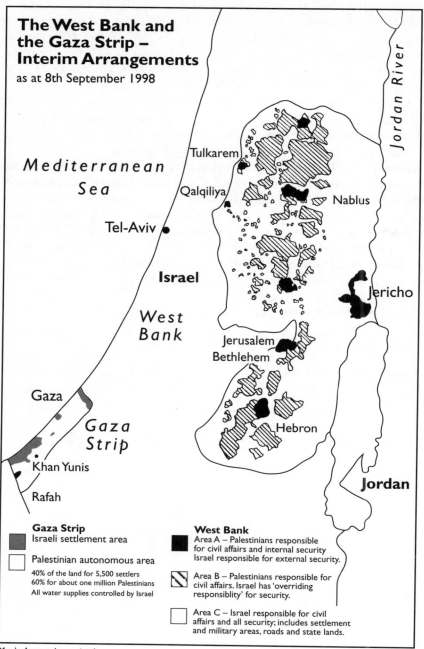

The West Bank and the Gaza Strip – Interim Arrangements

as at 8th September 1998

Jordan River

Mediterranean Sea

Tulkarem

Qalqiliya

Nablus

Tel-Aviv

Israel

Jericho

West Bank

Jerusalem
Bethlehem

Gaza

Gaza Strip

Hebron

Khan Yunis

Rafah

Jordan

Gaza Strip

Israeli settlement area

Palestinian autonomous area

40% of the land for 5,500 settlers
60% for about one million Palestinians
All water supplies controlled by Israel

West Bank

Area A – Palestinians responsible
for civil affairs and internal security
Israel responsible for external security.

Area B – Palestinians responsible for
civil affairs. Israel has 'overriding
responsiblity' for security.

Area C – Israel responsible for civil
affairs and all security; includes settlement
and military areas, roads and state lands.

Map by Amnesty International

APPENDIX

The Balfour Declaration

On 2nd November 1917, Lord Balfour, the British Foreign Secretary, wrote this letter to Lord Rothschild, the most prominent member of the British Jewish community:

Dear Lord Rothschild,

I have much pleasure in conveying to you, on behalf of His Majesty's Government, the following declaration of sympathy with Jewish Zionist aspirations which has been submitted to, and approved by the Cabinet:

'His Majesty's Government view with favour the establishment in Palestine of a national home for the Jewish people, and will use their best endeavours to facilitate the achievement of this object, it being clearly understood that nothing shall be done which may prejudice the civil and religious rights of the existing non-Jewish communities in Palestine, or the rights and political status enjoyed by Jews in any other country.'

I should be grateful if you would bring this declaration to the knowledge of the Zionist Federation.

Yours sincerely

Arthur Balfour

The effects of this letter, which became known as the Balfour Declaration, have been as far reaching as those of any document in history; and several points should be noted in connection with it:–

(1)   It was the Zionists themselves, led by Chaim Weizmann, who had inspired the letter and drafted the text.

225

(2)   The wording was deliberately ambiguous. Both the British Government and the Zionists, whose policy was founded on Theodore Herzl's book *Der Judenstaat (The Jewish State)*, knew what was meant by "national *home*". Edwin Montagu, the only Jew in the government, knew and disapproved.

(3)   Apart from the fact that the "non-Jewish communities" in Palestine were then ninety-two per cent of the population and that that was a dismissive, derogatory way of referring to the indigenous inhabitants – the Palestinians – the proviso concerning their "civil and religious rights" (there was no mention at all of their *political* rights) was soon thrown overboard by the Zionists; while the "rights and political status" enjoyed by Jews in some other countries were undermined: notably in the Arab world. (The terrorist means used to entice Iraqi Jews to Israel are described by David Hirst in *The Gun and the Olive Branch*, pp 155–164.)

(4)   Britain had absolutely no authority to make such a statement. Palestine was not ours to dispose of. It was, as usual, under foreign occupation: at that time, that of the Ottoman Turks. Part of the "fertile crescent" of the Arabian peninsular, it was a land "flowing with milk and honey", at the meeting-point of Europe, Asia, and Africa, and sacred to three great religions – Judaism, Christianity, and Islam – and has for millennia been the victim of conquest.

(5)   Britain was then at war with both Germans and Turks. Jews in Germany, it was hoped, would be inspired to undermine the German war effort. And grateful Europeans, settled near the Suez Canal, would surely help to safeguard our route to India.